Reflections on the 2019 South African General Elections

Reflections on the 2019 South African General Elections is a critical reflection on the key lessons of Elections 2019 in South Africa, focusing on the future of the country's electoral democracy.

The volume engages questions on land, election campaigns, voter turnout, voter apathy, and how opposition parties will be forced to co-exist in the context of declining electoral dominance the ANC once comfortably held. An important reflection on the lessons of the 2019 South African General Elections, the contributors ask: Quo Vadis South Africa? The 2019 General Elections marked a watershed in South Africa's political landscape. The ANC under the banner of a narrative of regeneration and getting back on the moral path dipped below the 60% mark for the first time in South Africa's democratic history. This decline in electoral support for the party may be interpreted as a degeneration of the ANC through the loss of its moral stature, the erosion of its integrity and disillusionment with its performance as a governing party. Opposition political parties could not capitalise on this seeming disillusionment with the ruling ANC. Caught in their own factional battles and in the midst of corruption scandals, opposition parties were unable to successfully increase their share of the vote, and capture the undecided and disillusioned voter.

Considering the future of South Africa's electoral democracy at 25 years of democracy, *Reflections on the 2019 South African General Elections* will be of great interest to scholars of African Studies, South Africa, Governance, and Elections.

The chapters in this book were originally published as a special issue of *Politikon: South African Journal of Political Studies*.

Joleen Steyn Kotze is Senior Research Specialist in Democracy and Citizenship at the Human Science Research Council's Developmental, Capable, and Ethical State Research Programme and Research Fellow at the Centre for Gender and African Studies, University of the Free State, Bloemfontein, South Africa.

Narnia Bohler-Muller is Divisional Director at the Human Science Research Council's Developmental, Capable, and Ethical State Research Programme and Research Fellow at the Centre for Gender and African Studies, University of the Free State, Bloemfontein, South Africa.

Reflections on the 2019 South African General Elections

Quo Vadis?

Edited by
Joleen Steyn Kotze and Narnia Bohler-Muller

Routledge
Taylor & Francis Group

LONDON AND NEW YORK

First published 2021
by Routledge
2 Park Square, Milton Park, Abingdon, Oxon, OX14 4RN

and by Routledge
52 Vanderbilt Avenue, New York, NY 10017

Routledge is an imprint of the Taylor & Francis Group, an informa business

British Library Cataloguing-in-Publication Data
A catalogue record for this book is available from the British Library

ISBN13: 978-0-367-46805-7

Typeset in Myriad Pro
by codeMantra

Publisher's Note
The publisher accepts responsibility for any inconsistencies that may have arisen during the conversion of this book from journal articles to book chapters, namely the inclusion of journal terminology.

Disclaimer
Every effort has been made to contact copyright holders for their permission to reprint material in this book. The publishers would be grateful to hear from any copyright holder who is not here acknowledged and will undertake to rectify any errors or omissions in future editions of this book.

Contents

Citation Information

The following chapters were originally published in the *Politikon*, volume 46, issue 4 (2019). When citing this material, please use the original page numbering for each article, as follows:

Chapter 1
Quo Vadis? Reflections on the 2019 South African General Elections
Joleen Steyn Kotze and Narnia Bohler-Muller
Politikon, volume 46, issue 4 (2019) pp. 365–370

Chapter 2
Do Election Campaigns Matter in South Africa? An Examination of Fluctuations in Support for the ANC, DA, IFP and NNP 1994–2019
Cherrel Africa
Politikon, volume 46, issue 4 (2019) pp. 371–389

Chapter 3
Voting Preferences of Protesters and Non-protesters in Three South African Elections (2014–2019): Revisiting the 'Ballot and the Brick'
Carin Runciman, Martin Bekker and Terri Maggott
Politikon, volume 46, issue 4 (2019) pp. 390–410

Chapter 4
Land Reform and Belonging in South Africa: A Place-making Perspective
Leslie J. Bank and Tim G. B. Hart
Politikon, volume 46, issue 4 (2019) pp. 411–426

Chapter 5
Coexistence as a Strategy for Opposition Parties in Challenging the African National Congress' One-Party Dominance
Isaac Khambule, Amarone Nomdo, Babalwa Siswana and Gilbert Fokou
Politikon, volume 46, issue 4 (2019) pp. 427–442

Chapter 6
Election of the National President: South Africa's Approach and Its Implications for Presidentialism
Dirk Kotze
Politikon, volume 46, issue 4 (2019) pp. 443–461

Chapter 7

The Decline of Partisan Voting and the Rise in Electoral Uncertainty in South Africa's 2019 General Elections
Collette Schulz-Herzenberg
Politikon, volume 46, issue 4 (2019) pp. 462–480

Chapter 8

The Unconvinced Vote: The Nature and Determinants of Voting Intentions and the Changing Character of South African Electoral Politics
Benjamin J. Roberts, Jarè Struwig, Steven L. Gordon and Yul Derek Davids
Politikon, volume 46, issue 4 (2019) pp. 481–498

For any permission-related enquiries please visit:
http://www.tandfonline.com/page/help/permissions

Contributors

Cherrel Africa Department of Political Studies, University of The Western Cape, South Africa.

Leslie J. Bank Economic Performance and Development, Human Sciences Research Council, Cape Town, South Africa. Department of Social Anthropology, Walter Sisulu University, Mthatha, South Africa.

Martin Bekker Centre for Social Change, University of Johannesburg, South Africa.

Narnia Bohler-Muller Democracy, Governance and Service Delivery Research Programme, Human Science Research Council, Pretoria, South Africa. Centre for Gender and African Studies, University of the Free State, Bloemfontein, South Africa.

Yul Derek Davids Democracy, Governance & Service Delivery (DGSD), Human Sciences Research Council (HSRC), Durban, South Africa.

Gilbert Fokou Democracy, Governance, and Service Delivery Research Programme, Human Sciences Research Council, Cape Town, South Africa.

Steven L. Gordon Democracy, Governance & Service Delivery (DGSD), Human Sciences Research Council (HSRC), Durban, South Africa.

Tim G. B. Hart Economic Performance and Development, Human Sciences Research Council, Pretoria, South Africa. Department of Sociology and Social Anthropology, Stellenbosch University, Matieland, South Africa.

Isaac Khambule School of Built Environment and Development Studies, University of KwaZulu-Natal, Durban, South Africa.

Dirk Kotze Department of Political Studies, UNISA, Pretoria, South Africa.

Joleen Steyn Kotze Democracy, Governance and Service Delivery Research Programme, Human Science Research Council, Pretoria, South Africa. Centre for Gender and African Studies, University of the Free State, Bloemfontein, South Africa.

Terri Maggott Centre for Social Change, University of Johannesburg, South Africa.

Amarone Nomdo Democracy, Governance, and Service Delivery Research Programme, Human Sciences Research Council, Cape Town, South Africa.

Benjamin J. Roberts Democracy, Governance & Service Delivery (DGSD), Human Sciences Research Council (HSRC), Durban, South Africa.

Carin Runciman Centre for Social Change, University of Johannesburg, South Africa.

Collette Schulz-Herzenberg Department of Political Science, Stellenbosch University, Matieland, South Africa.

Babalwa Siswana Democracy, Governance, and Service Delivery Research Programme, Human Sciences Research Council, Cape Town, South Africa.

Jarè Struwig Democracy, Governance & Service Delivery (DGSD), Human Sciences Research Council (HSRC), Durban, South Africa.

Introduction: Quo Vadis? Reflections on the 2019 South African General Elections

Joleen Steyn Kotze and Narnia Bohler-Muller

The 2019 General Elections marked a watershed in South Africa's political landscape. The ANC under the banner of a narrative of *regeneration* and *getting back on the moral path* dipped below the 60% mark for the first time in South Africa's democratic history. Just a mere three years before the General Elections, the ANC suffered punishing losses in the 2016 Local Government Elections where the party lost power in three major South African municipalities, that of Tshwane, Johannesburg, and Nelson Mandela Bay. The party only managed to secure 55.68% of the vote in this election compared to 63.65% in the 2011 Local Government Elections (IEC 2016, 2011).

This decline in electoral support for the party may be interpreted as a degeneration of the ANC through the loss of its moral stature, the erosion of its integrity and disillusionment with its performance as a governing party.[1] It could also potentially signal the decline of party dominance, an enduring characteristic of South Africa's democratic political system. The procedural integrity of South Africa's democracy has been undermined by an increase in corruption,[2] a lack of accountability[3] extending to lower levels of government where state resources have been used to fund party paraphernalia during Local Government Elections in some municipalities[4], demonstrating that the line between party and state has become increasingly blurred.

As South Africa marks 25 years of democracy, one cannot ignore that the *Dream of '94* (Steyn-Kotze 2017) remains elusive for ordinary South Africans. South Africa remains a highly divided society, in terms of class, race and gender. Two seemingly enduring legacies of apartheid characterise the socio-political realities of today: the seeming permanence of apartheid-constructed socio-political identities, and the concentration of poverty amongst the black African population. In assessing progress made towards achieving a non-racial, non-sexist South Africa, the ANC (2012) noted, 'a major policy weakness in the last 18 years has been a failure to significantly transform the colonial industrial structure and ownership of the economy'. This lack of transformation is rooted in the view that the implementation of its policy agenda has not sufficiently delivered on the vision of South Africa as captured in the Freedom Charter. In the 2019 General Elections campaign, issues of economic redress through a narrative of (radical economic) transformation, land redistribution, and a commitment to economic justice dominated the electoral narrative and messaging in political parties' electoral campaigns.

The run-up to the 2019 General Elections campaign was characterised by factionalism within the ANC that culminated with the reluctant resignation of Jacob Zuma as president of the country. In what can be seen as yet another *battle for the soul of the ANC*, the 2018 ANC Elective Conference marked a turning point for the party. In highly contested internal party leadership elections, Cyril Ramaphosa rose to become the new ANC president. He campaigned on the promise of a new dawn, a return to moral stature, and a need to regain the trust of ordinary South Africans following Zuma's *nine wasted years*. Under Ramaphosa's leadership, the ANC had daunting task a mere five months before South Africans went to the polls; rebuilding trust in the ANC brand with Cyril Ramaphosa as the face of the campaign to *get South Africa back on track* under his presidency.

Similarly, South Africa's largest opposition party, the Democratic Alliance succumbed to factional politics, most notably in the City of Cape Town, the proverbial crown jewel in the its electoral narrative of good governance and the delivery of social and economic goods to *create a better life* for all South Africans (Prevost, Steyn-Kotze, and Wright 2014). Internal party politics saw a breakdown in the relationship between City of Cape Town mayor, Patricia De Lille, who became increasingly vocal on issues of corruption. Further tensions arose as *party bosses* sought to entrench control of the DA to the detriment of free expression and debate on the political and policy trajectory of the political party, and a seemingly embedded culture of racism that effectively silenced, excluded, and undermined black leadership – and the rise of black leadership – in the party. Following a very public internal battle, 'Aunty Pat' left the DA to create the GOOD Party to contest the 2019 General Elections, similar to the birth of her Independent Democrats fifteen years earlier. This move divided the support base the DA counted on to increase their share of the vote in the 2019 General Elections. And, in a surprise turn of events, the conservative Freedom Front Plus rose to become the fourth largest party in Parliament. Many speculate the uncertainty around land coupled with the internal dynamics of the DA, saw the conservative vote find a new political home in this electoral season. However, the re-emergence of Helen Zille and the exit of Mmusi Maimane as the leader of the DA could lead to a return to the fold of those voters lost to the FF+, but may also lead to an exodus of progressive black voters who are seeking a new political home.

The EFF went to the polls under a banner of controversy, most notably around the VBS scandal, regarded as the *most unsophisticated bank heist* (Mantshantsha 2018). Key allegations centre around family members of the EFF's leaders, most notably Julius Malema and Floyd Shivambu, who are said to have received approximately R20 million (Mantshantsha 2018).

In addition to alleged personal benefit EFF leadership capitalised on from the VBS looting scandal, it emerged that

> … the ANC fired 14 mayors in municipalities across Limpopo and the North West for allegedly instructing officials to deposit municipal funds with the bank (illegally). Some municipalities lost as much as R234m as VBS ran out of cash and went into business rescue in March. In Gauteng, the ANC is said to be pressuring two mayors to resign, as it is illegal to deposit municipal funds with a mutual bank. The ANC has also had to admit it benefited to the tune of more than R2m in sponsorships by Vele and VBS, which hired buses to ferry members to its December 2017 elective conference.

The EFF dismissed the VBS scandal as 'propoganda' (Head 2018), and went to the polls under the populist banner of jobs and land (now!). It would seem that the VBS scandal did not diminish the electoral performance of the party as the EFF was the only political party, second to the Freedom Front Plus, to increase its share of the vote from just over 6% in 2014 to almost 11% in 2019.

Central issues that characterised the 2019 General Elections campaign were job creation, economic reinvigoration to create a vibrant economy, unemployment reduction, poverty alleviation and eradication, land redistribution, the comabtting of corruption, and restoring trust in political parties, government institutions and to some extent, democracy itself. This particular election came at a time where South Africa faced multiple challenges: a stagnant economy; the increasing politicisation of race; protests around the delivery of basic services; increased corruption and a flagrant lack of accountability (most notably under the Zuma Administration); and pressure to restore investor and international confidence in the future developmental trajectory of South Africa. This election, for us, signalled the first time the ANC could no longer rely solely on their rich liberation history. Citizens were no longer interested in rhetoric, but wanted to see concrete socio-economic change for the better. There is no doubt that party loyalty will not necessarily remain the deciding factor in future elections as South Africans become more *issue based* voters.

In this special issue we consider the fate of South Africa's electoral democracy. What lessons can we tease out from the 2019 General Elections; the campaign, voter turn-out, electoral behaviour, the construction and meaning of land, the decline in voter participation, protest and voting choices, lessons we can draw from coalitions moving forward, and our unique approach to '*electing*' a president. We engage the question *quo vadis South Africa*, with a focus on South Africa's electoral democracy and its future.

Cherrel Africa considers a very important, but often neglected question in South African electoral politics: Do campaign matter? She argues that in a one-party dominant context, such as that of South Africa, political parties campaign fiercely, but given the racialised nature of electoral politics, voters may not necessarily be seen as active participants when political parties campaign. They are ' ... guided primarily by symbolic or identity concerns ... ', a view that is strongly challenged, as Africa notes. Examining the campaigning strategies of the ANC, the DA, the IFP and the NP (before its eventual demise in 2004) since the birth of democracy, Africa concludes that political parties need high levels of credibility to perform at the polls, but, consistency in their political message over time and internal party dynamics also matters. In answering whether campaigns do matter in a South African electoral context, she notes the complex interplay between interparty political dynamics, context, the crux of the party's campaign message when engaging voters, and how voters perceive political leaders and the party. She concludes that South African ' ... voters emerge as active agents consuming relevant political information ... ', and as such, ' ... we should pay far more attention to the quality of choices offered to voters via campaigns ... [especially] the extent to which they provide voters with the basis to make informed choices and scrutinise the conditions under which campaigns enhance the quality of democracy'.

We often draw a correlation between what Booysen (2007, 2012) constructs as the *ballot and the brick* to engage the tension between protesting and voting in explaining the ANC's continued electoral dominance. Runciman, Bekker, and Maggot revisit this important question, which is built on the assumption that protest becomes another means of political engagement for ANC supporters, who whilst protesting against the governing party, will continue to vote for the party because of political loyalty. Runciman *et. al.* demonstrate, however, that the ANC has suffered electoral loss when protest activity has increased, and that party loyalty may be a less binding factor to sustained electoral support. Importantly, Runciman *et. al.* demonstrate that while the ANC ' ... remains a party of choice ... ' for voters who had and had not engaged in protests, ' ... opposition parties are, to a greater extent, characterised by voting protestors'.

Perhaps one of the most emotive issues in post-apartheid South Africa is that of land. Indeed, most political parties launched their campaign with either land as the key focus of their messaging or as an important discursive component in the campaign narrative. In their article, Bank and Hart engage land as belonging and place-making in contemporary South Africa. Drawing on an anthropological perspective, Bank and Hart demonstrate that political messaging political parties use in constructing land reform does not necessarily resonate with the electorate. Land and its meaning is complex, and as such, Bank and Hart conclude that one cannot debate land as development without engaging the meaning of land and place-making for people. This may go some way to explaining why, despite the loud political and media rhetoric, citizens are not as concerned about land as they are about unemployment, crime and corruption (South African Social Attitudes Survey).

Following the 2016 Local Government Elections, commentary on coalition government and cooperation between political parties emerged as a key scholarly conversation. This is not surprising given that none of the parties could attain an outright majority in three key metropolitan municipalities, that of Tshwane, Johannesburg and Nelson Mandela Bay. The DA was able to form coalition governments in these three metropoles, but not without much instability and, at times, administrative and political paralysis in the local councils. Khambule, Nomdo, Siswana, and Fokou provide a compelling analysis of coalition politics at local government level and expand on lessons learned. Central to their analysis is the strategies opposition parties use in structuring coalitions and informal partnerships as a means of coexistence to challenge the politically dominant position of the ANC. Khambule *et. al.* conclude that if the possibility of a national coalition government arises in future General Elections, consensus-based governance needs to be characteristic of political cooperation between political parties. If opposition parties are unable to draw on coexistence as a political strategy to challenge ANC electoral dominance, subsequent political paralysis could undermine accountability.

The 2019 General Elections saw political parties use the faces of their leaders to entice the electorate to cast their vote for the leader *as president*, most notably Ramaphosa, Maimane and Malema. Kotze provides a timely analysis of South Africa's unique approach to 'electing' a president. He rightly notes that research on the role of the president in South Africa is severely limited, and as such, given the 2019 election campaign that called for South Africans to *elect their president*, Kotze demonstrates that a *president is elected* not by the electorate, but rather by the internal party dynamics and a balance of power between political parties in Parliament. The Constitution guides all of these processes of a representative democracy. For Kotze, the electoral system shapes the relationship between the executive and the legislature, giving Parliament substantial power that shapes ' ... a relationship of direct presidential accountability to Parliament and gives an unusually strong combination of powers to Parliament to remove the President from office'. In addition, Kotze demonstrates that opposition parties tended to compete for the role of the Speaker in Parliament as opposed to the presidency because ' ... a symbiotic relationship exists between their party position and government positions'. Kotze concludes that while there may be an appetite to elect the South African presidential directly, it could potential undermine the oversight role Parliament plays over the Executive; ' ... thereby making the President less accountable and more powerful'. A number of experts, however, are calling for electoral reform to enable more direct accountability to constituencies.

Voter apathy, a politically disengaged youth, and voter abstention proved an issue of great concern in the 2019 General Elections. Many reasons are proffered to explain the decline in voter participation in General and Local Government Elections. These range from disillusionment due to anorexic service delivery to a lack of trust in political parties, which has been declining over the past 25 years. These issues, coupled with an increasingly disengaged electorate, proved the outcome of the 2019 General Elections to be less predictable than in the past. In previous elections, the outcome was generally premised on the view of *by how much the ANC would win*. Following the 2016 Local Government Election and the ANC's sharp electoral decline, the outcome of the 2019 General Election focused on the question of *whether or by what margin the ANC would win*.

Schulz-Herzenberg engages the question of electoral uncertainty in her contribution focussing on the decline of partisanship in South Africa. She demonstrates that a decline in partisan support over the last 25 years contributed to the uncertainty that shaped electoral behaviour in the 2019 General Elections. An increase in abstention, voters shifting their vote to another party, vote splitting, and late vote decisions, were key indicators of ' ... shrinkage in partisan loyalties ... ', which culminated in an unpredictability. This unpredictability was shaped by more short-term political concerns as opposed to ' ... long-standing, traditional party loyalties'.

Similarly, Roberts, Struwig, Gordon, and Davids engage voter turn-out and disengagement that was particularly pronounced in the 2019 General Elections. They interrogate factors that may impact on voter behaviour of decided voters, abstainers, and undisclosed and undecided voters. Partisan political attachment emerged as a key motivator to get voters to the polls, and party attachment and feelings of closeness to a political ideology do indeed matter in motivating voters to cast a vote. However, feeling close to a political party is not the *only* motivator to go to the polls. Other factors include a sense of civic duty, interest in politics, and a perceptions of efficacy. Indeed, Roberts *et. al.* conclude that 'compared to decided voters, abstainers are less interested in politics, less convinced that their vote makes a difference or that the elected are responsive to their needs, and possess a weaker sense of moral obligation to vote'.

Another compounding factor that impacts on voter turn-out is age, and as Roberts *et. al.* show, younger voters are less motivated to cast their votes. South Africa's electoral democracy will be negatively affected by continued disengagement: ' … if indecision combines with a mounting sense of psychological disengagement, there remains a real possibility that this could fuel the rising tendency towards electoral abstention in future'. Race continues to play a prominent role in voter behaviour, but age and educational attainment also matter as Roberts *et. al.* demonstrate. In looking towards electoral participation in the future, the authors conclude that questions of political efficacy, trust and accountability will shape the development of political culture and significantly impact on South Africa's electoral future.

The 2019 General Elections proved to be a turning point in the country's electoral history. There is a real possibility that we see the beginning of the decline of a dominant ANC in the electoral playing field. However, this does not mean that opposition political parties are able to capitalise on the declining support for the ANC. Instead of casting a vote for opposition parties, voters abstain from participating in elections. This could be related to the political messaging and campaign rhetoric that the opposition draws on in order to entice voters to cast a ballot for them. Yet, it would appear that campaign rhetoric and political messaging do not necessarily resonate with the political intentions or views of South Africa's electorate. Simply put, how effective are political parties in capturing a disillusioned voter? It is indeed time to reflect on South Africa's democratic journey. This issue is the first step towards looking at some key dynamics that shaped *Elections 2019*. However, there are some caveats. How do we explain the increase of support for the populist EFF in the midst of a major corruption scandal? Do the internal factional battles of the DA that impacted on their electoral performance show us that the official opposition may now be a party in search of an identity? Has the ANC outlived its ability to capitalise on its liberation credentials? How will our electoral democracy progress? Will we follow a path of apathy that opens the space for populist politics as seen in other countries?

Quo Vadis South Africa?

Notes

1. Afrobarometer time series demonstrates that trust in the ANC remains precarious. One quarter of South Africans in 2002 did not trust the ruling party at all. By 2018, this sentiment increased to 36%. When compared to data on whether South Africans trust the president, one notes a correlation between decline in trust for the ruling party and trust in the president. In 1999 37% of South Africans indicated a measure of trust in the president, and by 2018 only 30% said they trusted the president a little. Of interest is that in 1999 15% of South Africans did not trust the president at all. By 2018 27% of South Africans expressed this sentiment (See Afrobarometer 2019a, 2019b).
2. There have been various corruption scandals in South Africa's democratic history. The most notorious scandal is government spending in excess of R200 million on upgrades to former President Zuma's Nkandla homestead which included a swimming pool and an amphitheatre. The Zondo Commission, a judicial commission of enquiry, is currently investigating allegations of state capture and fraud in the public sector (https://www.sastatecapture.org.za). This commission's mandate is to 'inquire, make findings, report on, and make recommendations … '

following the former Public Protector, Thuli Madonsela's report entitled *State of Capture*, which investigated

> … complaints of alleged improper and unethical conduct by the president [Jacob Zuma] and other state functionaries relating to alleged improper relationships and involvement of the Gupta family in the removal and appointment of ministers and directors of State Owned Entities resulting in improper and possibly corrupt award of state contracts and benefits to the Gupta family's businesses. (Public Protector 2016)

3. Many municipalities and departments are unable to achieve a clean audit status. The Auditor-General regularly finds evidence of maladministration, irregular spending, and wasteful expenditure. It has also become common practice for government tenders to be awarded to companies in which government officials have a direct stake and as such are able to unduly benefit. This has now become known as 'tenderperneurship'. Key issues highlighted by the Auditor General include corruption, poor leadership, and unqualified and incompetent officials who occupy key leadership position (Nombembe 2012).

4. See http://www.heraldlive.co.za/metro-pays-for-anc-items.

References

Afrobarometer. 2019a. "Trust in the Ruling Party." Accessed January 12, 2019. http://www.afrobarometer.org/online-data-analysis/analyse-online.

Afrobarometer. 2019b. "Trust in the President." Accessed January 12, 2019. http://www.afrobarometer.org/online-data-analysis/analyse-online.

ANC. 2012. "A Second Transition? Building a National Democratic Society and a Balance of Forces." Accessed May 13, 2016. http://www.anc.org.za/docs/discus/2012/transition.pdf.

Head, T. 2018. "EFF Responds to Allegations That They Looted R1.8 Million from VBS Bank." Accessed November 4, 2019. https://www.thesouthafrican.com/news/eff-response-vbs-bank-scorpio/.

IEC. 2011. "Results Summary 2011 Local Government Elections: All Ballots." Accessed September 1, 2017. http://www.elections.org.za/content/LGEPublicReports/197/Detailed%20Results/National.pdf.

IEC. 2016. "Results Summary – All Ballots: 2016 Local Government Elections." Accessed September 2, 2017. http://www.elections.org.za/content/LGEPublicReports/402/Detailed%20Results/National.pdf.

Mantshantsha, S. 2018. "Scandal of the Year: VBS – a Most Unsophisticated Bank Heist." *Business Day Online*, December 21. Accessed November 4, 2019. https://www.businesslive.co.za/fm/features/cover-story/2018-12-21-scandal-of-the-year-vbs--a-most-unsophisticated-bank-heist/.

Prevost, G., J. Steyn-Kotze, and B. Wright. 2014. "'The Battle for the Bay': The 2011 Local Government Elections in the Nelson Mandela Bay Municipality." *Politikon* 41 (1): 59–83.

Public Protector. 2016. "The State of Capture: *A Report of the Public Protector*." Accessed January 30, 2019. http://saflii.org/images/329756472-State-of-Capture.pdf.

Steyn-Kotze, J. 2017. *Delivering an Elusive Dream of Democracy: Lessons from Nelson Mandela Bay*. Stellenbosch: African Sun Media.

Susan, Booysen 2007. "With the Ballot and the Brick: The Politics of Service Delivery in South Africa." *Progress in Development Studies* 7 (1): 21–32.

Susan, Booysen. 2012. "'The Ballot and the Brick' Enduring but Under Duress." In *Local Elections in South Africa: People, Parties, Politics*, edited by Susan Booysen. Stellenbosch: SUN Press.

Do Election Campaigns Matter in South Africa? An Examination of Fluctuations in Support for the ANC, DA, IFP and NNP 1994–2019

Cherrel Africa

ABSTRACT
Election campaigns in democratic South Africa have been eventful affairs. Despite the electoral dominance of the African National Congress (ANC) since 1994, political parties in South Africa have campaigned fiercely. At face value then, it would appear that election campaigns constitute an integral and valuable part of South Africa's democratic system. Yet, at the same time, following the 1994 elections and given the racialized dynamics of South Africa's electoral landscape, a view has emerged that does not regard South African voters as active agents consuming relevant political information. This view, which sees voters as guided primarily by symbolic or identity concerns, was strongly challenged by several analysts. However, the question as to whether election campaigns are relevant in the South African context still remains. In this article, I examine the relevance of campaigning in the South African context. I focus on the African National Congress (ANC), the Democratic Party (DP)/Democratic Alliance (DA), Inkatha Freedom Party (IFP) and the National Party (NP) /New National Party (NNP). I argue that campaign messaging and party credibility are important contributors of performance at the polls. Inconsistent and contradictory campaign messages, poor decisions and destructive behaviour had substantial repercussions for parties at the polls.

Introduction

The central question addressed in this paper is 'Do election campaigns matter in South Africa?' Since 1994, the ANC has won every national election with a clear majority. However, there have been interesting fluctuations in party support. The DA experienced a slow but steady upward trajectory from 1994 to 2014 and then declined slightly in 2019. The IFP has been on a downward trajectory since 1994 with a steady decline in its vote share, although its support increased marginally in 2019. The NNP's demise represents the most dramatic shift in political fortunes. I ask whether an examination of campaigning is able to enhance our understanding of the fluctuations in the support of the ANC, DA, IFP and NNP.

More specifically I examine the consistency of campaign messaging over time as well as the internal congruency of the messages. Given the need to examine the campaigns historically rather than focusing on one particular point in time, I chose to focus on the ANC, DA, IFP and NNP. Ideally the Congress of the People (COPE) and Economic Freedom Fighters (EFF) would also have been included, however given space constraints, I chose to focus on 'older parties' that contested in 1994 to enable a more thorough longitudinal analysis.

Campaign relevance: the debate on behavioural motivations of South African voters

Following the 1994 elections and considering the racialized dynamics of South Africa's electoral landscape, a view emerged that did not regard South African voters as active agents consuming relevant political information. Schlemmer (1994, 162), for example, relegated voters to being overwhelmed by 'some very vague, pervasive and powerful symbolic features'. Following the 1999 General Elections, Giliomee, Myburgh, and Schlemmer (2001, 162) argued that, while they were not suggesting 'that African voters are motivated by crude racism' … 'the outcomes have all the effects of racial solidarity in political behaviour'. According to Mattes and Piombo (2001, 102), prevailing analyses of voter motivations in South Africa see voting as a desire to express communal solidarity with political parties, or as a means to maintain or obtain government patronage. The view which sees voters as guided primarily by symbolic or identity concerns was strongly challenged by several analysts. The counter-argument (see for example Eldridge and Seekings 1995; Mattes 1995; Mattes and Piombo 2001) is that voting behaviour is complex with many interlinked factors having important effects on partisan support.

If those who argue that election outcomes in South Africa are essentially pre-determined by the demographic composition of the electorate are correct, then what role can campaigns really play in the South African context? Embedded in the perspective that sees voting primarily as an expression of racial solidarity is the idea that campaigns can be of little value in the South African context. Identity-based interpretations of voting behaviour leave little room for information and campaigns to play a role in voters' decisions, other than to reinforce racial modes of behaviour. Even the more nuanced analysis of Friedman has important ramifications for election campaigns and the way parties convey messages to voters. Friedman (2004, 3) argues that 'voter preferences are shaped by considerations other than competing technical solutions to economic and social problems', and to 'claim that a ballot will be decided by this or that "issue" is to misunderstand the electorate and the campaign'.

The focus of these analyses has been on the demographic features and the decision-making process of the voter. However, as Sniderman (2000, 68–69) argues, the focus should be shifted from 'citizens as choosers' to political institutions as 'the organizers of political choice'. While voters' decision-making processes are critically important, they are only one part of the electoral equation; political parties and the choices they offer constitute the other part. These two sides of the electoral equation meet up in a particular historical economic and social context where national, provincial and local developments play a role. Little attention has been paid to the quality of the 'supply side' of election campaigns, i.e. the quality of choices offered to voters. It is therefore important that micro-level analyses of voters be supplemented with systematic research on the quality of information and choices offered to voters by political parties.

Election campaigns: credibility, consistency and congruency and impact on party support

A good quality campaign is characterised by several dimensions including the calibre of the message content as well as the credibility and accessibility of the communication channels. However, it is beyond the scope of this paper to comprehensively assess each campaign on each dimension. Instead I focus on the consistency of campaign messaging over time as well as the congruence of messaging. I also look at contextual factors and internal party dynamics because they affect perceptions of trustworthiness which in turn impacts the way messaging is received by the electorate.

Campaign messages should be credible, compelling, internally congruent and consistent over time. While voters need competing information to make choices between parties, each party should:

(1) Keep their campaign messages short, simple and direct (Schnur 1999);
(2) Ensure that messages are consistent; in other words, not at odds with each other (Weaver 1996); and,
(3) Integrate their messages by means of a carefully devised campaign theme (Marquette 1996).

According to Marquette (1996, 151–153), a theme should rarely change and should fit all salient issues into an overarching message and should focus on unifying rather than divisive concerns. Marquette argues that the best themes are often emotive as well as urgent, and, once established must be used to formulate a clear and simple thematic statement.

The trustworthiness of the source plays an important role in the persuasiveness of a message. According to Newman and Perloff (2004, 27), 'persuasion experts unquestionably agree that the source of a message can significantly influence political attitudes'. Lupia and McCubbins (2000, 48) also assert that 'without trust there is no persuasion, without persuasion, people cannot learn from others and without learning from others it is very difficult for citizens to learn what they need to know'. The logical extension of these arguments is that voters will be less likely to pay attention to campaign messages coming from a party or leader they see as untrustworthy. Thus, campaigning is of little worth if the recipients of the campaign see the messages as 'tainted' by the characteristics of the source of the message. Messages from an untrustworthy source will either be interpreted through a negative mental schema or simply ignored. The result will be rejection or limited engagement with the substance of the message.

Farrell and Web (2000, 124) also emphasise that

> it is one thing to think that a politician has a good policy for alleviating unemployment, but it is quite another to believe that he or she is likely to (a) keep their word if returned to office or (b) prove competent to follow through on the promised intent of the policy

and 'therefore it is rational and important for any organisation campaigning for office to concentrate part of its efforts on fostering a reputation for integrity, veracity and competence'. Voters can use their prior knowledge and experience of political parties to enhance their assessment of the information provided by parties during the campaign period. Examples of questions voters could ask could include: Is the message consistent with the party's previous actions? Why should it be believed? Is it worthwhile to pay attention and store the information? How should the message be interpreted?

Clearly then a political party can expect to perform well if they have high levels of credibility (and are therefore trusted by voters) *and* the party weaves its campaign messages together into a well-blended and internally consistent theme, congruent with previous campaigns. This does not suggest that a party should stick rigidly to a theme or message if the context suggests that a change in messaging is required. At the very least there needs to be continuity in the approach.

Credibility, consistency and congruency: election campaigns, political developments and impact on party support in South Africa 1994–2019

What campaign messaging did political parties in South Africa present to voters since 1994? Were they consistent over time? Were the messages congruent or in contradiction with each other? Furthermore, how did the messaging intersect with the political context as well as the behaviour and strategic choices of political parties? Can we infer an impact on party fortunes? It is to this task I now turn.

The ANC

Since 1994 the ANC has won every national election with a clear majority. As demonstrated in Table 1, the ANC's national vote share increased from 62.7% in 1994, to 66.4% in 1999 to 69.7% in 2004. In 2009, the ANC's vote share at national level dropped to 65.9%. In 2014, the ANC's support slipped further obtaining 62.2% of the national vote. The ANC's worst national performance was in the 2019 elections. For the first time it received less than 60% by obtaining 57.5% at the national level.

The ANC took control of seven provinces in the 1994 Founding and 1999 General Elections. In 2004 the ANC obtained a plurality of the vote in the Western Cape and took control of the province (which was under NP rule in 1994 and 1999). The party also gained substantial support in KwaZulu-Natal in 2004, obtaining 47% of the provincial vote. In 2009, the ANC lost ground in all provinces, particularly the Western Cape, which the DA won through an outright majority. This was counterbalanced through gains in KwaZulu-Natal which it won with an outright majority of 63%. Indeed the downward trend in ANC support from 2009 would have been worse had it not been for the increased support in KwaZulu-Natal. In 2019 the ANC lost support in all the provinces, narrowly winning Gauteng with 50.2% of the provincial vote and 54.2% in KwaZulu-Natal. Support for the ANC also declined to 28.6% in the Western Cape (Chilenga-Butao 2019, 191–192).

The ANC's campaign messaging has showed significant consistency since the 1994 Founding Elections. Not only has the ANC's campaign messaging been consistent across elections, its messaging has been subsumed under a clear overarching campaign

Table 1. National results of the ANC, DA, IFP and NNP, 1994–2019[a].

Party	Percentage of votes					
	1994	1999	2004	2009	2014	2019
African National Congress	62.7	66.4	69.7	65.9	62.2	57.5
Democratic Party/Democratic Alliance	1.7	9.6	12.4	16.7	22.2	20.8
Inkatha Freedom Party	10.5	8.6	6.9	4.6	2.4	3.4
National Party/New National Party	20.4	6.9	1.7	NA	NA	NA

[a] National percentages cited in the balance of this article are also drawn from Schultz-Herzenberg (2019).
Source: Schultz-Herzenberg (2019).

theme. It has over time woven together its campaign messages into a simple, well-blended and internally coherent theme. Variation came in the extent to which the party contrasted itself with the opposition parties and negative or attack campaigning occurred outside of the formal campaign material. As Butler (2009, 43) shows, the ANC has proven to be a formidable campaigner built on a methodical and professional approach to campaigning. In its formal messaging the ANC has stuck to its script, irrespective of the political context and internal challenges. As will be discussed in more detail below, the political context changed dramatically in South Africa between 2004 and 2009. At the same time the ANC's credibility and perceptions of trust in the party declined dramatically due to changes in the political context and internal ANC dynamics. The ANC's messaging served it well in 1994, 1999 and 2004; however, from 2009 the messaging alone was unpersuasive to voters. The ANC's messaging started to ring hollow after the changes in the political context and the destructive path taken by the ANC in 2009.

Since 1994 the main thrust of the ANC's campaign has been that it is the only legitimate party that had the competence to improve the lives of ordinary people in South Africa. A key message related to its partnership with 'the people' in pursuing this goal. The theme of 'A better life for all', the presentation of the role of the ANC in ending apartheid as well as the importance of contracts and partnerships with various social actors form a golden thread that occurs throughout the campaigns of the ANC. This is evident in their election manifesto and campaign slogans. ANC posters typically feature its presidential candidate. Since 1994, the ANC has run its campaign around the following key tenets:

(1) Outlining the apartheid past and the ANC's contribution to overcoming apartheid;
(2) The achievements of the ANC since coming into power, in particular emphasising the fact that the achievements since the advent of democracy, delivered by the ANC, should be celebrated;
(3) Acknowledging challenges and shortcomings in relation to their goals and providing reasons for them;
(4) Drawing attention to the ANC's unique strength, experience and commitment to deal with the pressing social and economic challenges facing South Africa; and,
(5) Setting out their future plans for dealing with their stated goals.

With the founding elections of 1994 the ANC focused on their role in securing freedom and the end of apartheid. These were encapsulated in the slogan *Now is the time*, with posters that read, *Mandela for President: The People's Choice*. The campaign also included an 'Attack, Contrast and Endorsement' component which consisted of attacks on the NP and contrasted the ANC's Reconstruction and Development Programme (RDP) to the NP's purported lack of a plan as well as the endorsement of the ANC by community leaders at rallies and in the press (Eldridge and Seekings 1995, 15). Attention was given to the NP's past in terms of forced removals, corruption and involvement in third force activities, such as covert operations undertaken by the NP. As Mattes (1995, 12) argues, in 1994 voters overwhelmingly made judgements about the perceived responsibility of the ANC in securing their political freedom and dignity.

After the 1994 Founding Elections, voters watched the country change from a racist, deeply divided, authoritarian society into a more humane and democratic one. The

Mandela-era ushered in a new constitutional framework and by 1999 South Africa's government had undergone a fundamental and radical overhaul (Calland 1999, 1). In 1999, a theme of optimism was evident in slogans and press advertisements which stated 'our fight for change is showing results' and 'together we can speed up change' (Lodge 1999, 71). The 1999 manifesto title page was captioned '1999 manifesto: Forward to 5 years of accelerating change, partnership with the people, building a new patriotism and working together for a better Africa and world'. Thabo Mbeki, in his message accompanying the manifesto, emphasised that 'the days of darkness' of apartheid were over and that even greater change needed to be advanced through social discipline, as well as the advancement of national unity and reconciliation (African National Congress 1999). ANC election posters, featuring a smiling Mbeki, simply read 'Mbeki for President' and 'Vote ANC: A better life for all'.

In 2004 the ANC ran its campaign around the theme of celebrating ten years of democracy. The party highlighted its achievements, acknowledged its shortcomings and emphasised its strength, experience and commitment. The main thrust of the ANC's 2004 campaign was that it was the only legitimate party that had the competence to improve the lives of ordinary people in South Africa. A key message was its partnership with 'the people' in pursuing this goal. The message that 'the tide has turned' became institutionalised and indicated to voters that the ANC-led government was successful in ushering in change in South Africa (Booysen 2005, 131). Data from the Comparative National Elections Project (CNEP) cited by Africa (2008) reveals that in 2004 two thirds (66%) of the South African electorate saw the ANC as being trustworthy 'always' or 'most of the time' compared to majorities who saw all opposition parties as being trustworthy 'only some of the time' or 'never'. Additionally it was not only people who identified with the ANC that said the ANC was trustworthy. Among independent voters, a majority of 54% felt that the ANC was trustworthy. It should hardly be surprising that between 1994 and 2004, the ANC was on an upward trajectory at the national level.

Following the 2004 General Elections and in the lead up to the 2009 General Elections many events affected the credibility of the ANC. The fact that Jacob Zuma was able to ascend to the presidency of the ANC and then the presidency of the country despite the controversy linked to him severely tarnished the party. Zuma was asked to relinquish his role as deputy-president in 2005 after Durban businessman, Schabir Shaik, was convicted on two counts of corruption and one of fraud relating to alleged irregular financial dealings with him. This, as Southall (2009, 3) argues, left Zuma with his party platform from which to campaign for the presidency of the ANC to be decided at the ANC's 52nd national conference, known as the Polokwane conference. The Polokwane conference represented a turning point for the ANC. Despite impending fraud and corruption charges, Zuma was elected as the ANC's new president, defeating Mbeki in his bid to remain party president. As Booysen (2009, 90) observes, the ANC 'entered a spiral of contestation between Jacob Zuma and Thabo Mbeki centering on issues of succession and incumbency'. The culmination of this contestation was the removal of Mbeki as president of the Republic. This storm of controversial internal ANC processes was televised to the South African public. According to Butler (2009, 69), this unprecedented defeat of an incumbent ANC president was followed by a wave of instability where office-bearers were 'recalled' and perceived Mbeki-loyalists were purged. The 2009 campaign was therefore destined to be a more difficult one for the ANC (Butler 2009, 66).

In 2009, the party continued to focus on previous themes and projected a positive message that focused on a social contract. The manifesto was entitled 'Working Together We Can Do More' and posters with a smiling Zuma simply read 'Vote ANC'. Despite Zuma being at the centre of much of the challenges facing the ANC, in 2014 the ANC campaigned under the theme 'A Better Life For All: Together We Move South Africa Forward' and placed Zuma on its campaign billboards. Even though the ANC continued to run high-quality campaigns, the messages were 'tainted' because voters no longer saw the ANC as trustworthy.

After the 2009 General Elections, growing economic, social and political challenges resulted in widespread protest action. This included what has become known as the 'Marikana Massacre' which saw 34 mineworkers shot and killed by police officers in August 2012. The ANC increasingly received strong internal criticism, so much so that ANC stalwarts, Ronnie Kasrils and Nozizwe Madlala-Routledge, among others, embarked on the 'Sidikiwe, Vukane – We are fed up' campaign, to either spoil one's vote or vote for a small party. The party also faced condemnation from its alliance partner, the Congress of South African Trade Unions (Cosatu), for the rollout of e-tolls on highways in Gauteng. Additionally, the National Union of Metalworkers of SA (NUMSA) decided not to endorse the ANC in the 2014 General Elections. Nevertheless in 2014 the ANC stuck to its campaign script. The 2014 manifesto was entitled 'A people's contract to create work and fight poverty' stated that it was time to 'celebrate freedom'.

Zuma's dismissal of the finance minister Nhlanhla Nene in December 2015 was another tipping point which further tarnished perceptions of the ANC. After the South African currency, the Rand, plummeted and Zuma faced strong criticism for this decision, he was forced to reassign the newly appointed Finance Minister to another position four days later and appoint Pravin Gordhan as the new Finance Minister. Again, senior ANC members and past party leaders publicly criticised Zuma and supported calls by civil society organisations and the opposition for his resignation. To add to this in March 2016, the Constitutional Court ruled that Zuma had failed to uphold the constitution when he ignored the Public Protector's recommendation to repay a portion of public funds used to upgrade his private residence Nkandla in KwaZulu Natal. Zuma issued a public apology for the 'frustration and confusion' around Nkandla. In line with the Constitutional Court judgment, the National Treasury determined that Zuma needed to pay R7.8-million back to the state. Public opinion data from Afrobarometer demonstrate that Zuma lost significant citizen support over time. Their 2015 data showed a significant disapproval of the president's performance, perceptions of corruption in the Presidency were at their highest levels since Afrobarometer conducted its first survey in South Africa in 2000 while trust in President Zuma dropped by almost half between 2011 and 2015 (Afrobarometer 2015). However, while, on the one hand, much of the ANC's credibility woes related to former President Zuma, on the other hand, his support in KwaZulu Natal was most likely responsible for the increases in the province.

Jacob Zuma finally resigned as president in February 2018 after pressure from the ANC. A few days before his public resignation on broadcast on television, the ANC national executive committee (NEC), told Zuma to step down or face a vote of no confidence in parliament, which had been tabled by the EFF. Four commissions of inquiry related to the abuse of state resources had begun to reveal the damage inflicted on critical state-owned institutions as well some of the patronage networks that existed between political leaders and the private sector under his rule. The damage to Eskom, South Africa's only power utility, which contributed to an energy crisis and led to periods of loadshedding, further undermined the stability of the nation. In the run up to the 2019 General Elections, newly elected ANC president Ramaphosa admitted that members of the ANC were responsible for and allowed state capture (ENCA 2019). Indeed, as Schultz-Herzenberg (2019, 170) demonstrates, public trust in the ANC, and in its ability to govern effectively, had plummeted.

The 2019 General Elections saw a substantial change in the overall campaign theme of the ANC, whilst maintaining degrees of consistency with previous campaigns. Rather than emphasise twenty five years of democracy, the ANC campaigned under the promise of a 'New Dawn' under Cyril Ramaphosa. The 2019 manifesto was entitled 'Let's Grow South Africa Together'. Ramaphosa campaigned under the theme *Thuma Mina*, which means 'Send Me'. He cited the lyrics of a song by struggle and music icon, Hugh Masekela when he delivered his State of the Nation Address in 2018 and the theme was carried forward in the ANC's 2019 election campaign. The purpose was to galvanise and rejuvenate South Africans. The 2019 manifesto proclaimed that 'after a difficult time, we are on the cusp of a new era of hope and renewal – the New Dawn is upon us' (African National Congress 2019). The *Thuma Mina* campaign acknowledged the ANC's wrongdoing and promised organisational renewal. The focus on a new dawn, renewal and rebuilding that would eradicate corruption can ben seen as an admission that the ANC's failed in governance as well as the negative impact of the Zuma presidency. While a difficult and perhaps risky message to deliver to the electorate, it spoke to the reality that the ANC and the country faced.

According to Schultz-Herzenberg (2019, 182) the South African Citizens Survey (SACS) found that when Ramaphosa became president at the beginning of 2018, optimism about the future of the economy rose to 61%. Schulz-Herzenberg adds that in March 2018, SACS survey data shows a remarkable increase in public approval for the president from 22% as Jacob Zuma exited office, to 64% as Cyril Ramaphosa took over. The same data showed that Ramaphosa maintained a performance rating in the mid-sixties right up to the election. Thus, as Schulz-Herzenberg argues, positive evaluations of President Cyril Ramaphosa compensated for the decline in ANC partisanship and for the party's increasing trust deficit.

The Democratic Party/Democratic Alliance

The DA started out as a minor party known as the Democratic Party (DP) who only held only 1.7% of the national vote in 1994. Indeed, Welsh (1994, 106) observes, the 1994 Founding Election was an unmitigated disaster for the DP; so much so that the leader of the DP at the time, Zach de Beer, resigned on the day the election results became available. Following his resignation, the DP under its newly-elected leader, Tony Leon, built its strategy around 'robust opposition' (Schire 2001, 142). Thereafter the DA experienced a slow but steady upward trajectory from 1994 to 2014 but dropped support in 2019. Its share of the vote increased from 9.6% in 1999 to 12.4% in 2004. In the 1999 General Elections, the DP benefitted from the votes that the NNP lost, particularly in the Western Cape. In 2009 the DA increased its vote share to 16.7% nationally and it won the Western Cape with an outright majority of 51.5%. In 2014, the DA contested the general elections with

Helen Zille as leader and consolidated its support base in the Western Cape, obtaining an increased majority of 59.4% for the provincial legislature. At national level the DA's vote share increased to 22.2%. However in 2019 the DA's support at national level dropped down slightly to 20.8% and at provincial level in the Western Cape, support declined from 59.4% to 55.4% (Chilenga-Butao 2019, 214–215).

Since 1994 the DA maintained continuity in its campaigning messaging over time, particularly through its focus on the electoral dominance of the ANC. However, at times, its messaging has suffered from a lack of internal consistency. Southall and Daniel (2005, 50) correctly argue that adopting 'an unconvincing, somewhat populist platform to attract blacks' while simultaneously campaigning 'against black economic empowerment, affirmative action and minimum wages in favour of a largely unrestricted free market and more flexible labour laws' amounted to contradictory messages. The DA emphasised that the ANC lacked competence and integrity. Using its governance track record, the DA's campaigns typically set it out as South Africa's only serious alternative to the ANC. The DA has consistently emphasised the following key messages to the electorate:

(1) That the ANC's strength should be reduced and curtailed;
(2) That the ANC's policies are weak, they had performed poorly since coming into power and had failed South Africa in a number of key areas;
(3) That the ANC lacked integrity as illustrated by high levels of corruption
(4) That South Africans face a choice between an honest, capable, modern and orderly DA and a corrupt unaccountable ANC
(5) That other opposition parties lack the capacity to deal with these issues and to tackle the ANC.
(6) That a vote for other opposition parties simply served to fracture the opposition.
(7) That the DA had experienced and was continuing to experience significant growth; and
(8) That it had a series of workable policies that would deal with South Africa's problems.

In 1994 the DP, the predecessor of the DA, opted to attack both the NP and the ANC on their records in respect of human rights and economic management. Their 1994 election manifesto, entitled 'Protecting You from the abuse of Power', focused on 'the supreme worth of every individual'. According to Welsh (1999, 91), the DP in 1996 began to fashion a new approach to election campaigns which involved the presentation of two clear competing visions: the ANC's collectivism and the DP's democratic liberalism. In 1999, the DP cast a spotlight on the dangers of one-party dominance and a concentration of power under a two-thirds ANC majority. This formed the basis of its aggressive 'fight back' campaign in the 1999 General Elections. The 1999 manifesto, entitled 'Fight Back for a Better Future: The Democratic Party's plan for South Africa', spelt out its vision for an 'opportunity society', giving extensive details of its policy positions on a range of issues.

In the 2004 General Elections, the DA highlighted the fact that it was ready to take office and presented itself as an alternative government rather than just an opposition party (Booysen 2005, 137). The primary theme used by the DA during the 2004 campaign was 'South Africa deserves better'. According to Booysen (2005, 136) the party's approach was three-pronged, starting with the projection of DA strengths and its policy alternatives, to highlighting ANC weaknesses with reference to integrity and policy, as well as the weaknesses of other opposition parties. The DA in their manifesto, entitled 'A Better South Africa', gave a detailed outline of their policy positions. The message that the DA wished to highlight through its 'Coalition for Change', entered into with the IFP, was that it could challenge the ANC for government over the next five years through a multi-identity liberal movement (Booysen 2005). The DA also highlighted the fact that a vote for the NNP was as good as a vote for the ANC. The DA benefitted from the NNP's loss of support particularly in the Western Cape. After 2004 it also benefitted from the ANC's loss of support in the Western Cape. Its credibility grew steadily using its success in the Western Cape as the basis for its campaign communications.

The DA elected Helen Zille as the new party leader in 2007 and underwent a rebranding process (Jolobe 2009, 31). In 2009, under the leadership of Zille, the DA ran a well-organised and focused campaign under the banner 'One Nation One Future'. Its message could be summarised in the slogans of two campaign posters 'Vote to win' and 'Stop Zuma' (Daniel and Southall 2009, 237). Jolobe (2009, 141) observed 'the DA was able to present a comprehensive and coherent message which drew on its experiences in oppositional politics'. In the 2014 election many of the ANC's problems (the Public Protector's report on Nkandla in particular) provided the party with rallying points for its 'Western Cape Story' campaign. Much of the DA's strategy was focused on repudiating the ANC's 'good story' message while simultaneously highlighting the party's achievements in the Western Cape. In 2014, the DA also initiated the 'Know your DA' campaign emphasised its liberal and progressive roots and played up its part in the struggle against apartheid, in particular the roles of Helen Suzman and Helen Zille (Jolobe 2014, 63). The manifesto was entitled 'Together for Change, together for jobs'.

The DA campaigned under the theme 'One South Africa for all' in 2019. In its campaign the DA appealed to South Africans to bring a better future and 'help build one South Africa for all'. In the foreword to the manifesto entitled. 'The Manifesto for Change: One South Africa for All', the DA's new leader Mmusi Maimane asserted that 'South Africans face a choice between the corrupt, old, disorderly ANC and the honest, capable, modern and orderly DA'. In addition to a strong focus on the failings of the ANC, the party continued its campaign against small parties. In a series of radio advertisements and SMS messages, Maimane claimed that 'voting for smaller parties right now is tantamount to rearranging deck chairs on the Titanic. Smaller parties will not stop our demise under the ANC and blurs our focus on the biggest threat to our democracy: one-party dominance'. In Gauteng, the DA launched the 'The ANC Is Killing SA' campaign. The names of the people who died in the Marikana massacre, the Life Esidimeni tragedy, and children who had died after falling down pit toilets with the words 'The ANC is killing us' appeared on a massive billboard.[1] Meanwhile, in the Western Cape, posters and pamphlets appealed to voters to block an EFF/ANC coalition.

There are several problems that have hindered the DA's messaging. The first relates to the negativity of its messaging. The 1999 'Fight back' campaign and the key message of 2004 that 'South Africa deserves better' could be regarded as being unnecessarily dramatic or even unpatriotic. The slogan 'Vote DA for real change' raised questions about whether the change from apartheid to democracy was artificial. As Booysen (2005) argues these slogans were interpreted 'as being polarising'. In 2019, rather than recalibrating its messaging to align with the new political context, the DA continued its attack politics. The decision to create the #TheANCIsKillingSA billboard did it no favours. Families of the

Life Esidimeni victims said it had opened old wounds. Secondly appropriating struggle imagery from the ANC is a questionable approach. In 2019 a DA billboard in Gauteng proclaimed 'Honour Mandela's vision to build one South Africa for all'. The third issue relates to the disjuncture between messaging and the reality. Appeals to block an EFF/ANC coalition rang hollow given the DA's coalition arrangements with the EFF in the metros of Tshwane and Johannesburg. Fourthly the DA's continued campaign against small parties' revealed insecurity to voters. Finally the DA has, at times, struggled with the congruency of its messages as it attempted to appeal to divergent constituencies with opposing interests leading to ambivalence on key issues. As Gumede (2019) argues, black voters were repelled by perceptions that strong black leaders were marginalised in the party and that it was not serious about the existential black issues of black economic empowerment (BEE) and affirmative action.

Additionally between 2014 and 2019 the DA struggled with major internal divisions and leadership issues which affected its credibility. Mmusi Maimane, who was elected leader of the DA in 2015, faced immense challenges around the direction of the DA. A long and fractious battle with former DA mayor of the City of Cape Town Patricia De Lille, which played out in court and the media, hurt the image of the DA. Former DA leader and Western Cape Premier Helen Zille was asked to vacate various decision-making structures of the party and was embroiled in controversy after she tweeted that 'colonialism was terrible but its legacy is not only negative'. The DA was also unable to maintain control in Nelson Mandela Bay with the ousting of former mayor Athol Trollip. Trollip's ousting was filled with controversy and drama. The resignation of Solly Msimanga as Tshwane Mayor as well as the resignation of the DA's policy head, Gwen Ngwenya, with a leaked resignation letter that alleged the party didn't take policy seriously, raised further concerns. To add to all of this, Maimane considered standing as Western Cape Premier. Curiously, former party leader Tony Leon started providing public commentary on these events and this was not done in a way that built up the party's reputation. On a governance level, the DA was severely criticised for its management of the drought in the Western Cape as fears and concerns about 'day zero' consumed citizens of the province through most of 2017.

In 2019, the DA saw a slight reversal of fortunes. The drop in DA support can be explained by its ambivalence on key issues, its leadership challenges and its poor management of the water crisis in the Western Cape. The DA's strategic choices around the handling of Patricia de Lille and its poor management of the water crisis in the Western Cape undermined its messaging and damaged its brand as the best-run province with the best story to tell.

The IFP

The IFP has been on a downward trajectory since 1994 although it experienced a measure of growth in the 2019 General Elections. In 1994, the IFP obtained 10.5% of the national vote and an outright majority of 50.3% in KwaZulu-Natal. The party's national vote share declined steadily thereafter from 8.6% in 1999, to 7% in 2004, 4.6% in 2009, and down to 2.4% in 2014. The IFP lost their majority in KwaZulu-Natal, obtaining 41.9% in 1999. In 2004, the party obtained 36.8% at the provincial level, 22.4% in 2009 and 10.9% in 2014. In 2019 the IFP experienced a marginal increase to 3.4% at the national level and also gained in KwaZulu-Natal, increasing its vote share to 16.3% (Chilenga-Butao 2019, 204–206).

The IFP has been consistent in terms of messaging and its messages are internally coherent. However the IFP has struggled with credibility issues since 1994. The IFP's pre-election stance regarding participation in the 1994 elections tarnished campaign messages developed thereafter. The loudest message that voters received from the IFP in 1994 was not through its formal campaign messages. As Southall and Daniel (2005, 51) indicate, the IFP had 'imperilled the democratic transition by threatening to boycott the founding elections'. This stance tarnished IFP campaign messages developed thereafter. Additionally the IFP has been constrained by the fact that its support base is strongest in KwaZulu-Natal. As Piper (2014, 90) shows, 90% of the party's national vote is located in the province. The IFP struggled to project itself as a nationally strong party. Between 1994 and 2019 campaign communications have generally centred on Chief Mangosuthu Buthelezi, who featured on most IFP election posters in all democratic elections. It is likely that building the campaign primarily around Buthelezi was a strategically adverse decision. As Piper (2005, 156) argues, the IFP has been overly reliant on the statesmanlike appeal of Buthelezi.

The IFP's campaign messaging was consistent and internally coherent after 1999. Typically the party presented its track record in KwaZulu-Natal and offered a series of comparative messages contrasting its policies against its critique of ANC policies. The IFP has emphasised the following key messages to the electorate:

(1) That it had a series of workable policies that would deal with South Africa's social and economic problems;
(2) That the ANC's strength should be reduced so as to avoid the risk of sliding into one-party authoritarianism;
(3) That the ANC had performed poorly since coming into power and had failed South Africa in a number of key areas – most notably HIV/Aids, corruption, crime, unemployment and poverty;
(4) That on previous occasions those that were dissatisfied with the ANC's performance should not abstain from voting; and
(5) That KwaZulu-Natal had performed better than other provinces under the leadership of the IFP and this demonstrated the capacity and the will of the IFP in dealing with critical issues.

Little can be said about any Inkatha Freedom Party (IFP) campaign in the 1994 Founding Elections. While election rallies were held and the IFP put up posters urging voters to vote for the IFP 'when the time comes', the IFP agreed to participate a mere week before the elections (Hamilton and Mare 1994, 81–82). In elections thereafter, the IFP ran its campaigns by contrasting itself against the ANC around the theme of government performance. Manifestos and official communications focused on what it deemed as governance failures of the ANC, arguing that the ruling party had performed poorly since coming into power and had failed South Africa in a number of key areas. The IFP also argued that the ANC's strength should be reduced so as to avoid the risk of sliding into one-party authoritarianism.

The IFP's 1999 campaign emphasised 'a revolution of goodwill'. It focused on federalism and policy issues such as crime, unemployment and corruption. The IFP's 1999 manifesto was entitled 'How the IFP will make South Africa governable'. In 2004, the IFP's campaign emphasised 'making a difference together'. The IFP manifesto, entitled 'Real Development Now: Let Us Make a Difference –Together' manifesto provided an extensive outline of the IFP's policy positions (Inkatha Freedom Party 2004). At the end of March 2004, the IFP released a series of pledges around job creation, clean governance and safety. The IFP also sought to communicate that it had strengthened its position through its alliance with the DA. A key message of the IFP was that KwaZulu-Natal was in a better position than other provinces due to the leadership of the IFP. Buthelezi gave the example of how the IFP-led provincial government of KwaZulu-Natal ensured the distribution of Nevirapine to all HIV-positive pregnant women in the province and how it defended this decision against the central government in the Constitutional Court. This, he argued, gave South Africans an opportunity to see how they would govern the entire nation.

In 2009, the IFP campaigned under the theme 'The Tried and Tested Alternative', which also highlighted ANC failings. The manifesto asserted that the IFP wanted to 'make things better, fix what is broken, and stop the rot: not to reinvent the wheel'. After the 2009 elections the party experienced a split. As Piper (2014, 89) indicates the failure of the party to respond to the heavy losses of 2009 led the national chairperson, Zanele kaMagwaza-Msibi, to leave and form the National Freedom Party (NFP) which took more than 35% of the IFP's support in the 2014 election. The 2014 manifesto, entitled 'The Power is Your's!', invited voters to partner with the IFP to heal the nation (Inkatha Freedom Party 2014).

In 2019, the IFP campaigned around the theme 'Trust us'. In his foreword message to the manifesto, Buthelezi claimed that the 2019 manifesto was a blueprint for fixing problems so that the social and economic justice South Africa deserves could be created (Inkatha Freedom Party 2019). As Africa (2019, 124) indicates the IFP's change in fortune is most likely due to a number of contextual factors. The first one can be linked to the internal leadership battles within the NFP. When the NFP's leader, Zanele kaMagwaza-Msibi, took ill, former IFP members who were in the NFP 'went back home' to the IFP. Secondly, dissatisfaction with the ANC worked to the IFP's favour. Given the problems in the ANC, a substantial proportion of voters in KwaZulu returned to the IFP or abstained from voting. This is reflected in the provincial results of KwaZulu-Natal where the ANC won with a narrow margin of three percentage points.

The NP/NNP

The NNP, formerly the NP, no longer exists. In the 1994 Founding Elections, the NP emerged as the second largest party in the country in 1994 obtaining 20.4% of the national vote. It won the Western Cape with 53.3% of the provincial vote in 1994. In 1999, the NNP only received 6.9% of the national vote and lost its majority status in the Western Cape, obtaining 38.4% in the province. In 2004, the NNP was decimated at the polls, receiving a paltry 1.7% of the vote at the national level and 10.9% in the Western Cape (Schultz-Herzenberg 2005, 170–171).

The NP/NNP's campaign messages of 1994, 1999 and 2004 were inconsistent with each other. This is particularly evident when the 1994 campaign messaging is contrasted against the 2004 messaging. Schultz-Herzenberg (2005, 168) correctly points out that since 1994 the NNP struggled with questions of tactics and strategy, mainly revolving around the dilemma of choosing a more constructive or more robust opposition stance in relation to the ANC.

The NP's 1994 campaign painted a bleak future for South Africa under an ANC-led government. It depicted the ANC as a dangerous, violent, dictatorial, politically intolerant party unfit to govern (Giliomee 1994; Eldridge and Seekings 1995). In 1994 the dominant theme of the NP's campaign was that the economic policy of the ANC and SACP would bring the country to its knees, but that the NP had the experience and the ability to create order and economic prosperity out of chaos (Giliomee 1994, 62). The NP's campaign consisted of the following steps:

(1) To hammer home the message that freedom and the end of apartheid already had been achieved;
(2) to ensure free and fair elections through spreading the message that the ballot would be secret;
(3) present the 'new' NP's philosophy and policy programme; and (iv) to depict the ANC as a dangerous party (Giliomee 1994, 56).

The vast series of endorsements which the NP ran utilised images of terrorism, intimidation, burning of collaborators, boycotts and strike action. Arguably the NP lacked credibility as the architect of apartheid, however in the 1994 elections it was able to tap into the fears of voters predominantly in the Western Cape.

The NP's 1994 campaign messages were undermined by the reality that unfolded after 1994. Following the ANC's victory in 1994, the dire predictions of the NP for South Africa under ANC-rule failed to materialise. Additionally the credibility of the NNP was undermined when in May 1996, then NP President FW de Klerk informed a packed press conference that he was taking the NP out of the Government of National Unity's cabinet (Calland 1999, 6). Calland notes that this was not a unanimous decision, with many NP leaders wanting to stay in power. In September 1997, De Klerk resigned and was replaced by Marthinus Van Schalkwyk (Southall 1998, 462). According to Breytenbach (1999, 119), De Klerk's absence as the party leader weakened the NNP and worsened divisions within the party, resulting in the resignation of Roelf Meyer who had played a central role in developing the interim constitution and the negotiation process. The woes inflicted on the NNP through organisational problems and defections were exacerbated by the disclosure of atrocities committed by the apartheid government at the Truth and Reconciliation Commission (TRC) (Welsh 1999, 91). As Breytenbach (1999, 119) indicates, some NNP supporters were 'shamed by the revelations of the TRC'.

In the 1999 General Elections the NNP's campaign messaging could not rely on the type of fear-mongering it had drawn on in the founding election. Instead the 1999 NNP manifesto professed that the party was the most multiracial party in South Africa, representing 'a broad and inclusive South African patriotism that transcends race, language and religion' (New National Party 1999, 213). According to Breytenbach (1999, 121) the issues addressed in its 1999 manifesto 'were rather general' and 'the party seemed unsure how to campaign for the election without a clear identity'.

In June 2000, the New National Party (NNP) and the Democratic Party (DP) announced that they would join together as the Democratic Alliance with the DP's Tony Leon as the national leader and NNP's Marthinus Van Schalkwyk as the deputy leader. The merger was never institutionalised and by November 2001 the alliance had sprung apart (Lodge 2002, 157). The merger and subsequent split with the DP had stretched its resources and the DA had effectively absorbed the NNP's grassroots structures (Schultz-Herzenberg 2005, 166). The NNP then entered into an alliance with the ANC.

By 2004 the party's campaign messaging was completely at odds with each other. The NNP also expounded a campaign message that completely contradicted its messages of 1994 and 1999 because it had gone into alliance with its former nemesis, the ANC. In the 2004 campaign, the NNP contrasted the aggressive style of the DA against itself as the mediator between voters and the ANC. The NNP's primary campaign theme was that they provided a voice for voters via their coalition arrangement with the ANC. In his introduction to the NNP manifesto, entitled 'You Deserve a Fair Share', Van Schalkwyk framed the NNP as the only opposition party that could ensure a voice in a multi-party government for opposition voters (New National Party 2004). He argued that the NNP's consensus politics would be influential in dealing with the ANC and would encourage stability while the aggressive style of the DA encouraged instability. The 2004 election manifesto set out the key policy positions of the NNP and then listed areas for negotiation. The manifesto's account of past NNP performance framed the party as having taken the initiative to transform South Africa by listing the NNP's 'timeline of courage'. The manifesto also outlined how voters would benefit from the NNP's dialogue with the ANC but also took pains to indicate how the NNP differed from the ANC (on issues such as the death penalty, abortion, affirmative action and Zimbabwe).

The collaborative arrangement with the ANC, as well as the assertion that this would benefit voters, essentially communicated to voters that the NNP had erred in its previous assessment of the ANC. Not only was the 2004 campaign in stark contrast with previous campaigns but there was also a lack of internal consistency between the NNP messages presented to voters in the 2004 campaign. The messages that the NNP had strengthened its position through its alliance with the ANC but that it was distinct from and would hold the ANC to account were at odds with each other. As Southall and Daniel (2005, 48) state the messages of:

(1) The NNP being committed to constructive opposition, reconciliation and political consensus;
(2) Differing from the ANC on key aspects such as being tougher on crime and the handling of Zimbabwe; and
(3) Its presence in government giving important leverage to minority groups was as confusing as it was unconvincing.

It is therefore not surprising that in 2004 trust in the NNP was low – only 16% of CNEP respondents said that the party could be trusted 'always' or 'most of the time' while 65% of respondents said the party could be trusted only some of the time or not at all (Africa 2008).

The NNP's demise was finalised by internal organisational difficulties, outlandish inconsistencies in its campaign rhetoric, lack of congruence between its messages as well as its poor strategic choices. The party scored low on credibility, message consistency and congruence of its messages. It paid dearly at the polls in 2004.

Conclusion: campaigns matter but should be the end of a productive inter-campaign period

For a party to perform well they need high levels of credibility, general consistency of messaging over time as well congruency of messages in a given election campaign. What then accounts for electoral trends of these parties since 1994? The answer to this question is complex and multi-faceted. An examination of electoral trends electoral trends, the consistency and congruency of campaign messages as well as the ways in which these messages intersect with internal party dynamics and broader political dynamics reveals that campaigns do indeed matter and are relevant in the South African context. However, a good campaign is only the starting point or rather it should be the end of a productive inter-campaign period. What happens between elections are also important to voters. As previously indicated, perceptions of political parties and party leaders are the lens through which campaign communications are evaluated and have far-reaching effects in terms of voter choices.

Poor decisions and destructive behaviour resulted in negative perceptions that had harmful repercussions for party performance at the polls. Indeed the fluctuations in party support and the specific trends since 1994 should not be seen as a surprise. The ANC had consistent and internally coherent messaging but was affected by credibility issues after the 2004 General Elections. This coincided with its upward trajectory between 1994 and 2004 as well as its decreased support since 2009. The DA managed to maintain elements of consistency in its messaging, however, it has faced serious messaging challenges as well as credibility challenges in the run up to the 2019 General Elections. Again, coincidentally the DA experienced a drop in support in 2019 after an extended period of incremental growth. The IFP's messaging was consistent over time and coherent but it has struggled with credibility issues since the 1994 Founding Elections – the IFP has been on a downward trajectory since 1994 with a marginal improvement in 2019. The NP/NNP had major problems with credibility, message consistency and message coherence.

Viewed in this way South African voters emerge as active agents consuming relevant political information. As Key (1967, 1) said more than 60 years ago, 'Voters are not fools'. This is not to say that sociological and identity-related dynamics are unimportant. Indeed, Mattes (1994, 12) argues, long-term factors shape the way in which we filter information and perceive and evaluate political reality. However from these trends we can infer that political parties through their choices, behaviour and campaigns as well as concurrent political developments, are primarily responsible for the changes in these parties' political fortunes.

If campaigns do matter, we should pay far more attention to the quality of choices offered to voters via campaigns. We should ask questions about the extent to which they provide voters with the basis to make informed choices and scrutinise the conditions under which campaigns enhance the quality of democracy.

Note

1. The death of scores of people vulnerable and mentally ill people moved by the Gauteng's health department from specialised care facilities to unlicensed organisations became known as the Life Esidimeni tragedy.

Disclosure statement

No potential conflict of interest was reported by the author.

References

Africa, C. 2008. "The Impact of the 2004 Election Campaign on the Quality of Democracy in South Africa." Unpublished thesis., University of Cape Town.

Africa, C. 2019. "The Smaller Parties: Who's in and Who's Out?" In *Election 2019: Change and Stability in South Africa's Democracy*, edited by C. Schulz-Herzenberg, and R. Southall, 113–131. Johannesburg: Jacana Media.

African National Congress. 1999. *Manifesto: Together Fighting for Change: A Better Life for All.*

African National Congress. 2019. *Election Manifesto: A People's Plan for a Better Life for All.* Accessed January 13, 2019. https://www.politicsweb.co.za/documents/the-ancs-2019- election-manifesto.

Afrobarometer. 2015. *South Africans have Lost Confidence in Zuma, Believe he Ignores Parliament and the Law.* Accessed October 3, 2019. http://afrobarometer.org/publications/ad66-south-africans-have-lost-confidence-zuma-believe-he-ignores-parliament-and-law.

Booysen, S. 2005. "The Democratic Alliance: Progress and Pitfalls." In *Electoral Politics in South Africa: Assessing the First Democratic Decade*, edited by J. Piombo, and L. Nijzink, 129–147. New York: Palgrave Macmillan.

Booysen, S. 2009. "Congress of the People: Between Foothold of Hope and Slippery Slope." In *Zunami! The 2009 South African Elections*, edited by R. Southall, and J. Daniel, 85–113. Johannesburg: Jacana Media.

Breytenbach, W. 1999. "The New National Party." In *Election '94: The Campaigns, Results and Future Prospects*, edited by A. Reynolds, 114–124. Cape Town: David Philip.

Butler, A. 2009. "The ANC's National Election Campaign of 2009: Siyanqoba!." In *Zunami! The 2009 South African Elections*, edited by R. Southall, and J. Daniel, 113–131. Johannesburg: Jacana Media.

Calland, R. 1999. "Democratic Government, South African Style 1994–1999." In *Election '99: From Mandela to Mbeki*, edited by A. Reynolds, 1–15. Cape Town: David Philip.

Chilenga-Butao, T. 2019. "Provincial Dynamics and Results in Elections 2019." In *Election 2019: Change and Stability in South Africa's Democracy*, edited by C. Schulz-Herzenberg, and R. Southall, 65–84. Johannesburg: Jacana Media.

Daniel, J., and R. Southall. 2009. "The National and Provincial Outcome: Continuity with Change." In *Zunami! The 2009 South African Elections*, edited by R. Southall, and J. Daniel, 190–218. Johannesburg: Jacana Media.

Eldridge, M., and J. Seekings. 1995. *An Uphill Battle: Voter Attitudes and ANC Strategy in the 1994 South African Elections.* Cape Town: Centre for African Studies, University of Cape Town.

ENCA. 2019. *Ramaphosa Admits the ANC Allowed State Capture.* April 29. https://www.enca.com/news/ramaphosa-admits-anc-allowed-state-capture.

Farrell, D. M., and P. Web. 2000. "Political Parties as Campaign Organisations." In *Parties Without Partisans: Political Change in Advanced Industrial Democracies*, edited by R. J. Dalton, and M. P. Wattenberg, 102–128. Oxford: Oxford University Press.

Friedman, S. 2004. "Why We Vote: The Issue of Identity." *Election Synopsis* 1 (2): 2–4.

Giliomee, H. 1994. "The National Party's Campaign for a Liberation Election." In *Election '94: The Campaigns, Results and Future Prospects*, edited by A. Reynolds, 43–71. Cape Town: David Philip.

Giliomee, H., J. Myburgh, and L. Schlemmer. 2001. "Dominant Party Rule, Opposition Parties and Minorities in South Africa." *Democratization* 8: 161–182.

Gumede, W. 2019. "The DA's Campaign Battle Plan was Simply Wrong." Accessed May 19. https://www.news24.com/elections/voices/the-das-campaign-battle-plan-was-simply-wrong-20190519

Hamilton, G., and G. Mare. 1994. "The Inkatha Freedom Party." In *Election '94: The Campaigns, Results and Future Prospects*, edited by A. Reynolds, 73–87. Cape Town: David Philip.

Inkatha Freedom Party. 2004. *IFP National Manifesto January 2004*. Real Development Now: Let's make a Difference – Together.

Inkatha Freedom Party. 2014. *National Election Manifesto of The Inkatha Freedom Party*. Accessed June 3, 2019. http://ifp.org.za/wp-content/uploads/2014/ManifestoEnglish.pdf.

Inkatha Freedom Party. 2019. *Inkatha Freedom Party 2019 Election Manifesto*. Accessed March 10, 2019. http://www.ifp.org.za/wp-content/uploads/2019/03/IFP-Election-Manifesto-for-2019.pdf.

Jolobe, Z. 2009. "The Democratic Alliance: Consolidating the Official Opposition." In *Zunami! The 2009 South African Elections*, edited by R. Southall, and J. Daniel, 131–146. Johannesburg: Jacana Media.

Jolobe, Z. 2014. "The Democratic Alliance Election Campaign: 'Ayisafani'?" In *Elections 2014 South Africa: The Campaigns, Results and Future Prospects*, edited by C. Schulz-Herzenberg, and R. Southall, 57–71. Johannesburg: Jacana Media.

Key, V. O. 1967. *The Responsible Electorate: Rationality in Presidential Voting*. Cambridge: Harvard University Press.

Lodge, T. 1999. "The African National Congress." In *Election '99: The Campaigns, Results and Future Prospects*, edited by A. Reynolds, 64–87. Cape Town: David Philip.

Lodge, T. 2002. *Politics in South Africa: From Mandela to Mbeki*. Cape Town: David Philip.

Lupia, A., and M. D. McCubbins. 2000. "The Institutional Foundations of Political Competence: How Citizens Learn What They Need to Know." In *Elements of Reason: Cognition, Choice and the Bounds of Rationality*, edited by A. Lupia, M. D. McCubbins, and S. L. Popkin, 47–66. Cambridge: Cambridge University Press.

Marquette, J. 1996. "Developing a Campaign Theme." In *Campaign Craft: The Strategies, Tactics, and Art of Political Campaign Management*, edited by D. M. Shea, 147–156. Westport: Praeger Publishers.

Mattes, R. B. 1995. *The Election Book: Judgement and Choice in South Africa's 1994 Election*. Cape Town: Institute for Democracy in South Africa.

Mattes, R. B., and J. Piombo. 2001. "Opposition Parties and the Voters in South Africa's General Election of 1999." *Democratization* 8 (3): 101–128.

New National Party. 1999. *Our Blueprint for Real Democracy*. South Africa: New National Party.

New National Party. 2004. *Manifesto 2004: New National Party: You Deserve a Fair Share*. South Africa: New National Party.

Newman, B. I., and R. M. Perloff. 2004. "Political Marketing: Theory, Research and Applications." In *Handbook of Political Communication Research*, edited by L. L. Kaid, 17–46. New Jersey: Lawrence Erlbaum Associates Inc.

Piper, L. 2005. "The Inkatha Freedom Party: Between the Impossible and the Ineffective." In *Electoral Politics in South Africa: Assessing the First Democratic Decade*, edited by J. Piombo, and L. Nijzink, 148–165. New York: Palgrave Macmillan.

Piper, L. 2014. "Inkatha Freedom Party: The elephants' graveyard." In *Elections 2014 South Africa: The Campaigns, Results and Future Prospects*, edited by C. Schulz-Herzenberg and R. Southall. Johannesburg: Jacana Media.

Schire, R. 2001. "The Realities of Opposition in South Africa: Legitimacy, Strategies and Consequences." In *Democratization Special Issue: Opposition and Democracy in South Africa*, edited by R. Southall, 138–145.

Schlemmer, L. 1994. "South Africa's First Open Election and the Future of its New Democracy." In *The Bold Experiment: South Africa's New Democracy*, edited by H. Giliomee, and L. Schlemmer, 149–167. Cape Town: Southern Book Publishers.

Schnur, D. 1999. "Greater Than the Sum of Its Parts: Co-Ordinating the Paid and Earned Media Message." In *Handbook of Political Marketing*, edited by B. I. Neuman, 143–158. Thousand Oaks: Sage Publications.

Schultz-Herzenberg, C. 2005. "The New National Party: The End of The Road." In *Electoral Politics in South Africa: Assessing the First Democratic Decade*, edited by J. Piombo, and L. Nijzink, 166–186. New York: Palgrave Macmillan.

Schultz-Herzenberg, C. 2019. "The 2019 National Election Results?" In *Election 2019: Change and Stability in South Africa's Democracy*, edited by C. Schulz-Herzenberg, and R. Southall, 170–189. Johannesburg: Jacana Media.

Sniderman, P. M. 2000. "Taking Sides: A Fixed Choice Theory." In *Elements of Reason: Cognition, Choice and the Bounds of Rationality*, edited by A. Lupia, M. D. McCubbins, and S. L. Popkin, 67–84. Cambridge: Cambridge University Press.

Southall, R. 1998. "The Centralization and Fragmentation of South Africa's Dominant Party System." *African Affairs* 97 (389): 443–469.

Southall, R. 2009. "The Democratic Alliance: Consolidating the Official Opposition." In *Zunami! The 2009 South African Elections*, edited by R. Southall, and J Daniel. Johannesburg: Jacana Media.

Southall, R., and J. Daniel. 2005. "The State of Parties Post-Election 2004: ANC Dominance and Opposition Enfeeblement." In *State of the Nation South Africa: 2004–2005*, edited by J. Daniel, R. Southall, and J. Lutchman, 34–57. Cape Town: HSRC Press.

Weaver, M. R. 1996. "Paid Media." In *Campaign Craft: The Strategies, Tactics, and Art of Political Campaign Management*, edited by D. M. Shea, 201–218. Westport, Conn.: Praeger Publishers.

Welsh, D. 1994. "The Democratic Party." In *Election '94: The Campaigns, Results and Future Prospects*, edited by A. Reynolds, 88–100. Cape Town: David Philip.

Welsh, D. 1999. "The Democratic Party." In *Election '99: From Mandela to Mbeki*, edited by A. Reynolds, 1–15. Cape Town: David Philip.

Voting Preferences of Protesters and Non-protesters in Three South African Elections (2014–2019): Revisiting the 'Ballot and the Brick'

Carin Runciman ⓘ, Martin Bekker and Terri Maggott

ABSTRACT
This article examines the relationship between protest and voting by revisiting Booysen's 'ballot and the brick' thesis. Booysen argued that, in South Africa, protest forms part of a 'dual repertoire' that poor communities use to fight for service delivery between elections but that protesters, ultimately, remain loyal to the African National Congress (ANC). Since Booysen first elaborated this argument the political landscape has altered considerably. The ANC has suffered declines in electoral support at a time when protest across many social spheres has been increasing. Yet, there is little scholarship that attempts to examine the relationship between these two phenomena. This article addresses this gap through the analysis of data collected in three surveys of South African voters. Our analysis reveals that while the ANC remains the party of preference of both voters who have not engaged in protest and those that have not, we find that opposition parties are, to a greater extent, characterised by voting protesters. We suggest that party loyalty to the ANC has become a much less binding constraint on voting protesters' indirect and direct political actions.

Introduction

In South Africa, it has become common that in the months preceding an election for there to be threats to boycott elections should demands around 'service delivery' not be met (see Mkhize and Raubenheimer 2014; Ntshobane 2016; Khumalo 2019). Yet, come election day, few of these boycotts seem to materialise. This has led to a general view, supported and furthered by Booysen's (2007, 2012) 'ballot and the brick' thesis that, in South Africa, protest forms part of a 'dual repertoire' that poor communities use to fight for service delivery between elections but that protesters, ultimately, remain loyal to the party of liberation, the African National Congress (ANC) at election time. When Booysen first made this argument over a decade ago, electoral results seemed to support this thesis.[1] However, much has altered from the time when Booysen first made this argument. Community protests have increased in scale (Alexander et al. 2018), the Economic Freedom Fighters (EFF) emerged as an opposition party and the trade union movement fractured over its support for the ANC (Gentle 2015). Although the ANC has retained power, it has done so with a declining share of the electorate's vote, suggesting a significant weakening and fragmenting of its hegemony. The purpose of this article is to explore the relationship between voting and protesting and to consider whether the 'dual repertoire' thesis holds over a decade since it was first made.

To consider the relationship, the article first examines the scale of protest activity, particularly community protests, in South Africa. The analysis highlights the contentious nature of South Africa's democracy and considers to what extent the escalation in protest may have shaped the ANC's electoral performance. In particular, the article assesses the claim made by some analysts (see Municipal IQ cited in Ntshidi 2019), that protests increase prior to an election. Using data from the Centre for Social Change (CSC), University of Johannesburg, which counts media-reported community protests (MRCPs), we demonstrate that there is no robust evidence to suggest that community protests do indeed increase prior to an election.

Having considered the possible relationship between protest and voting at a general level, the article then moves on to consider individual voter and protest behaviour based on an analysis of three exit polls of South African voters, conducted on the day of the 2014 and 2019 national and provincial elections as well as the 2016 local government elections by the CSC. In contrast to most scholarship on South African elections, which relies heavily on aggregate results (see Booysen 2012; Friedman 2015; Schulz-Herzenberg 2016), the three surveys provide a rare view into the decisions of individual voters in a range of townships and informal settlements predominantly in Gauteng, areas of historically strong ANC support and protest.

Our analysis reveals that while the ANC remains the party of preference of both voters who engage in protest and those who do not, we find that opposition parties are to a much larger extent characterised by voting protesters. This suggests that party loyalty to the ANC has become a much less binding constraint on voting protesters at the polls. We argue that, in the current context, there is a need to revisit the notion of protest as a largely ANC-supporting repertoire.

The relationship between protesting and voting

The relationship between protest and voting is generally recognised as an area that has been under-researched (McAdam and Tarrow 2010; Galais 2014). What research that does exist has tended to concentrate in established democracies where analysis demonstrates that protesting and voting are often compatible and complementary forms of political participation. Saunders (2014) finds that those who engage in demonstrations more frequently were more likely to participate in electoral politics than those who participated less frequently in demonstrations. Similar findings have been made by Norris (2002) and Schussman and Soule (2005), who found that being registered to vote had a positive relationship on the likelihood of protesting. In third wave and developing democracies the picture has arguably been more mixed. Research in Argentina and Bolivia (Moseley and Moreno 2010) supports the findings made by Saunders and others above, while scholars in Brazil and South Africa (see Power and Roberts 1995; Runciman 2016) have argued that protesters may be more likely to abstain from electoral politics.

Booysen's (2007, 2012) 'dual repertoire' thesis views protesting and voting as complementary forms of political action that ultimately result in the continued support for the ANC. However, as Runciman (2016) has argued elsewhere, part of Booysen's argument rests on her interpretation of South Africa as a multi-party democracy, as opposed to the conventional view that South Africa has a dominant party system (see Giliomee, Myburgh, and Schlemmer 2001; Habib and Schulz-Herzenberg 2011). She therefore argues that dissatisfaction with the ANC can be expressed at the ballot box through voting for opposition parties. However, a lack of feasible opposition parties may make this option undesirable, if not wholly impracticable. The main opposition party, the Democratic Alliance (DA), although witnessing some electoral growth, remains for many voters an unfeasible electoral alternative. The legacy of apartheid means that, as Mattes (2014) highlights, 'race' continues to play an important role in South Africa's electoral politics. Numerous studies have demonstrated that a key attribute that voters examine in South Africa is whether a party is perceived to be racially and ethnically inclusive. In the South African National Election Survey, only 39% of respondents considered the DA to be racially inclusive (cited in Mattes 2014, 183). The formation of the EFF arguably represents a more viable alternative to the ANC for black working-class voters. However, as EFF leader, Julius Malema, has admitted, the militaristic and macho culture displayed by the EFF has been off-putting to many women voters (Gouws 2014; Cilliers 2018).

South Africa's contentious democracy and fragmenting ANC hegemony

The period between 2014 and 2019 has been a turbulent one for the ANC. Former Minister of Arts and Culture, Pallo Jordan, has said that the repercussions of the state's involvement in the Marikana massacre has led to a loss of legitimacy for the ANC (cited in Saul and Bond 2014, 244). This has been further compounded by various corruption scandals at various levels within the party, most notably, the corruption scandals that have centred on former President Jacob Zuma and his links to the Gupta family. The influence of the Gupta family on President Zuma is implicated in his decision to replace former Finance Minister Nhlanhla Nene in December 2015 and in the cabinet reshuffle in March 2017. The 2017 cabinet reshuffle galvanised nationwide protests against Zuma's leadership under the banner #ZumaMustFall. What was significant about these protests was that, perhaps for the first time under the democratic dispensation, both black and white middle class citizens were brought out to the streets (Runciman, Nkuna, and Frassinelli 2017). These protests together with ongoing community protests and widespread student protests meant that under Zuma's leadership, South Africa became a more 'contentious democracy' (Runciman 2016, 420–422; Paret 2017, 8–10).

Protest has become an everyday part of the South African political landscape. Although there are debates regarding how protests should be counted, by most measures, protest has been increasing since 2005 (Alexander et al. 2018). Figure 1 provides the number of MRCPs recorded in the CSC database. While Runciman and her colleagues (2016) estimate, through comparisons with police data, that the media records only a quarter of community protests they have also found that the recording of media data does provide a somewhat reliable indicator in the trends of protest. Looking at the trends, we can see that the number of MRCPs has been increasing since 2005. Between 2014 and 2017, there has been an average of 379 MRCPs a year. It is therefore likely that the true average number of community protests was closer to 1500 per year or an average of 4 community protests a day. Through comparisons with the Armed Conflict Location and Event Data (ACLED), a database that monitors political violence and protest across Africa (see ACLED 2019), we can demonstrate that this level of community protests is significantly higher than elsewhere

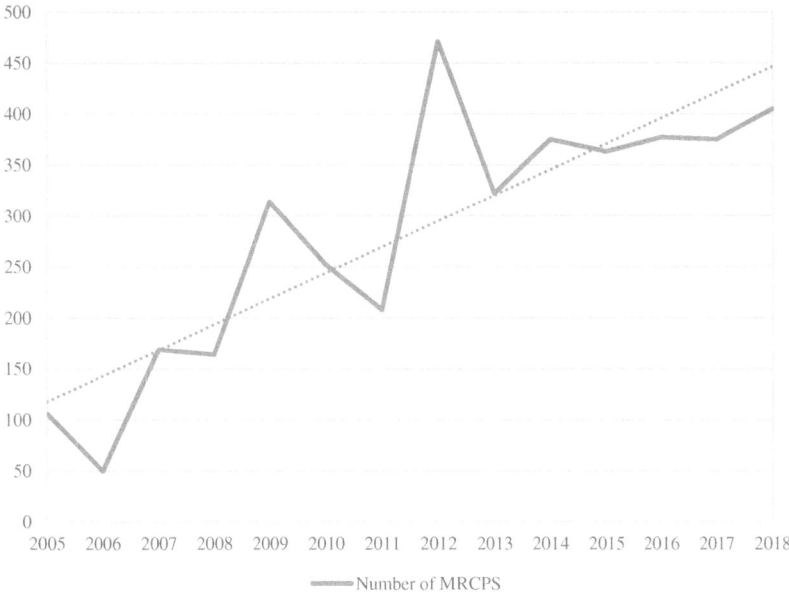

Figure 1. Number of MRCPs 2005–2017 (Source: CSC database).

in the continent (Alexander 2019). This seems to bear out the assertion that South Africa is experiencing a 'rebellion of the poor' (Alexander 2010, 25).

Whether there has been a commensurate 'rebellion of workers' (Alexander 2015) is debatable. The 2014 General Elections were held in the midst of the 5-month platinum sector strike but, as Bhorat and Tseng (2014) demonstrate, South Africa's level of strike activity is consistent or, indeed lower, than many other middle-income or, indeed, high-income countries. That said, there has been a rising proportion of unprotected strikes; strikes that do not follow the provisions set out in the Labour Relations Act. Between 2000 and 2010, a third of strikes, on average, were unprotected. In recent years, the percentage of unprotected strikes has grown considerably. Between 2012 and 2016 half of all strikes, on average, were unprotected (Runciman 2018). This suggests rising levels of worker militancy, where workers are prepared to go on strike without the legal protection against dismissal afforded by protected strike action.

In the same period, nationwide student protests emerged organised under the banner of #RhodesMustFall and #FeesMustFall. While far from the first time students organised to protest across South Africa's campuses, the protests were distinctive for their national character and the way in which they pressed their demands not just to university management but also to the governing ANC (see Booysen 2016; Heffernan and Nieftagodien 2016). These different forms of protest activity, taken together, mean that South Africa can be regarded as a contentious democracy.

Some commentators argue that a feature of this contentious democracy is that there is a marked increase in the numbers of community protest prior to elections (see Municipal IQ 2019; cited in Ntshidi 2019). To assess this claim we analysed the number of protests per month between January 2014 and April 2019 and calculated the average number of protests per month for the same period (see Figure 2). When we consider the average number of protests, it is important to observe the pattern of seasonal variation. In general, protest tends to increase and peak from April to July, the winter months, and regardless of whether there is an election or not. Protests tend to decline from October onwards.

In 2014, while January and February registered more MRCPs than average, the months immediately prior to the 2014 national elections had a lower than average number of MRCPs and lower than the preceding months. In 2016, the number of MRCPs steadily grew from January until May, consistent with or slightly above the average trend. However, in the month before the 2016 local government election, the number of MRCPs declined, consistent with the general patterns in protest activity. Similarly, in 2019, in the 2 months prior to the 2019 national elections the numbers of MRCPs declined in comparison to January and February and were lower than the average number of protests. While we cannot measure the extent to which protests may be under-reported in the run up to an election due to coverage of election campaigning, the data presents us with no grounds to assert that community protests increase in the run up to an election. This, of course, does not mean that communities do not choose to strategically protest around election time, but it does contradict the assertion that this is a dominant trend in protest activity.

Over this same period, there has been a decline in electoral participation. Table 1 analyses the registration of voters, the turnout and results of the 2014 and 2019 national elections both by the registered population and the eligible voting age population (EVAP). The table shows that there has been a slight decline in the percentage of the EVAP registered to vote from 77.7% in 2014 to 74.6% in 2019. The voter turnout amongst both the registered population and the EVAP has similarly declined, amongst registered voters the turnout declined to 66.0% in 2019, representing only about half of all those eligible to vote. Correspondingly, voter abstention has risen from 42.9% amongst the EVAP in 2014 to 50.7% in 2019. While amongst registered voters, the percentage that chose not to vote grew from 26.5% in 2014 to 34.0% in 2019.

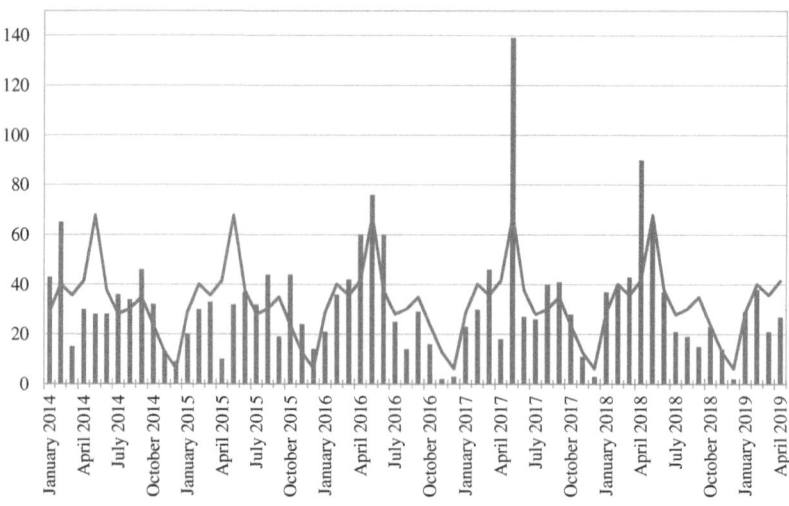

Figure 2. Number of MRCPs per month and average number of MRCPS per month, January 2014–April 2019 (Source: CSC database).

Table 1. National election results 2014 and 2019 South African elections 2014–2019 (Source: Schulz-Herzenberg 2019a).

	2014	2019
EVAP	32,687,600	35,868,190
Registered voters	25,390,150	26,756,649
% of the EVAP registered to vote	77.70	74.6
Total votes cast (incl. spoilt votes)	18,654,771	17,671,616
Turnout of EVAP	57.10	49.3
Turnout of registered voters	73.50	66.0
% of abstaining registered voters	26.50	34.0
% of abstaining voters in EVAP	42.90	50.7
% of valid votes for the ANC	62.10	57.5
% of EVAP vote for ANC	35.00	28.0
% of valid vote for opposition parties	37.30	44.0
% of EVAP vote for opposition parties	21.30	20.7

When analysing the results, Table 1 provides the results both by the actual results and by the percentage of the EVAP vote. The decline in support for the ANC amongst voters is well documented, but Table 1 also reveals the decline in support amongst the EVAP. It demonstrates that in 2014, 35.0% of the EVAP voted for the ANC. In 2019, support amongst the EVAP for the ANC declined to 28.0%. While opposition parties have increased their share of the vote from 37.3% in 2014 to 44.0% in 2019, it is interesting to note that the support for opposition parties amongst the EVAP has more or less remained the same. This suggests that while some voters who may be dissatisfied with the ANC are voting for opposition parties; some are simply choosing not to vote at all.

Voter abstention is an under-studied phenomenon in South Africa and across the continent generally (although see Lodge 2003; Ryabchuck 2016; Schulz-Herzenberg 2019b). Voter abstention is most commonly seen as a result of a combination of voter apathy, particularly among young people, and institutional barriers (see Kersting 2007; Oyedemi and Mahlatji 2016). Indeed, the HSRC voter participation surveys (2014, 25) highlight that apathy, conceptualised as 'disinterest and disillusionment', and administrative barriers, such as not being registered, are the most common reasons for not intending to vote. However, as Runciman (2016) has argued elsewhere, a limitation of this survey is that respondents are only presented with what could be characterised as 'negative options' to explain disinterest and disillusionment. What is excluded is an option in which abstention can be considered as an active political choice to signal political dissatisfaction.

In the run up to an election, there are often calls by different communities to boycott elections. This strategy was, amongst others, prominently used by the Landless Peoples' Movement in 2004, mobilising around the slogan 'No Land! No Vote!' Later, in 2006, a similar campaign was taken up by the Anti-Eviction Campaign and Abahlali baseMjondolo around the slogan 'No Land, No House, No Vote'. In the build-up to the 2014 elections, former minister of intelligence Ronnie Kasrils led the SidikiweVukani (Vote No) campaign. Although this was widely misunderstood as a call for a vote boycott, Kasrils and others actually called for a vote against the ANC (Nicolson 2014). Threatening to boycott elections has also been a common strategy across a range of different communities in pursuit of demands around service delivery (see Mkhize and Raubenheimer 2014; Ntshobane 2016; Khumalo 2019). In practice, few of these boycotts appear to materialise. One notable exception occurred in Vuwani in 2016 when four of the district's 56 voting stations recorded no votes (Mabena 2016), illustrating, in practice, the limited appeal of boycotting elections. However, Runciman (2016) has argued, in areas of intense protest there is evidence to suggest that there are higher rates of voter abstention. This could suggest higher rates of disillusionment within protesting communities, but may also represent a conscious and political choice not to vote. As voter abstention increases, this is becoming an area of inquiry in need of further research. While, within this article, we are unable to offer further insight into the motivations of non-voters, we are able to shed light on voting preferences of protesting and non-protesting voters.

Methodology

This study is based on three exit poll surveys of voters conducted by the CSC on the day of the 2014 national and provincial government election (7 May), the 2016 local government election (3 August) and the 2019 national and provincial government election (8 May). In the 2014 survey, 15 sites were surveyed, in 2016, 11 sites were surveyed and in 2019, 23 sites were surveyed (see Appendix 1). Only 8 sites have been repeated in all 3 rounds of the survey. The selection of research sites was not intended to be nationally representative but rather focused primarily on urban, black working-class townships and informal settlements, many of which we have been able to determine as protest hotspots due to the information captured in the CSC database. Other sites were chosen based on various research interests within the overall research team or, in 2019, with partner organisations that participated in the survey (see Paret and Runciman 2019).

Conventionally, nationally representative exit polls employ systematic sampling (Bautista et al. 2008, 4). However, as this was not a nationally representative survey, convenience sampling was employed outside voting stations after votes had been cast. The reason convenience sampling was used was to increase the survey response rate in order to generate a sample that would be large enough to be representative of the voting districts sampled (see below). In 2014, 3782 respondents were surveyed, 4313 in 2016 and 5337 in 2019, for a combined sample of 13,432. In 2014 and 2016, the survey was interviewer-administered using paper-based surveys and, in 2019, digitally with Personal Digital Assistants, an increasingly common data-gathering method which allows for automatic geo-tagging, pre-configured skip structures and real-time data collection (see Tomlinson et al. 2009).

In the analysis we present here we use findings from the combined sample. While we recognise that national and provincial elections have different political dynamics from local government elections, our data illustrates that there is a broadly consistent profile of 'those who vote'. There are, therefore, more commonalities than differences in voter profiles across the different types of elections. Although the arguments put forth in this article would hold without the inclusion of the 2016 local government election exit poll data, we believe that the inclusion of this data makes for a more robust argument and guards against drawing conclusions based on potentially transitory trends between the two national elections.

The limitation of this exit poll is that the data collected is not nationally representative, which must temper the conclusions that can be drawn from it. However, the primary focus on collecting data within predominantly black townships and informal settlements, particularly areas with a high incidence of protest, provides a rare insight into areas that have historically been important constituencies for the ANC. The dataset provides the only, to our knowledge, South African election-day exit poll data that asks questions about social background, protest activity and voting decisions and, therefore, provides a unique dataset through which to analyse the relationship between protest and voting. The following section compares our dataset to the national picture in order to highlight the strengths and weaknesses of our sample.

Comparing the sample to the national picture

Table 2 presents key demographic data from each of the three surveys and compares this to data from the 2011 census. Our 2019 data ranged between less than six percentage points from the expected proportional sizes of the age cohorts. Similarly, the percentage of women surveyed appeared to be close to that in the actual population, the variance less than one percentage point. However, turning to the linguistic and ethnical composition of our sample, it is clear how the working-class and 'township-centred' nature of site selection is reflected. We have sampled a larger proportion of isiZulu, isiXhosa, Setswana, Sesotho and 'Black Other' (including Venda and Ndebele) than their expected proportions of the national population.

Table 3 compares employment and unemployment data from the Quarterly Labour Force survey from Statistics South Africa with our sample of voters. We see that our sample contains a higher proportion of people in employment than found in the population and a lower proportion of the unemployed. Given the areas that the survey was conducted in, this is perhaps a surprising finding and it could suggest that the employed are more likely to vote than the unemployed. However, this also highlights the caution that must be exercised in generalising the findings to the population.

Table 4 provides an analysis of voter choices captured in our sample and the actual election results. As the table shows, about a quarter of respondents refused to answer the question about their voting choice. Despite this refusal rate, our survey results provide an approximation to the actual results. When we compare the voting choices of our sample to the actual election results in Gauteng, where most of the sites were

Table 2. Comparing survey data with census data South African elections 2014–2019 (Source: CSC exit poll dataset and Statistics South Africa).

	2014 (%)	2016 (%)	2019 (%)	2011 Census (%)
Age cohorts				
18–24	23.03	22.40	18.53	21.91
25–34	25.70	25.04	26.16	27.00
35–44	19.94	20.22	21.96	19.02
45–54	12.77	16.88	16.06	14.42
55+	12.48	14.31	16.54	17.64
Gender				
Women	48.89	48.20	51.85	51.30
Language/Ethnicity				
Zulu	20.68	23.86	25.26	24.70
Xhosa	19.59	18.22	19.28	15.60
Afrikaans/English	8.81	5.26	8.30	20.50
Pedi	7.96	6.07	6.88	9.80
Tswana	16.53	18.20	12.24	8.90
Sotho	12.27	17.32	10.87	8.00
Tsonga	5.63	4.71	3.95	4.00
Black-other	7.27	5.70	12.50	6.70

Table 3. Employment and unemployment rates, national and sampled voters South African elections 2014–2019 (Source: Quarterly Labour Force Survey and CSC exit poll dataset).

	2014 (%)	2016 (%)	2019 (%)
QLF			
Employed	42.7	42.5	42.6
Unemployed	25.5	26.6	27.6
Sampled voters			
Employed	56.8	61.2	59.9
Unemployed	15.3	14.9	16.2

Table 4. Actual elections results and survey results for Gauteng, indicating the top three political parties by support, South African elections 2014–2019 (Source: CSC exit poll dataset).

	Actual result (%)			Survey result (%)			Difference*		
	ANC	EFF	DA	ANC	EFF	DA	ANC	EFF	DA
2014	54.9	10.3	28.5	49.5	12.5	10.4	−5.4	2.2	−18.1
2016	45.8	11.3	37.2	43.1	17.5	9.6	−2.7	6.2	−27.6
2019	53.2	13.5	24.5	44.5	16.4	7.9	−8.7	2.9	−16.6

Note: *Difference is indicated in percentage points. The refusal rate in the CSC exit poll survey was 20%, 24.5% and 25% in the years 2014, 2016 and 2019, respectively.

surveyed, we see that our results provide a fairly accurate representation of the vote share for the ANC and EFF. Although, in all three iterations of the survey, we slightly under-represent ANC voters and over-represent EFF voters. However, when we compare our sample of DA voters, we see that we have considerably under-sampled DA voters when compared to the provincial picture. Given that the sites we sampled are predominantly in townships and informal settlements, we would not expect to capture as many DA voters. However, when we compare our results to the actual results of the voting districts the survey was carried out in, we see that there is a much smaller variance between our sampled DA voters and the actual results. In 2016, we under-sampled DA voters by 3.1 percentage points and in 2019, by 2.4 percentage points. (Paret 2016, 8; Paret and Runciman 2019, 4–5) Therefore, our sample provides a close approximation of the voting patterns of townships and informal settlements, our key area of interest. This analysis demonstrates that, while not without its limitations, our dataset provides a robust sample through which to consider the relationship between protest and voting.

The profile of a voting protester

Our instrument included three questions asking whether respondents have participated in a community protest, protest at the workplace, and student protest, each 'in the last five years'. The question about student protests was only included in the 2016 and 2019 surveys. Figure 3 presents the percentage of respondents who participated in each form of protest over the three election cycles. Our survey demonstrates that in the sites sampled, community protest was the most common of the three protest types. 28.2% of respondents had participated in at least one protest in 2014, 19.7% in 2016 and 27.3% in 2019. The percentage of respondents who said they had engaged in a workers' protest in the last five years was the same in 2014 and 2019, 16.8%, but increased slightly in 2016–21.5%. In 2016, 19.7% of our respondents said they had engaged in a

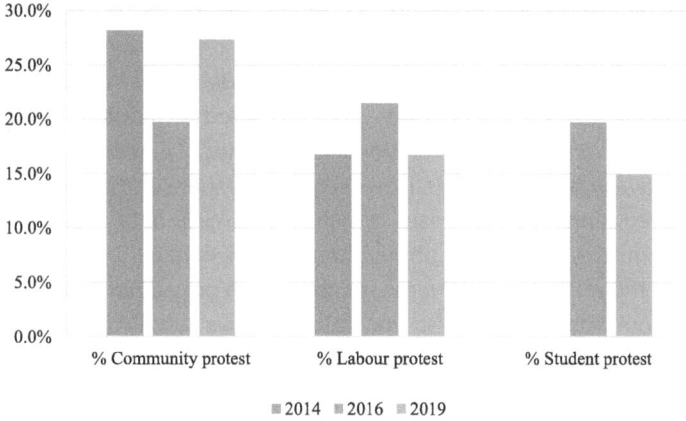

Figure 3. Percentage of respondents who participated in a community, labour or student protest (Source: CSC exit poll dataset).

student protest, this figure declined in 2019 to 15.0%. This decline may be related to the fact that many of the students who had participated in the #FeesMustFall protests have since graduated and were therefore less likely to be respondents in our survey.

We combined the three forms of protest into a category 'Any protest', into which 42% (5660) of our combined sample fell. This is a large number of sampled protesters compared to publicly available databases that include commensurate categories. Figure 4 presents the percentage of sampled voters who reported participation in a protest in the last five years. In 2014, only about a third of voters reported participation in a protest while in 2016, nearly half of the sampled voters were protesters. In 2019, just over a third of sampled voters had participated in a protest.

The high level of protest participation in our sample is reflective of the areas that were sampled, many of which were chosen for their propensity to protest. Therefore, the level of protest activity amongst voters cannot be taken as nationally representative. In order to understand our sample better, we compared our data to HSRC's South African Social

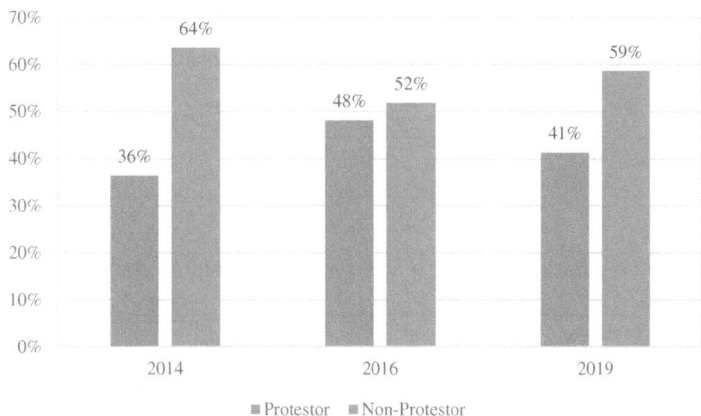

Figure 4. Percentage of protesters and non-protesters (Source: CSC exit poll dataset).

Attitudes Survey (SASAS), a weighted sample survey based on 3 079 responses, which in 2016 included a question asking 'During the last 12 months, have you taken part in a protest march or demonstration?'. A total of 266 respondents answered yes, representing 8.6% of the population. When this data was cross tabulated with people who self-reported to have voted in the then recent 2014 National and Provincial Elections, 205 people (6.7%) answered affirmative in both instances. However, once responses that include refusals and blanks are removed, only 199 responses remain. The SASAS data provides a good indication of the extent to which, in the population, citizens engage in both voting and protesting. However, the relatively small *n* means that it can provide only a limited picture of protesting and non-protesting voters. Our dataset, while not without its limitations, is therefore able to provide a more comprehensive picture than has previously been available.

Table 5 provides an insight into the gender of voting protesters, more voting protesters were men and, conversely, more voting non-protesters were women. In contrast, the SASAS sample found that more women than men were voting protesters, 56% women and 44% men. This finding is particularly interesting considering that compared to the population (see Table 2 above), the SASAS sample underrepresents women as only 46% of their sample were women.

When the type of protest was analysed by gender, some interesting patterns emerged, as Table 6 demonstrates below. More than half of voters who had engaged in community protest were men. As we may expect, voters who had engaged in a labour protest were predominantly men, although it is interesting to note that the proportion of women voters engaged in labour protests increased in 2019, almost double that of 2014. Participation of voters in student protests was evenly divided between men and women.

When considering the mean age of voting protesters, we found the average was 36.6 years. This was markedly younger than the average age of a non-protesting voter, which was 38.9 years (considering the average age overall in the sample, 37.9 years). These findings were considerably lower than the average age in the SASAS data of 44.2 years. Part of the reason for this may be the inclusion of sample sites within the campuses of the University of Johannesburg and the University of the Witwatersrand, which included a number of voters who had participated in student protests. Indeed, the average age of a student protester in

Table 5. Profile of voting protesters by gender South African elections 2014–2019 (Source: CSC exit poll dataset).

	Men	Women	Prefer not to say	Total
Count	3229	2410	21	5660
Percentage	57.0	42.6	0.4	100

Table 6. Type of protest participation by year and gender South African elections 2014–2019 (Source: CSC exit poll dataset).

	Community		Work		Student	
	Men (%)	Women (%)	Men (%)	Women (%)	Men (%)	Women (%)
2014	55.8	43.7	75.9	23.5	NA	NA
2016	56.8	43.2	67.1	32.9	52.3	50.9
2019	53.7	46.0	59.4	39.8	49.5	49.2

Table 7. Full-time employment and unemployment among non-protesting voters and protesting voters, South African elections 2014–2019 (Source: CSC exit poll dataset).

	2014 (%)	2016 (%)	2019 (%)
Non-protesting voters			
Full time employed	29.1	34.6	37.8
Unemployed	15.8	15.8	17.4
Protesting voters			
Full time employed	45.4	37.8	39.7
Unemployed	14.5	14.0	14.4

our sample is 28.6 years, notably lower than the sample mean or when compared to the means for community or worker protest, 37.5 and 39.8 years respectively.

Table 7 considers our sample by employment status. For ease of analysis here, we focus only on those who reported their status as in full time employment or unemployed. Apart from 2014, the employment and unemployment rates of non-protesting voters and protesting voters were similar. The higher rate of full-time employed protesting voters in 2014 can most likely be explained by the fact that one of our survey sites was located in the Platinum Belt. The 2014 national elections took place against the backdrop of the 5-month platinum sector strike, and our survey is likely to have included a number of striking miners. As discussed above, the data more closely approximates the percentage of the population that is employed while it under-represents the unemployed.

While our data on employment and unemployment may not be representative of the population as a whole, we can use the SASAS dataset to see if this data may be representative of protesting voters. In comparison, from the 199 voting protester respondents in the SASAS dataset, a mere 13 (6.5%) were employed full-time, and 30.7% were unemployed and looking for work. The SASAS data significantly under-represents the employed and more closely approximates the percentage of the population that is unemployed. It is difficult to account for the significant differences in these findings other than them being reflective of the different methodologies and sampling deployed. It further illuminates the strengths and weaknesses of each of these datasets and the cautions we must exercise in our analysis.

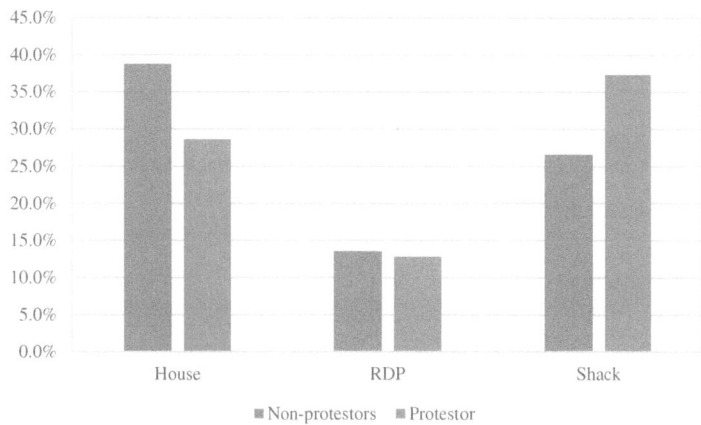

Figure 5. Housing type for protesters and non-protesters (Source: CSC exit poll dataset).

Analysing protesting and non-protesting voters by their housing type revealed some interesting differences, as shown in Figure 5 below. It should be noted that different housing categories were used in the three iterations of the survey. The data presented below provides a summary of some of the housing options and, therefore, totals do not add up to 100%. Most protesting voters lived in a shack while most non-protesting voters lived in a house. It is instructive to note that amongst voters who lived in a government-built Reconstruction and Development Programme (RDP) house, the percentage of protesting and non-protesting voters was very similar.

The analysis of the data above provides a profile of the differences and similarities between voting protesters and non-protesters. On the whole, there are few significant differences between the demographics of protesting and non-protesting voters in our sample with the exception of housing. This suggests, as we may expect, that those living in shacks are in the greatest need of service delivery and therefore may be more likely to take to the streets.

Voting preferences of protesters and non-protesters

Having considered the demographic and socio-economic differences and similarities between voting protesters and non-protesters, as well as how the data relates to the national picture, we now turn to considerations of voting behaviour. In this section, we consider the differences in voting preferences between protesting and non-protesting voters and whether these differences are statistically significant.

Figure 6 provides an analysis of the party choice of protesters and non-protesters for each survey year. It demonstrates that for both protesters and non-protesters, the ANC was the most popular party but that it received higher levels of support among non-protesters. On average, non-protesters reported voting for the ANC 8.8% more than protesters in the sample. In 2014, the most popular opposition party for non-protesters was the DA, while protesters favoured the EFF. In 2016 and 2019, the EFF was the most popular

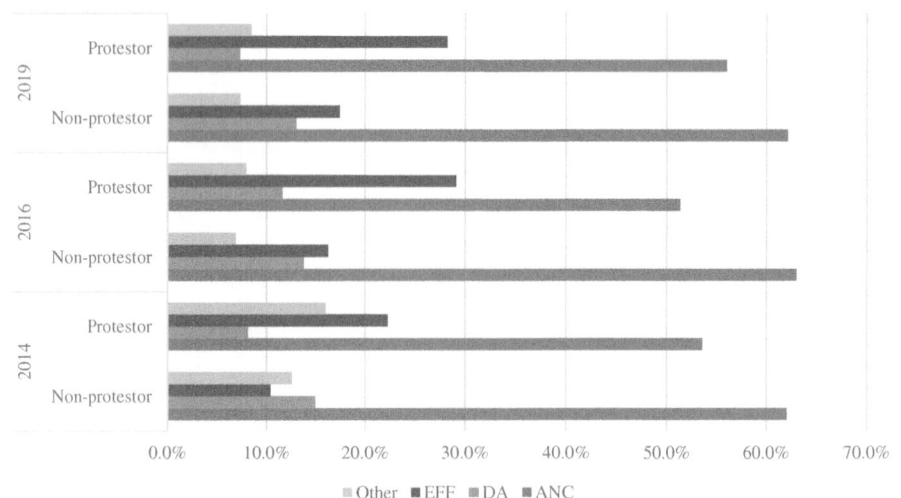

Figure 6. Party choice by voting protesters and non-voting protesters, South African elections 2014–2019 (Source: CSC exit poll dataset).

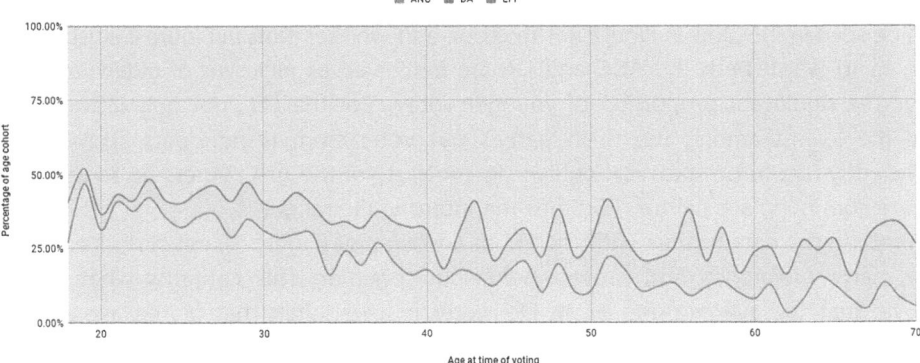

Figure 7. Party preference by voter age, 2019 South African National elections (Source: CSC exit poll dataset).

opposition party amongst both protesters and non-protesters, but support amongst protesters sampled was an average of 11.7% higher than non-protesters.

Figure 7 examined party preference by the age of the voter, aggregated by the three largest parties. This shows that the EFF's support is concentrated at the younger-end of voting ages. That the ANC captures roughly 75% of votes among 70 years-olds, but not much over 50% of the votes of 18–20 year-olds, is also illustrated. As might be expected, the EFF performs better among a younger age profile. Among the 'youth cohort' (ages 18–35), the EFF captured more than 25% of the vote, steadily declining as voter ages increase. It appears that while the EFF is a relatively young political party, it is worth remembering that for a person turning 25 in 2019, the EFF has been a political option for as long as they have been able to vote. Moreover, as Figure 7 illustrates, the younger the voter, the more likely they are to vote for the EFF.

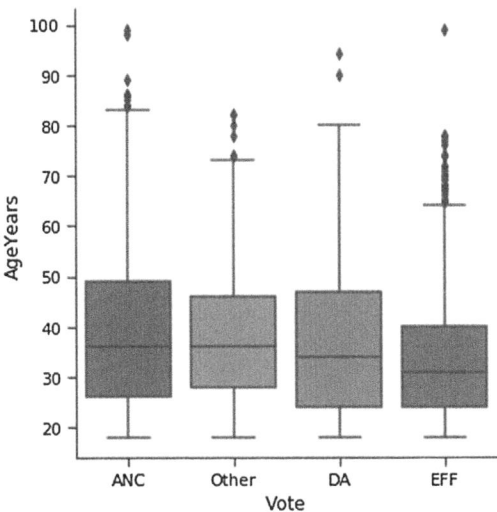

Figure 8. Box plots depicting ages of voters by party preference, South African elections 2014–2019 (Source: CSC exit poll dataset).

The median age of EFF voters is thus also notably lower than that of the ANC and DA, as can be seen in the plots in Figure 8. These box-and-whisker plots in Figure 8 illustrates the degree to which both the ANC and DA are perceived as inclusive of older voters, but 'losing' a significant proportion of younger voters. For the EFF, not only is their mean age the lowest among the main parties but votes from respondents above 65 are sufficiently rare to be statistical outliers. In contrast, for the ANC, voters up to the age of 84 are commonplace (within 1.5 times the interquartile range).

Probing the data further, with the aid of a violin plot (Figure 9), enables us to analyse age, party preference and protest behaviour together. This confirms what we saw above, that the average age of an EFF voter is lower than that of the average ANC voter. For the ANC violin plot, we can see that the age distribution of ANC voters is broadly the same for protesters and non-protesters, although older age cohorts are, perhaps unsurprisingly, less likely to report having recently participated in protests. The asymmetry between the respective halves of each of the violin plots illustrates how the protester portions tends to be younger than the non-protester portions. This observation holds true for the DA and EFF plots, just as it does for the ANC, indicating that, as expected, protesters tend to fall in the younger cohorts, regardless of their party preference. Overall, we see that there is variance between the protesting and non-protesting halves of the plots – for the ANC, DA and EFF, it is their younger members who participate in protests. It is also clear that protesters are rarely older than 60 years.

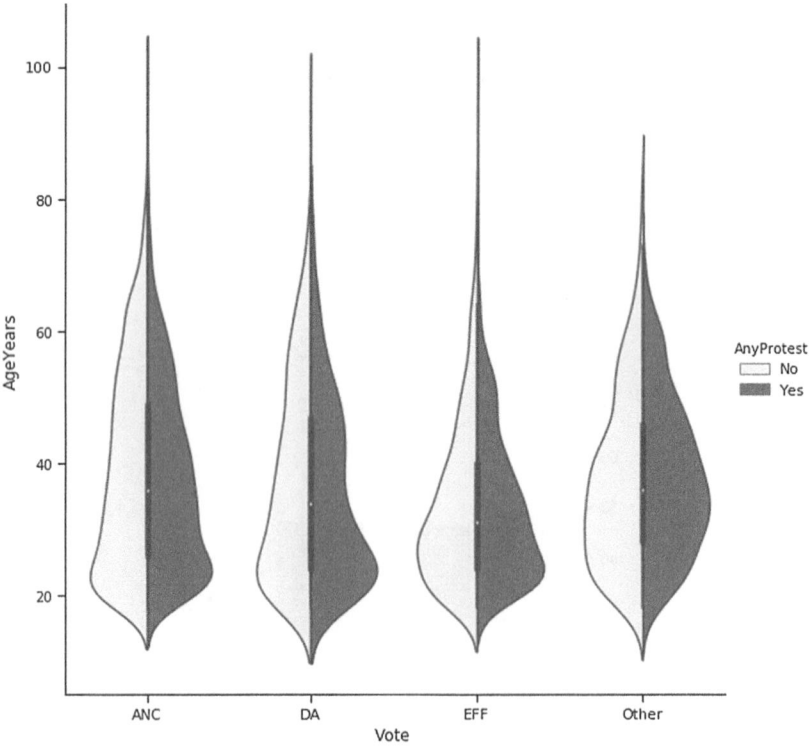

Figure 9. Violin plots presenting differences in age, party preference and protest behaviour, South African elections 2014–2019 (Source: CSC exit poll dataset).

While these findings demonstrate some differences between the voting preferences of protesters and non-protesters, we wanted to examine whether there was a statistically significant relationship regarding the difference in protest patterns between the various political parties. Assuming independence of samples and acceptable proportional sizes, we apply the standard test for independent sample proportions. Formally, considering the position of whether a person's party preference is a predictor of their likelihood to have participated in protest, one might suggest a null hypothesis that

$$H_0: p_{ANC} - p_{Others} = 0$$

with the alternative hypothesis that

$$H_a: p_{ANC} - p_{Others} \neq 0$$

Where p represents the proportion of voters having participated in protest (against all voters for the ANC or Others). One may even extend this so that 'Others', the aggregating of all non-ANC voters, could be replaced with preference for the EFF, to see if the proportions are maintained. The limited number of observations for the DA implied that comparing the ANC and DA directly would not return a robust test.

Using the test statistic for the hypothesis test for the difference of two population proportions:

$$Z = \frac{(\hat{p}_1 - \hat{p}_2) - 0}{\sqrt{\hat{p}(1 - \hat{p})((1/n_1) + (1/n_2))}}$$

Where

$$\hat{p} = \frac{Y_1 + Y_2}{n_1 + n_2}$$

We find the following Z-scores in Table 8. In the case of the null hypothesis being true, we would expect the Z-score to be between 2 and −2, that is, a difference of less than two standard deviations between the proportions being compared. Moreover, the large sample n provides additional surety that the comparison is robust. From the table, we note that the returned Z-scores are, statistically speaking, markedly more than 2, which compels us to reject the null hypothesis. The difference in proportion between ANC voting protesters and non-ANC voting protesters and EFF voting protesters are indeed statistically significant beyond the 99.9% confidence level. Unfortunately, the sample yielded insufficient observations of DA voters overall for the same test to be repeated between the ANC and DA. However, the two comparisons suggest that the profile of the opposition party-voting protester and the ANC-voting protester is, at least since 2014, at strong variance.

Table 8. Z-Scores of differences in proportions of voting patterns related to various political parties in South Africa, 2014–2019.

	2014	2016	2019
ANC compared to Others, i.e. All non-ANC	4.72	6.74	3.92
ANC compared to EFF only	8.83	54.89	7.36

Note: 'Others' denote all parties expect the ANC (including but not limited to the DA and EFF), which indicates that there is a greater likelihood for a non-ANC voter to have participated in protest (vis-à-vis a ANC voters). The second measure compares the two extreme cases – the ANC against the ostensibly protest-prone EFF.

Conclusion

This article has examined the relationship between voter preferences and protesting over the course of three South African elections. Community protests have, since 2005, been increasing in frequency and during the period under consideration here, 2014–2019, we estimate that there were at least 4 community protests a day. During the same period, nationwide student protests emerged, and significant strikes occurred, such as the 2014 platinum sector strike. Illustrating that South Africa has become a 'contentious democracy' (Runciman 2016, 420–422; Paret 2017, 8–10).

Contrary to the common perception, we have demonstrated that there is no firm evidence to suggest that community protests increase prior to an election. In fact, we mostly see the opposite, that community protests continue along an annual rhythm, sometimes even translating into a decrease in the month or months prior to an election. Some commentators have described community protests as 'popcorn protests', reflecting the way they appear to rapidly spring up but, often, equally rapidly subside suggesting that they leave no lasting impression on the political landscape (Bond and Mottiar 2013, 289). While it is not possible to draw a causal relationship, we suggest that the decline in voter turnout is not unrelated to the increase in contentious politics encapsulated in various forms of protest activity. Our analysis shows that amongst the EVAP, that support for the ANC has declined from 35.0% in 2014 to 28.0% in 2019. Yet, notably, there has been no corresponding rise in support for opposition parties amongst the EVAP. This suggests that those that are dissatisfied with the ANC are perhaps more likely to choose not to vote at all, rather than vote for an opposition party. This raises the need for further research on the reasons as to why citizens choose to abstain from voting.

For those that do choose to vote, this article has examined the differences between voting protesters and non-protesters. While not providing a nationally representative picture, the data collected provides a unique insight into the individual protest and voting behaviours of a selection of voters, predominantly located in the townships and informal settlements of Gauteng and thus offers insight into a key constituency of the ANC's support base, the black working class.

The article found that there were few demographic differences in the profile of voting protesters and non-protesters except that protesting voters were more likely to live in a shack. Overall, the findings demonstrate that, as we would expect, on average, a voter is more likely to have cast their ballot in favour of the ANC than an alternative party, regardless of whether they have previously participated in protests. However, our analysis also provides caution against hasty conclusions drawn from the above – we demonstrate that opposition parties are to a much larger extent representative of protesters. Moreover, voting protesters, as persons driven by circumstance to direct political action, have now found political homes to both the left and right of the ANC - and these may be considered, to some degree, as 'parties of protest'. This notwithstanding, it may still be true that 'bricks' are used as part of a dual repertoire of political signalling, albeit under circumstances of party loyalty being much less of a binding constraint on the voting protester's cross at the polls.

Note

1. Elsewhere Runciman (2016) has critiqued Booysen for her interpretation of the election results to support her argument.

Disclosure statement

No potential conflict of interest was reported by the authors.

ORCID

Carin Runciman ⓘ http://orcid.org/0000-0002-5177-8889

References

Alexander, Peter. 2010. "Rebellion of the Poor: South Africa's Service Delivery Protests – A Preliminary Analysis." *Review of African Political Economy* 37 (123): 25–40.

Alexander, Peter. 2015. *South Africa's Twin Rebellions: Bifurcated Protest*. Accessed August 14, 2018. https://www.opendemocracy.net/en/south-africas-twin-rebellions-bifurcated-protest/.

Alexander, Kate. 2019. *From Rebellion of the Poor to Revolution of the People?*. Public lecture delivered at Centre for Social Change Colloquium, Social Change from Below, University of Johannesburg, Johannesburg, June 12.

Alexander, Peter, Carin Runciman, Trevor Ngwane, Boikanyo Moloto, Kgothatso Mokgele, and Nicole van Staden. 2018. "Frequency and Turmoil: South Africa's Community Protests 2005–2017." *South African Crime Quarterly* 63: 27–42.

Armed Conflict Location & Event Data Project. 2019. *What is ACLED?* Accessed July 3, 2019. https://www.acleddata.com/about-acled/.

Bautista, Rene, Mario Callegaro, Vladimir Paniotto, Natalya Kharchenko, and Fritz Scheuren. 2008. "Exit Poll Methodologies Across Nations: Some Constraints and Measurement Problems." Paper presented at the 3MC conference, Berlin, Germany, June 25–28.

Bond, Patrick, and Shauna Mottiar. 2013. "Movements, Protests and a Massacre in South Africa." *Journal of Contemporary African Studies* 31 (2): 283–302.

Booysen, Susan. 2007. "With the Ballot and the Brick: The Politics of Attaining Service Delivery." *Progress in Development Studies* 7 (1): 21–32.

Bhorat, Haroon, and David Tseng 2014. *South Africa's Strike Data Revisited*. Accessed October 23, 2019. https://www.brookings.edu/blog/africa-in-focus/2014/04/02/south-africas-strike-data-revisited/.

Booysen, Susan. 2012. "The Ballot and the Brick – Enduring Under Duress." In *Local Elections in South Africa: Parties, People, Politics*, edited by S. Booysen, 295–312. Bloemfontein: Sun Media.

Booysen, Susan. 2016. *Fees Must Fall: Student Revolt, Decolonisation and Governance in South Africa*. Johannesburg: Wits University Press.

Cilliers, Charles. 2018. "Women Don't Vote for EFF, because we Don't Make Any Sense." *The Citizen*, August 9. https://citizen.co.za/news/south-africa/1993470/women-dont-vote-for-eff-because-we-dont-make-any-sense-malema/.

Friedman, Steven. 2015. "Archipelagos of Dominance: Party Fiefdoms and South African Democracy." *Comparative Governance and Politics* 9: 139–159.

Galais, Carol. 2014. "Don't Vote for Them: The Effects of the Spanish Indignant Movement on Attitudes About Voting." *Journal of Elections, Public Opinion and Parties* 24 (3): 334–350.

Gentle, Leonard. 2015. "What About the Workers? The Demise of COSATU and the Emergence of a New Movement." *Review of African Political Economy* 42 (146): 666–677.

Giliomee, Hermann, James Myburgh, and Lawrence Schlemmer. 2001. "Dominant Party Rule, Opposition Parties and Minorities in South Africa." *Democratization* 8 (1): 161–182.

Gouws, Amanda. 2014. "Women and the Election: The 'Not So Good' Story to Tell." In *Election 2014 South Africa: The Campaigns, Results and Future Prospects*, edited by C. Schulz-Herzenberg, and R. Southall, 122–127. Auckland Park: Jacana.

Habib, Adam, and Collette Schulz-Herzenberg. 2011. "Democratization and Parliamentary Opposition in Contemporary South Africa: The 2009 National and Provincial Elections in Perspective." *Politikon* 38 (2): 191–210.

Heffernan, Anne, and Noor Nieftagodien. 2016. *Students Must Rise: Youth Struggle in South Africa Before and Beyond Soweto '76*. Johannesburg: Wits University Press.

Human Sciences Research Council. 2014. *IEC Voter Participation Survey 2013/14: An Overview of Results.* Accessed July 3, 2019. https://www.elections.org.za/content/Documents/Research-and-Statistics/Voter-Participation-Surveys/Slide-Presentation-of-HSRC-2013-Voter-Participation-Survey-(PDF)/.

Kersting, Norbert. 2007. "Electoral Reform in Southern Africa: Voter Turnout, Electoral Rules and Infrastructure." *Journal of African Elections* 6 (1): 134–151.

Khumalo, Siphumelele. 2019. "We Will Not Vote, Say Residents." *The Star*, April 11.

Lodge, Tom. 2003. "Voter Abstention in the South African General Election of 1999." *Representation* 39 (2): 105–118.

Mabena, Sipho. 2016. "Vuwani: The No Show Counts." *The Times*, August 5.

Mattes, Robert. 2014. "The 2014 Election and South African Democracy." In *Election 2014 South Africa: The Campaigns, Results and Future Prospects*, edited by C. Schulz-Herzenberg, and R. Southal, 20–41. Auckland Park: Jacana.

McAdam, Doug, and Sidney Tarrow. 2010. "Ballots and Barricades: On the Reciprocal Relationship Between Elections and Social Movements." *Perspectives on Politics* 8 (2): 529–542.

Mkhize, Vumani, and Graeme Raubenheimer. 2014. *Bekkersdal Vows to Boycott Voter Registration.* Accessed July 3, 2019. http://ewn.co.za/2014/02/08/Bekkersdal-vows-to-boycott-voter-registration.

Moseley, Mason, and Daniel Moreno. 2010. "The Normalization of Protest in Latin America." *Americas Barometer Insight* 42: 1–7.

Nicolson, Greg. 2014. "Kasrills and the 'Vote No' Campaign: Point of No Return." *Daily Maverick.* Accessed July 3, 2019. https://www.dailymaverick.co.za/article/2014-04-15-kasrils-and-the-vote-no-campaign-point-of-no-return/.

Norris, Pippa. 2002. *Democratic Phoenix: Reinventing Political Activism.* New York: Cambridge University Press.

Ntshidi, Edwin. 2019. "Protests to Spike Ahead of Election, Warns Municipal IQ." *EWN*, April 12. Accessed July 2, 2019. https://ewn.co.za/2019/04/11/municipal-iq-warns-of-spike-in-service-delivery-protests-across-sa.

Ntshobane, Sikho. 2016. "Mayors say sorry after protests and threat to snub poll." *Daily Dispatch*, March 14.

Oyedemi, Toks, and Desline Mahlatji. 2016. "The 'Born-Free' Non-Voting Youth: A Study of Voter Apathy Among a Selected Cohort of South African Youth." *Politikon* 43 (3): 311–323.

Paret, Marcel. 2016. *Local Government Elections 2016: Some Preliminary Findings from an Exit Poll of Voters.* Accessed September 30, 2019. https://www.uj.ac.za/newandevents/Documents/LGE%202016%20Report%20CR%2011%2001_Final%20Cover%20Included.pdf.

Paret, Marcel. 2017. "Southern Resistance in Critical Perspective." In *Southern Resistance in Critical Perspective: The Politics of Protest in South Africa's Contentious Democracy*, edited by M. Paret, C. Runciman, and Luke Sinwell, 1–18. London: Routledge.

Paret, Marcel, and Carin Runciman. 2019. *Who Votes? Preliminary Findings from an Exit Survey of Voters in the 2019 National Elections.* Accessed September 30, 2019. https://www.uj.ac.za/contact/Documents/Final%202019%20election%20report.pdf.

Power, Timothy J., and Timmons J. Roberts. 1995. "Compulsory Voting, Invalid Ballots and Abstention in Brazil." *Political Research Quarterly* 48: 795–826.

Runciman, Carin. 2016. "The "Ballot and the Brick": Protest, Voting and Non-Voting in Post-Apartheid South Africa." *Journal of Contemporary African Studies* 34 (4): 419–436.

Runciman, Carin. 2018. "New Amendments to Labour Legislation are Likely to Increase Unprotected Strikes." *Business Day*, February 8. Accessed September 30, 2019. https://www.businesslive.co.za/bd/opinion/2018-02-08-new-amendments-to-labour-legislation-are-likely-to-increase-unprotected-strikes/.

Runciman, Carin, Peter Alexander, Mahlatse Rampedi, Boikanyo Moloto, Boitumelo Maruping, Eunice Khumalo, and Selaphi Sibanda. 2016. *Counting Police Recorded Protests: Estimates Based on SAPS Data.* South African Research Chair in Social Change: Johannesburg University of Johannesburg.

Runciman, Carin, Linah Nkuna, and Pier Paulo Frassinelli. 2017. "Survey Sheds Light on Who Marched Against Zuma and Why." *The Conversation Africa*, April 20. Accessed September 30, 2019. https://theconversation.com/survey-sheds-light-on-who-marched-against-president-zuma-and-why-76271.

Ryabchuck, Anastasia. 2016. "Voter Abstention in South African 2014 Elections: Beyond the Apathy Argument." *Transformation* 92: 37–59.

Saul, John S., and Patrick Bond. 2014. *South Africa - The Present as History: From Mrs Ples to Mandela and Marikana*. Rochester, NY: Boydell & Brewer Ltd.

Saunders, Clare. 2014. "Anti-Politics in Action? Measurement Dilemmas in the Study of Unconventional Political Participation." *Political Research Quarterly* 67 (3): 574–588.

Schulz-Herzenberg, Collette. 2016. "Shifting Electoral Trends, Participation and Party Support." *Journal of Public Administration* 51 (3): 487–512.

Schulz-Herzenberg, Collette. 2019a. "Trends in Voter Participation: Registration, Turnout and the Disengaging Electorate." In *Election 2019: Change and Stability in South Africa's Democracy*, edited by C. Schulz-Herzenberg, and R. Southall, 44–65. Auckland Park: Jacana Media.

Schulz-Herzenberg, Collette. 2019b. "To Vote or Not? Testing Micro-Level Theories of Voter Turnout in South Africa's 2014 General Election." *Politikon* 46 (2): 139–156.

Schussman, Alan, and Sarah A. Soule. 2005. "Process and Protest: Accounting for Individual Protest Participation." *Social Forces* 84: 1083–1108.

Tomlinson, Mark, Wesley Solomon, Yages Singh, Tanya Doherty, Mickey Chopra, Petrida Ijumba, Alexander C. Tsai, and Debra Jackson. 2009. "The Use of Mobile Phones as a Data Collection Tool: A Report From a Household Survey in South Africa." *BMC Medical Informatics and Decision Making* 9 (1): 1–8.

Appendix 1: Sites sampled in 2014, 2016 and 2019 exit surveys.

2014 sites

Site	Municipality	Province
Alexandra	City of Johannesburg	Gauteng
Bekkersdal	Rand West City	Gauteng
Bokfontein	Madibeng	North West
Brixton	City of Johannesburg	Gauteng
Diepkloof Extension	City of Johannesburg	Gauteng
Dube hostel	City of Johannesburg	Gauteng
KwaThema	Ekurhuleni	Gauteng
Motsoaledi	City of Johannesburg	Gauteng
Noordgesig	City of Johannesburg	Gauteng
Potchefstroom	Tlokwe	North West
Rustenberg	Rustenburg	North West
Thembelihle	City of Johannesburg	Gauteng
University of Johannesburg (Auckland Park Kingsway Campus)	City of Johannesburg	Gauteng
Zamdela	Metsimaholo	Free State
Zandspruit	City of Johannesburg	Gauteng

2016 sites

Site	Municipality	Province
Alexandra	City of Johannesburg	Gauteng
Balfour	Dipaleseng	Mpumalanga
Brixton	City of Johannesburg	Gauteng
Freedom Park	City of Johannesburg	Gauteng
Hammanskraal	City of Tshwane	Gauteng
Marikana	Rustenburg	North West
Motsoaledi	City of Johannesburg	Gauteng
Potechstroom	Tlokwe	Gauteng
Thembelihle	City of Johannesburg	Gauteng
University of Johannesburg (Auckland Park Kingsway Campus)	City of Johannesburg	Gauteng
Zamdela	Metsimaholo	Free State

2019 sites

Site	Municipality	Province
Alexandra	City of Johannesburg	Gauteng
Bekkersdal	Rand West City	Gauteng
Brixton	City of Johannesburg	Gauteng
Cato Manor	Ethekwini	KwaZulu Natal
Diepkloof Ext	City of Johannesburg	Gauteng
Dube Hostel	City of Johannesburg	Gauteng
Fourways	City of Johannesburg	Gauteng
Freedom Park	City of Johannesburg	Gauteng
Kamhlushwa	Nkomazi	Mpumalanga
Kimberly	Sol Plaatje	Northern Cape
Kuruman	Ga-Segonyana	Northern Cape
KwaThema	Ekurhuleni	Gauteng
Kwazakhele	Nelson Mandela Bay	Eastern Cape
Marikana, Philipi	City of Cape Town	Western Cape
Motsoaledi	City of Johannesburg	Gauteng
Noordgesig	City of Johannesburg	Gauteng
Mkhondo	Mkhondo	Mpumalanga
Thembelihle	City of Johannesburg	Gauteng
University of Johannesburg (Auckland Park Kingsway Campus)	City of Johannesburg	Gauteng
University of the Witwatersrand (Braamfontein Campus)	City of Johannesburg	Gauteng
Wonderkop	Rustenburg	North West
Zamdela	Metsimaholo	Free State
Zandspruit	City of Johannesburg	Gauteng

Land Reform and Belonging in South Africa: A Place-making Perspective

Leslie J. Bank ⓘ and Tim G. B. Hart ⓘ

ABSTRACT
Political debate around South African land reform peaks in the run up to the national elections. 2019 was no exception. Escalating urban 'land grabs' in 2017 had already increased emotion, tension and political urgency on the issue. However, the debate again carried surprisingly little weight at the polls. It was overshadowed by the burning issues of jobs, housing, crime, corruption and service delivery. We offer some insights into the racial and cultural topography of the attachment to land in South Africa, and how historical processes of settlement affect the nature of land hunger and demand in South Africa today through a place-making lens. The article is based on our own experiences, research and observations in rural and urban and urban areas, along with two recent studies of urban and rural land hunger we jointly undertook in 2017 and 2018. In retrospect it seems that, despite the perversely unequal nature of the South African spatial economy, there is an uncanny stability to local settlement patterns. Despite urbanisation, the homelands remain favoured spaces for African homemaking, while white South Africans cling to the coastline as a preferred place of investment. The debate about the productive use of land for development, we argue, should not be abstracted from an appreciation of the complex way in which land is inhabited, used and valued.

Introduction

Land reform remains a political and emotive lightning rod in South Africa and most of the rumpus around land seems to occur in the periods between national elections (Netsebeza and Hall 2007). Thus, land reform seems not to play much of a role in securing new votes or losing political party support. Indeed, Schwikowski (2019) observes, political commentators suggest that land reform is not the reason South Africans vote for a party or candidate: 'They are more interested in jobs, health and increased security'. In previous elections, political parties have always included some mandate about land reform, jobs and housing, but this has not necessarily been realised. More than four million houses have been built by the state in urban areas and only an estimated 8–10% of commercial land has been distributed – less than the desired target of 30%. The desire for land redistribution has politically waxed and waned since 1994, yet it remains an issue that cannot be ignored by major political parties because of the importance of land redistribution for nation building and addressing inequality. The 2019 General elections were no different in respect to the significance of land redistribution. Despite the furore over expropriation without compensation (EWC) during the two years preceding the 2019 General Elections and millions of Rands spent on determining if changing Section 25 of the Constitution was acceptable to the populace, no such change is in fact necessary (Netsebeza 2007; Ngcukaitobi 2018). Section 25 of the Constitution is quite clear on how land and other property can be expropriated in terms of existing law and allows for expropriation under certain circumstances, including those highlighted during the various workshops during 2018. The two new parties with land as a major political mandate and rallying point, the Black First Land First party and the Land Party, failed to secure seats in the National Parliament. The same fate befell the new Socialist Revolutionary Workers Party, also having land as a core part of its mandate.

With regard to land reform and party-political promised mandates in the 2019 General Elections, most of the key parties represented in Parliament had little new to add to their usual beliefs about land reform. These parties focused on rural areas, agricultural development and agrarian reform in these areas. Only the Democratic Alliance (DA) specifically mentioned urban areas, where the greatest need for land is felt by South Africans. The African National Congress (ANC) continued with its past rhetoric of focusing on agricultural production and economic development along with collaboration with established agribusinesses (Ngcukaitobi 2019). According to the ANC no structural shifts, as necessary as they are, were tabled (ANC 2019). The farming economic model remains unexplained or even challenged, despite its lack of success for most land beneficiaries. The ANC dismissed EWC as a harmless necessity for ensuring faster and better land reform within the rule of law; as if a change in the Constitution or how land is acquired will really make a difference to the outcomes. Much more is needed and requires not only an egalitarian focus and greater investment by the state, but also a clear understanding of the demand for land and intended use so that diverse needs can be understood and catered for. Ironically, Ms Thoko Didiza, the former minister who drove land reform towards its current inegalitarian pathways, has returned as Minister of Agriculture, Rural Development and Land Reform to lead land reform into the future. Such an appointment seemingly illustrates that the government is unaware of local land hunger and the diverse purposes for which land is demanded.

The DA's electoral promise on land reform starts by pointing out the corruption within the land reform programme, elite capture, lack of political will, post-acquisition support and training (DA 2019). The party then highlights the idea that EWC will negatively impact on the rights of all property owners and argues that they will protect these rights, despite their being enshrined in the Constitution. For the DA, the redress component of land reform and the emphasis on its importance for economic development is crucial. But much of what they have to say is almost an antithesis of the mandates outlined by the EFF and the ANC, while in other instances they like the ANC will work with existing farmers and agribusinesses (ANC 2019; DA 2019). They also don't envisage much structural change and are keen to push for share equity scheme farms – a partnership of commercial farmers and their workers (DA 2019). The DA, like the ANC, largely remains unclear about how what they will do will create jobs and bring about economic development.

The Economic Freedom Fighters (EFF) are against private property rights and want all land under the custodianship of the state, while certain game parks will be nationalised (EFF 2019). Since 2006, as part of the Proactive Land Acquisition Strategy (PLAS), recent land redistribution means that this redistributed land is already under state custodianship. Yet, as Hall and Kepe (2017) observe, there has been little fairness or justice in this process, which largely manifests as elite capture whereby multinational firms and local elites lease this land from the state at relatively low costs, as opposed to redistribution to the poor. The EFF is silent on how this can be prevented. Unlike the DA and the ANC, the EFF is committed to passing legislation that will affect land redistribution and agrarian reform, which may lead to tangible structural change in these policy areas (EFF 2019). They are also willing to address communal and customary land rights and the protection of indigenous people from dispossession of land rights. Rather than working with existing farmers and agribusinesses, the EFF's populist rhetoric wants to regulate these roleplayers (EFF 2019). Like the ANC, the EFF does not address corruption, which is as evident in land reform as elsewhere (AG 2019).

All three leading parties fail to address the plight of labour tenants and labour dwellers (farmworkers and their families). The DA might envisage them as part of their shared equity schemes, but these are actually very small in number and largely Western Cape-based. These schemes would not account for the numerous farmworkers and their families who become homeless by default when they resign or are dismissed. They are ignored by the ANC and the EFF.

While many academics and researchers have written about the inadequacies, inefficiency and even the historical continuities of land reform policy and practice in South Africa over the past 25 years (Aliber et al. 2013; Cochet, Anseeuw, and Fréguin-Gresh 2015; Cousins 2013; Cousins and Walker 2015; De Wet 1997; Greenberg 2010; Hebinck and Cousins 2013; James 2007; Kepe and Hall 2018; Weidman 2004), we consider a slightly different and less instrumentalist approach to understanding the contemporary 'land issue' in South Africa. Much has happened since 1995 that shapes the land reform debate. Policies and practices have changed, and financial resources allocated to the land reform budget has dropped significantly since 2008 (APLR&A 2019, 13).[1] Black South Africans now own farmland individually and have title deeds, and, despite training and infrastructure constraints, some of these farmers farm regularly and productively. South Africa experienced significant changes politically, economically, socially and culturally since the 1913 Land Act. We cannot simply return to a pre-1913 land status quo. Agriculture, the main driver of rural development in South Africa's rural countryside, has changed. Since the 1960s farming units have got larger through consolidation, while the number of farming units has decreased (Liebenberg 2013). There are now fewer farmers (landowners), more capital-intensive technology is being used, and labour has been consistently shed. In this article we avoid offering a solution to the many constraints that have negatively affected land reform in so many ways as this goes beyond the space available. We believe it is more helpful to explore what land means to South Africans in the twenty-first century. Our starting point is that land reform should be considered from the perspective of land and its connectedness to social belonging (homemaking), i.e. from a cultural and not simply economic perspective. For years political parties have ignored the land needs of South Africans and the significance of land. Similarly, they continue to ignore the consequences of policies and thereby continue with the same strategies., based on little evidence.

In exploring rural livelihoods in the former Transkei, Shackleton and Hebinck (2018) argue that when trying to understand farming practices in the southern Transkei, we should start from the premise of this place as a landscape of belonging. Here, they mean as a place for Xhosa home-making, where farming is still a critical component of multiple live-lihood strategies, but not a necessary condition for homestead building (see McAllister 2001), which in turn is the building block for a connection to place. In this context, they suggest that household involvement in agriculture in the former Transkei simply cannot be seen as either a linear process of *proletarianisation* (the shift from a peasantry to a rural working class) nor as a process of *de-agrarianisation* (marking a permanent shift away from agriculture as a livelihood strategy). Instead, they speak of the conditions under which both 'thick' and 'thin' farming persists in a region of belonging (Shackleton and Hebinck 2018, 277), where the former focuses on field production and the latter on keeping a garden plot and small livestock next to the homestead to save money on food expenditure and to use the savings for other purposes, such as clothing, health and education (see Hart 2011).

In this article we consider the implications of a wider focus on landscape and home-making as a lens for understanding of the implications of land reform in South Africa. We suggest that the process of investment in, and the struggles for land, are profoundly shaped by cultural and place-making considerations that have important implications for the capacity of land reform policy and practice to build a more inclusive and productive economy and society. We also argue that contemporary shallow and increasingly exploi-tative, exclusionary forms of rentier capitalism on the land undermines the longer-term prospects for growth and development through more productive land use. Such strategies also offer limited capacity to address the challenges of economic inclusion and inequality – in fact they tend to do the opposite. Political manifestos and policies continue to ignore these realities and remain focused on 1994 (ANC 1994) and 1997 (DLA 1997) ideals of land redistribution and ignore the importance of place-making and social relationships.

Methodology

This article is drawn from our experiences as anthropologists, each with more than 20 years of research in urban, peri-urban and rural areas. It is supported by two studies we undertook together on Land Hunger and Access to the City by the poor in 2017 and 2018, respectively. These two studies respectively drew on literature reviews and ethno-graphic fieldwork in nine rural districts and five urban metropoles across South Africa.

Homelands as 'heartlands'

The anti-apartheid discourse of the 1980s often presented the Bantustans or homelands as 'concentration camps', where 'surplus Africans' who could not be accommodated in the white economy were sent to die. This actually happened, as the ethnographies and reports from rural slums in places like QwaQwa, Bophuthatswana and the former Ciskei attest (Desmond 1971; Platsky and Walker 1985). Mass relocation camps were set up in the open veld without services, agricultural land or employment. The former homelands were also created through an earlier history of African resistance to colonialism and land alienation. They were places where African polities, clans and families dug in their heels in a desperate struggle to protect their sovereignty, land and homes from colonial dispossession. These places are simultaneously heartlands of great cultural and emotional significance and products of apartheid history.

Today, rural home-making in the former homelands is a multi-dimensional process linked to this history, as well as the challenges of the urban job market in the twenty-first century. The homesteads that Shackleton and Hebinck (2018) describe were embroiled in the system of labour migration throughout the twentieth century. The capacity to access the urban labour market as migrants and to bring wages home to supplement rural income and subsistence was always vital to the process of building a homestead; especially where households generally did not have sufficient land to produce enough food for their own subsistence (also see Wilson 1972; Wolpe 1972).

In a spirit of resistance, rural regimes of value were created to neutralise the alienating power of enforced wage labour, colonial control and a cash economy (Comaroff and Comaroff 1992; Coplan 1994). In the townships African men and women judged each other by the clothes they wore, the goods they purchased, the education they acquired, and even the cars they drove, but this was not the case in the countryside. Here, cash and consumerism were more ambiguous and often viewed as 'hot and dangerous', morally threatening and corrosive (see Bank 2011; Niehaus 2010). Hence, it created an imperative for labourers to convert their cash into cattle to anchor the security and prestige of rural homestead in traditional values and cater for the needs of social reproduction, which revolved around bride wealth payments and cattle exchanges (see Ferguson 1990; Kuper 1980; Murray 1980).

Attempts by the colonial state to cull cattle to protect the rural reserves from overstocking and soil erosion during the 1940s produced rural rebellions across the reserves in the 1950s, from the Eastern Cape to the North West and Limpopo (see Kepe and Ntsebeza 2011). In a context where rural patriarchs and chiefs were judged by the size of their herds, it was difficult to accept state-imposed limits to cattle keeping. Rural communities also revolted against the replacement of trusted traditional leaders, who upheld local rural regimes of value, with authorities selected by the apartheid government under the Bantu Authorities Act of 1951. Extreme force was used to restore order and shifted emphasis away from individualised patriarchal strategies of home building to a collective culture of shared poverty based on the reconstruction of ideas of tribe and ethnicity, which underpinned the homeland system.

In post-apartheid South Africa, as in the post-Soviet territories of Eastern Europe, older values have re-emerged as the repression and controls of the past ebbed away. The Soviet regimes of enforced collectivisation weakened and collapsed in many places when older social organisation, values and cultural capital resurfaced after socialism (see Hann 1996; Humphries 1996; Verdery 1998). In rural South Africa, the loyalties of tribe and ethnicity are no longer as important as in the past and have become articulated with new versions of South African and African nationalism in a globalised world. Similarly, as apartheid settlement and population controls fell away, many people reconnected with their histories, place-based identities and family tradition at 'home', while many family members urbanised.

Thus, despite the rapid urbanisation in South Africa since 1994, the former Bantustans have not lost their value as 'heartlands' and 'home-spaces'. In fact, Jacob Zuma almost lost his presidency when he scandalously used state funds to build a palatial rural family home in Zululand. For Africans, dignified and legitimate rural home-making comes with struggle and commitment, it cannot be built on ill-begotten state funds. Zuma's sleight of hand marked his political downfall. Nevertheless, the Zuma home-making project also confirmed the new aspirational template of post-apartheid, rural home-making, which is not anti-agrarian, but places greater value in the symbols of suburban citizenship and affluence than agrarian investment.

In this frame, modern houses and cars are the forms of value most coveted in the countryside. To be sure, gardening is still useful to symbolise tradition and keep consumption costs down at home, while social grants are vital for every day subsistence needs. The status of the rural homestead, however, rests now on the suburban look and feel of the main house matters – and also whether household members have smart phones, post-school educations, government jobs and personal cars – all of which are conspicuously displayed. They are also a source of great envy amongst neighbours and kin, which can be socially very divisive.

The vitality of the rural house as a symbol of modernity and citizenship in the former Transkei and Ciskei was confirmed by the general manager of the hardware chain store, BUCO, George Williams. He noted that sales in the rural Eastern Cape were, on average, 40% higher than in the Western Cape: 'Those from the old homelands are investing more in their country homes than in their city houses'. He also observed that BUCO stores in ex-homeland towns are among the top performers for the company, while the Eastern Cape is the best performing region in South Africa, despite the dire state of its productive economy: 'This is a growth market for us, stores like the one at Butterworth now does more than R4 million turnover a month' (Personal Communication June 2019).

Other industry representatives, like Cash Build, said that volumes in old Eastern Cape homelands have been increasing between 5% and 10%, year on year, over the past decade. Store managers also noted that flexible payment schemes allowed urban migrants to purchase goods in Johannesburg, Durban or Cape Town and have them collected at the store by a local builder or relative. To be sure, cattle still retain their residual value and remain a basis through which families can express their upward mobility and status in the rural sector (Bank and Kenyon 2019; Shackleton and Hebinck 2018). Fields are also still used, and gardens planted, sometimes only very occasionally.

Since the 2000s, the youth have left the rural areas in ever larger numbers to find urban jobs. They display little or no interest in low-status agriculture job at home, nor in making careers in farming. There primary aim is for urban education and employment. There is consequently little overt land hunger for crop farming in homelands because the focus of household investment and aspiration is not located in the agrarian economy. Moreover, where chiefs or headmen sell and barter land (illegally), it is mainly to families seeking residential plots close to towns, or for mining, rather than agricultural use.

The investment in brick and mortar in the former homelands and coloured rural reserves, particularly in rural villages, far exceeds the levels of investments in farming and cattle keeping (authors' own observations). Urban transfers and remittances are no longer primarily converted into 'goodly beasts', as much as they are into 'beastly goods'. Cash and commodities are also not hot and morally dangerous in the way they used to be, as they are now key markers of rural upward mobility and status differentiation. Family rituals are also much less about affirming wider social connection and sharing, than about demonstrating to neighbours and kin that migrant families continue to make invest-ments in rural home-making.

Reduced rates of marriage in rural and urban areas has also encouraged this aggrega-tion, because building a homestead of one's own is usually only expected after marriage. Until you are married, you remain part of the larger family and are socially obliged to work towards its well-being. Siblings now work together from the cities to build the dignity and status of their family homesteads. The insecurity of the urban labour market is another reason why building at home seems sensible to urban migrants and even immigrant. Rural areas remain places for anchoring in family, culture and tradition in an uncertain world (see Bank 2015a; Perry 2017).

The form that rural anchoring has taken since the end of apartheid has profoundly affected not only the urban property market, which has been slow to development in poorer communities, but also the demand for agricultural land in rural areas. Ineffective rural development policies are also to blame. Moreover, part of the intensity of the struggle for urban land today is related to the desire of urban household to use that land to raise rent (cash), which can be reinvested in rural home-building, affirming a per-vasive commitment to doubled rootedness in African communities. There is currently a development paradox in South Africa between urban dwelling and rural building, where the spirit of suburbanisation in the city is being enthusiastically embraced in the countryside. Thus, while the state imagines the former homelands as landscapes of pro-ductive, small-scale farms, the residents and migrants from there have prioritised turning family homesteads into suburban houses and compounds as a key post-apartheid development priority. They have chosen sub-urbanisation over agrarianism. So, to discuss the agrarian change in the former homelands today without an appreciation of the process of popular suburbanisation would be to ignore the current connections between *dwelling* and *building* (see Bank and Kenyon 2019; Sennett 2018).

Home-making in townships and suburbs

The existence of these practices and values in rural South Africa does not, of course, prevent people from urbanising or building permanent homes for themselves in the cities. This process is happening on a massive scale there too, especially as townships and suburbs have become the permanent and desired home of many Africans (Bank et al. 2018). The former apartheid urban settlements were initially rejected as match boxes on postage stamp plots – relative to what white South Africans had – but since the end of apartheid these have emerged as desirable and appropriate places for African home-making in the pursuit of urban permanence. Soweto is now so popular as a place that it has its own TV channel. Many of the classic old apartheid townships, like Soweto or Orlando in Johannesburg, Mamelodi in Pretoria, Mdantsane in East London, Umlazi and Kwa-Mashu in Durban, or even Khayelitsha in Cape Town have developed a new post-apartheid urban identity, charisma and style which sets them aside from the past. The capacity of these areas to transition from townships to African suburbs seem to be predicated on the stability of a social core of original families, which anchor the place. The identity of place here is associated with these families, with their unique politi-cal and social traditions of resistance to apartheid and to the cultures of their well-known streets, taverns and places.

Where home-making has not yet been achieved in the cities, it is generally seen in the new Reconstruction and Development Programme (RDP) settlements and sprawling shack areas, many of which have been transformed into dense, informal slums with minimal basic services. Ironically, and contrary to the intention of state housing policy, it is from within these peripheral spaces and the surrounding shack areas that the strongest impulses for rural home-making exist (see Bank 2015a). It is precisely where the post-apartheid state has promised new opportunities for urban access and opportunity that the least powerful desire exists to transform shacks and houses into homes. It is here that those with resources continue to look over their shoulders to rural villages and settlements for the possibilities of dignity and belonging after their struggle for survival in the city wears thin.

As research shows (Bank et al. 2018), most residents in informal settlements come from other urban settlements or shack settlements as they struggle for the best location in the city, yet this does not necessarily diminish their appetites for rural investment and retreat. In fact, the commodification of everyday life in these under-serviced slums, which are characterised by rising shack rents, rampant crime and extractive commercial and social practices, is that they remain *unsettled* and express a sense of *placelessness*, as well as the pain of *homelessness* that people here feel all the time. This is a driving factor to ensure home-making in rural areas.

Shack settlements often initially enjoy a sense of social cohesion based on ideas of struggle. They are frequently named through an insurgent language of land claim, referencing liberation icons such as Joe Slovo and Chris Hani, or alternatively through some hopeful reference of co-operation for survival, such as Imizamo Yethu (our effort) or Masiphumelele (hope for success). This sense of identity is usually lost in the process of their conversion of RDP settlements as only the chosen few get houses or services. Divisions emerge, which are exacerbated when the beneficiaries of RDP houses are transformed into rent seeking landlords, who transform their suburban lots into shack farms. The absence of the common Nguni (IsiXhosa and IsiZulu) prefix *Kwa* (meaning, place of), as in KwaMashu in Durban or Kwazekele in Port Elizabeth, in the naming of informal settlements is indicative of this feeling of urban alienation. New forms of urban alienation, dislocation and exclusion fuel feelings nostalgia for home and encourage rural investment in what Bank (2015a) calls the *displaced urbanism*.

Land hunger and coastal whiteness

So, what does this mean for land reform? The first point to make is that the desire of black South Africans is for a place they can call home in a society which has for more than 300 years tried to render them homeless – and still does to a considerable extent. Not surprisingly, many of these homes are made in the former homelands, where there is little demand for land for agrarian crop production. Range land for cattle is still needed, but people in these areas are generally less interested in crop and horticultural farming for a living (Hebinck and van Averbeke 2013). Families in these areas also generally cannot work much more than the land they have because so many of their family members are seeking a living in the cities (Hebinck and van Averbeke 2013). Since the main focus in individual and family livelihood strategies today centre on urban employment or wages, rather than rural production, land hunger has unsurprisingly been expressed through 'land grabbing' in the metros. In the old 'heartlands', there is no need to 'grab land' because access to residential land is not restricted or refused. And, as we have explained, because of the lower rates of marriage, families are mainly building new sub-urban-style homes on land their families already hold or control rather than opening up new Greenfield sites. In areas closer to thriving rural towns, where well-located land for settlement is scarce and valuable, there is now clear evidence of the commodification of communal land, as chiefs and headmen sell un-serviced sites for a once off fee (Bank 2015a).

There is a demand for the wealth and income of the white commercial farms, but there is currently little desire to transform this land into thriving commercial farms. Where communities have seized land in the rural areas, they have generally made new homes and accumulated new assets, rather than developing agricultural businesses. The startling figures of the failure of land reforms projects to generate large-scale economic returns is evidence of this trend. The reasons for failed land reform projects are, of course, the result of many other factors as well, such as a lack of inputs, training, refusal to subdivide land into accessible and pragmatic parcels, and poor administration of projects that seem to require continual funding (Aliber et al. 2013; Bank et al. 2017; Cochet, Anseeuw, and Fréguin-Gresh 2015). The home-making impulse is also a result of the generally enforced communalism of some of these projects, which makes it difficult for individual families and entrepreneurs to break out of the apartheid model of 'shared poverty' (Bank et al. 2017; James 2001).

A recent national scan of land needs and demands revealed that rural residents wanted to work land as families rather than as communities, and that their interest was primarily in small scale farming that could be incrementally supported by the state and developed over time (Bank et al. 2017). The mismatch between the desire for land reform and the redistribution process is plainly seen in the state's refusal to resize farms or offer individualised opportunities for low- and middle-income families, which stunts the ability of those who do want to farm in the rural areas from making a go of it.

Nevertheless, the bulk of land demand in South Africa is for urban land where poor families in shack areas and informal settlements seek alternative modes of accessing the city outside of the exploitative rental arrangements that earlier arrivals in the city have set up in the main receiving areas (Harber 2011). Some want land to escape these relations, others seek it to replicate them so that they can build resources to find a better place to live in the city or extract enough income from new arrivals to rebuild rural homes into the image of suburban life to which they aspire.

White South Africans' land hunger is also limited to the city and the coastal resorts to which they have migrated since the end of apartheid. In the Eastern Cape, for example, many white people with resources who owned or worked on farms under apartheid have moved to coastal towns, like Jeffreys Bay, Kenton-On-Sea or Port Alfred, to settle and set up guesthouses or small businesses. Farm murders are another reason for the coastal drift (Bank 2015b). The massive rise of agribusiness and the escalating size of farms in South Africa is thus not merely a function of the economic imperatives of globa-lisation and the concentration of capital. It is a product of the fact that many rural white South Africans no longer see farms as safe or even viable places for home-making. Outside of landscape niche areas, like the winelands of the Western Cape, parts of the Natal midlands or game farms, where lifestyle, tourist opportunity and farming intersect in mutually beneficial ways for white people, the desire is to leave the land for a good price and retire to a coastal town or city away from the vagaries of climate change, rising farm murders, and fear and insecurity in the heart of the country.

The investments white South Africans make in suburban and coastal landscape has as much to do with home-making as they do with profit seeking. It is often a form of exit, what some call 'semi-gration', from a society where they feel increasingly alienated and realise that seeking refuge is a better strategy than committing their capital to new economic ventures that are shrouded in uncertainty. The opportunity of extracting rent from property in the suburbs, or better still, from tourists at the coast or on a game farm seem to have far more appeal to them than reinvesting in growing the productive economy. The land expropriation without compensation decision offers a massive threat to the exit and new low-key accumulation strategies of the economically dominant class since it removes the capital on which their escape from black domination is predicated.

Agribusiness and the 'empty land'

New formats of more rapid rural land reform have been adopted where the state has acquired large farms in the former white countryside and then leased them to new elites, who hold the land under lease from the state. Hall and Kepe (2017) have criticised this state-led process as elitist, because it fails to effect fundamental transformations in the way the land is used, farmed and occupied. They suggest that the new version of the land reform programme, PLAS, looks like a thinly veiled attempt to reward and enrich politically connected elites, who use the state land leased to them to build their own asset portfolios, without actually farming it themselves. They explain, that the new mode of accumulation is predicted on rent extraction from agribusinesses which produce on land they do not own. Moreover, Hall and Kepe (2017) argue that the model contradicts the spirit and content of the post-apartheid land reform programme because it fails to address the needs of poor and emerging black farmers in any significant way. It excludes them completely.

However, the difficulties that the state is currently experiencing in finding enthusiastic young black farmers to transform the mainly white-owned commercial agricultural countryside are not only the consequences of these dynamics, nor simply a consequence of appropriate training, inputs and failures in policy administration. They also relate to the longer-term processes of colonial, apartheid and post-apartheid land alienation and the social 'thinning' of the connections that Africans have too much of the formerly white, commercial farmland.

Forced removals and homeland development after the 1960s was a direct response to what the apartheid perceived as a deepening attachment of black families to 'white land' in the context of increasing white urbanisation. In the early twentieth century, Afrikaner nationalists frequently argued that when Afrikaners trekked into the interior, they found that the land was 'empty' and thus they did not seize it as much as occupy it. They also argued that their forms of occupation and the domestication of land were beneficial to the country. Amongst others, they brought a social thickness to occupation which embedded particular pieces of land into the culture and history of God-fearing families who were sons of the African soil.

The absence of sufficient labour in Afrikaner families to produce significant surpluses for the market, encouraged them to partner with African tenants and sharecroppers, who in partnership with Afrikaner farmers modernised production in a labour-intensive model during the first half of the twentieth century. By the 1950s, the apartheid state was appalled by the continuing extent of the 'Beswarting van die platteland' – Afrikaans for the blackening of the countryside – (the title of an influential government report in 1950) and introduced massive new capital-intensive schemes to replace subsistence labour tenants with technologies and machinery across the sector, sponsored by the Land Bank and the state (Van Onselen 2005).

This resulted in massive forced removals across South Africa, which aimed to discon-nect black farmers from white land and re-domesticate them as land holders under tribal authority in the new homelands (Meredith 2006, 417). In 1994, the threat of land reform and enforced measures to shore up the security of tenure for blacks who remained on white land also resulted in farmers pushing their workers off the land and into small towns, thus effecting a new wave of social disconnection.

The effectiveness of these programmes in disconnecting black Africans socially and cul-turally from the white owned countryside and reconstituting it as 'empty land' should not be under-estimated in considering the current formats for land reform and limited success of the post-apartheid land reform programme. As many white farmers, especially in mar-ginal areas, now seek to cash in their land assets for profits that can assist them in making new homes in coastal locations, the state struggles to find appropriately qualified and committed black landowners who want to farm in the formats that the state requires. When land is transferred or seized, the most common response observed in the literature and empirical research is a process of social thickness and repossession rather than econ-omic transformation (Bank et al. 2018). Clearly the state has not got a suitable, pragmatic or economic plan to use the land it already has in its possession. Expropriation, without any pragmatic economic plan is going to negatively affect the countryside in multiple ways.

If land expropriation without compensation is to be predicated on the productive use of land for economic purposes and food security, then the current formats of opening the countryside to large-scale agribusiness, who use the land in partnership with black elites from the urban middle class, will be difficult to displace in the short term. To be sure, the transition from semi-feudal to capitalist farming by Afrikaners on the land in the twentieth century occurred in several phases, of which recreation of the countryside as *culturally white* was a critical precondition for the successful agrarian transition to state-subsidised capitalist farming under apartheid. The lack of success in the post-apart-heid era in reconnecting black Africans to the land constitutes a major threat to the new expropriation for production programme achieving both its political and economic objectives.

Conclusion

As South Africans seek new homes and reassert their connection to historic places of comfort in a society where new forms of home-making have proved challenging, it is likely that many of the farms transferred under land reform will be run by absentee land-lords or urban elites, and that agricultural production will not necessarily increase, under the pressures of climate change, to above the current 2.5% of GDP. Coastal and rural home-building will continue to be sponsored by a variety of forms of rentier capitalism, targeting vulnerable members of the aspirant urban working class at the margins, international agribusinesses and visiting tourists on holiday. In South Africa, both urban shack rentals and tourist accommodation are massively overpriced and seem to be destroying the very markets they rely on for survival. While the transfer of land to international investors in the Cape or renting it to international agribusinesses in the interior does very little to move an inclusive post-apartheid land reform agenda forward.

The persistence of the cultural legacies of colonial and apartheid land occupation and the current economics of home-making has created a stark disconnection between land, production and place-based economic development in South Africa. This limits the capacity of a rapid land reform to be able to fix South Africa's economic problems, create an inclusive economy, or meaningfully reduce poverty and inequality. History is not on the side of that kind of transition, and many opportunities for change have been wasted over the past 20 years. The failure of the ANC to acknowledge these failures recolonises the land issue as a question of lost racial assets and space, rather than a failure of appropriate forms of place-making (see Kepe and Hall 2018).

If the Zimbabwe style land reform process, with its disastrous economic consequences, directly resulted in half of Zimbabwe's population migrating to South Africa, then alternative strategies will need to be found in order to ensure simultaneous change in agrarian and urban social economies in South Africa. In the rural sector, there is a need to focus on new kinds of partnerships and on the redistribution of wealth and opportunity through farming. The creation of decent jobs on farms is critical, as well as a focus on profit sharing within arrangements which bolster productivity for market production, for food security and rural development. One of the critical questions raised by this paper is: will there an appetite for new forms of agrarian investment in the heartlands and beyond, once the current drive towards rural suburban, home improvement has run its course? With the support of technology and renewable energy, there must be new and innovative opportunities for investment in farming and other sectors, given that urban wages and capital continue to gravitate to the former homelands.

In the urban sector, it is critical that the government finally effects a real transition from providing housing and services to the poor to the creation of proper human settlements that encourage local investment, civic pride and drive long-term urban place-making. The current policy shift to township revitalisation must be extended and enlarged. Since urban land will be taken, the government, civic bodies and the private sector needs to proactively start preparing sites for settlement before they are invaded. Titling and ownership of urban land and dwellings by families living on that land must happen very rapidly, together with the promotion of new forms of civic organisation and popular participation in settlement formation and construction. In this area, the physical and infrastructural features of the settlement creation process (such as taps, sewers, toilets and cement) cannot be disconnected from the socio-cultural dimensions of.

The disjuncture between dwelling, building and belonging noted above lie at the heart of some of South Africa's most serious economic and social challenges. The fact that so few new productive and stable suburban communities have been able to take root in South Africa cities after apartheid and investment in home-making is still directed to the former homelands must be deeply concerning for the state. The current housing and settlement policies in South Africa seem unable to stablise urban communities in ways that allow them to out *a better life for all* in place. Shack farming in RDP settlements is a common way that housing beneficiaries now compensate for their failure to secure jobs and access to the city. This often undermines the possibilities of positive place-making in the long term.

Urban involution, community fracture, basic service breakdown, rising crime and violence are common outcomes of these processes of unplanned densification (Bank et al. 2018). In fact, the overheated rental market on well-located RDP sites drives new urban land invasions, to avoid rising rents, and accelerated rural home investment as the pathologies of place increase. The state has to find a way of creating space for the consolidation of urban communities without undermining the possibilities of positive place-making. Schools, parks, streets and other public infrastructure cannot be sacrificed for personal profit-seeking strategies by residents and councillors. The state must find incentives and strategies to convert the current forms of occupy urbanism into meaningful urban permanence. The state must try to prevent urban wages and income leaking out of the city on such a large scale to support rural home-making and suburban investment. The fact that political parties remain trapped in bifurcated discourses of communal versus freehold land tenure, formal versus informal settlements, or stolen land versus misused land denies them the possibility of meaningfully engaging with the complex ways in which land has been socialised, used and deployed in South Africa today.

It was Karl Marx who noted long ago that property is not a *relationship between people and things, but a relationship between people about things* (Marx 1990, 165). In the twentieth century, the brilliant Hungarian economist and anthropologist, Polanyi (2001) further enriched and developed these insights through his theories of substantive economics. These perspectives of socialised property seem lost to the EFF and even the ANC, as they both objectify land as a static racialized object, asset or thing that need only be released to ensure economic freedom for the majority. The belief of the DA that an extension of the way land is currently socialised will necessarily produce an inclusive economy is equally misguided. None of these political ideologies have worked. For land to become more productive in South Africa it must be re-socialised in new ways. Existing political mandates fail to realise this and remain focused on old and residual ways of doing things. In the light of more than a decade of state capture and corruption that has greatly reduced skills and resources, along with so many other policy mandates that the ANC has committed itself to, valuable and necessary land reform for the purposes of those who need it most (the rural and urban poor) remains major task that none of the political parties seem able to comprehend. Even those political parties that made small gains in the 2019 General Elections seem unaware that rural and urban South Africans want land for food security, settlement and close proximity to livelihoods. Political parties and their manifestos do not speak to the electorate and their relationships to land, nor do they appreciated that land reform will necessary require the restructuring of local level social relations, not merely the provision of support or the (re)allocated of assets.

Note

1. That this declining budget is evident after President Zuma came into power is not unsurprising in the light of the subsequent decade of State Capture and blatant corruption.

Acknowledgement

We thank the editor and the two anonymous peer reviewers for their insightful, provocative and relevant comments. We acknowledge the interaction with colleagues at the HSRC. This is our own original work and the views expressed do not reflect those of any other party.

Disclosure statement

No potential conflict of interest was reported by the authors.

ORCID

Leslie J. Bank ⓘ http://orcid.org/0000-0002-8506-7401
Tim G. B. Hart ⓘ http://orcid.org/0000-0003-0463-9947

References

AG (Auditor General). 2019. *Consolidated General Report on the Local Government Audit Outcomes, 2017–18*. Pretoria: Office of the Auditor General.

Aliber, M., T. Maluleke, T. Manenzhe, G. Paradza, and B. Cousins. 2013. *Land Reform and Livelihoods: Trajectories of Change in Northern Limpopo Province, South Africa*. Cape Town: HSRC Press.

ANC (African National Congress). 1994. *The Reconstruction and Development Programme*. Johannesburg: Umanyano Publications.

ANC (African National Congress). 2019. *Let's Grow South Africa Together: 2019 Election Manifesto*. Johannesburg: ANC.

Bank, L. J. 2011. *Home Spaces, Street Styles: Contesting Power and Identity in a South African City*. Johannesburg: Wits University Press.

Bank, L. J. 2015a. "City Slums, Rural Homesteads: Migrant Culture, Displaced Urbanism and the Citizenship of the Serviced House." *Journal of Southern African Studies* 41 (5): 1067–1081.

Bank, L. J. 2015b. "Frontiers of Freedom: Race, Landscape and the Coastal Cultures of South Africa." *Anthropology Southern Africa* 1&2: 30–55.

Bank, L. J., T. G. B. Hart, M. Patterson, A. Beukes, M. Gaqa, D. Grinaker, K. Gwala, et al. 2017. *Land Hunger in Rural South Africa (LHRSA): Towards a Strategic Land Needs and Use Assessment. Final Report*. Pretoria: Department of Rural Development and Land Reform.

Bank, L. J., and M. Kenyon. Forthcoming 2019. "Cattle After Migrant Labour? Emerging Markets and Changing Regimes of Value in Rural South Africa." In *Migrant Labour After Apartheid*, edited by L. Bank, D. Posel, and F. Wilson. Cape Town: HSRC Press.

Bank, L. J., M. Paterson, T. G. B. Hart, C. Ndinda, J. Visagie, N. Botha, E. Makhetha, et al. 2018. *Evaluating Interventions by the Department of Human Settlements to Facilitate Access to the City by the Poor*. Pretoria: Department of Human Settlements.

Cochet, H., W. Anseeuw, and S. Fréguin-Gresh. 2015. *South Africa's Agrarian Question*. Cape Town: HSRC Press.

Comaroff, J., and J. Comaroff. 1992. *Ethnography and Historical Imagination*. Emeryville: Avalon Publishing.

Coplan, D. B. 1994. *In the Time of Cannibals: The Words and Music of South Africa's Basotho Migrants*. Chicago: Chicago University Press.

Cousins, B. 2013. "Land Reform and Agriculture Uncoupled: The Political Economy of Rural Reform in Post-Apartheid South Africa." In *In the Shadow of Policy: Everyday Practices in South African Land and Agrarian Reform*, edited by P. Hebnick, and B. Cousins, 47–62. Johannesburg: Wits University Press.

Cousins, B., and C. Walker, eds. 2015. *Land Divided Land Restored: Land Reform in South Africa for the 21st Century*. Auckland Park: Jacana Media.

DA (Democratic Alliance). 2019. *The Manifesto for Change: One South Africa for All*. Cape Town: DA.

Desmond, C. 1971. *The Discarded People*. Hamondsworth: Penguin.

De Wet, C. 1997. "Land Reform in South Africa: A Vehicle for Justice and Reconciliation, or a Source of Further Inequality and Conflict?" *Development Southern Africa* 14 (3): 355–362.

DLA (Department of Land Affairs). 1997. *White Paper on South African Land Policy*. Pretoria: Government Printers.

EFF (Economic Freedom Fighters). 2019. *Our Land and Jobs Now: 2019 Election Manifesto*. Pretoria: EFF.

Ferguson, J. 1990. *The Anti-Politics Machine: Development, Depoliticization and Bureaucratic Power in Lesotho*. Cambridge: Cambridge University Press.

Greenberg, S. 2010. *Status Report on Land and Agricultural Policy in South Africa. Research Report 40*. Bellville: Institute for Poverty, Land and Agrarian Studies, University of the Western Cape.

Hall, R., and T. Kepe. 2017. "Elite Capture and State Neglect: New Evidence on South Africa's Land Reform." *Review of African Political Economy* 44 (15): 122–130.

Hann. 1996. "Introduction: Political Society and Civil Anthropology." In *Civil Society: Challenging Western Models*, edited by C. Hann, and E. Dunn, 1–26. London: Routledge.

Harber, A. 2011. *Diepsloot*. Jeppestown: Jonathan Ball Publishers (PTY) Ltd.

Hart, T. G. B. 2011. "The Significance of African Vegetables in Ensuring Food Security for South Africa's Rural Poor." *Agriculture and Human Values* 28 (3): 321–333.

Hebinck, P., and B. Cousins, eds. 2013. *In the Shadow of Policy: Everyday Practices in South African Land and Agrarian Reform*. Johannesburg: Wits University Press.

Hebinck, P., and W. van Averbeke. 2013. "What Constitutes the Agrarian in Rural Eastern Cape African Settlements?." In *In the Shadow of Policy: Everyday Practices in South African Land and Agrarian Reform*, edited by P. Hebinck, and B. Cousins, 189–204. Johannesburg: Wits University Press.

Humphries, D. 1996. *Forest Politics: The Evolution of International Cooperation*. London: Earthscan.

James, D. 2001. "Land for the Landless: Conflicting Images of Rural and Urban in South Africa's Land Reform Programme." *Journal of Contemporary African Studies* 19 (1): 93–109.

James, D. 2007. *Gaining Ground? 'Rights' and 'Property' in South African Land Reform*. Oxon: Routledge-Cavendish.

Kepe, T., and R. Hall. 2018. "Land Redistribution in South Africa: Towards Decolonisation or Recolonisation." *Politikon* 45 (1): 128–137.

Kepe, T., and L. Ntsebeza. 2011. "Introduction." In *Rural Resistance in South Africa: The Mpondo Revolts After Fifty Years*, edited by T. Kepe, and L. Ntsebeza, 1–18. Leiden: Brill.

Kuper, A. 1980. *Wives for Cattle: Bridewealth and Marriage in Southern Africa*. London: Routledge and Keegan Paul, Ltd.

Liebenberg, F. 2013. "South African Agricultural Production, Productivity and Research Performance in the 20th Century." Unpublished PhD thesis, University of Pretoria.

Marx, K. 1990. *Capital: A Critique of Political Economy*. Vol. 1. Translated by Ben Fowkes. New York: Penguin.

McAllister, P. 2001. *Building the Homestead: Agriculture, Labour and Beer in South Africa's Transkei (African Studies from the Netherlands Series 16/200)*. Aldershot: Ashgate Publishing.

Meredith, M. 2006. *The State of Africa: A History of Fifty Years of Independence*. Johannesburg: Jonathan Ball Publishers.

Murray, C. 1980. "Kinship, Continuity and Change." In *Transformations on the Highveld: the Tswana and Southern Sotho*, edited by W. F. Lye, and C. Murray, 106–121. Cape Town: David Philip.

Netsebeza, L. 2007. "Land Redistribution in South Africa: the Property Clause Revisited." In *The Land Question in South Africa. The Challenge of Transformation and Redistribution*, edited by L. Netsebeza, and R. Hall, 107–131. Cape Town: Human Sciences Research Council Press.

Netsebeza, L., and R. Hall, eds. 2007. *The Land Question in South Africa. The Challenge of Transformation and Redistribution*. Cape Town: Human Sciences Research Council Press.

Ngcukaitobi, T. 2018. "Land reform can be done reasonably." *Mail and Guardian*, March 9. Accessed March 21, 2019. https://mg.co.za/article/2018-03-09-00-land-reform-can-be-done-reasonably.

Ngcukaitobi, T. 2019. "2019.The land wars of 2019: Analysing the EFF and ANC Manifestos." *Mail and Guardian*, February 7. Accessed February 28, 2019. https://mg.co.za/article/2019-02-07-00-the-land-wars-of-2019-analysing-the-eff-and-anc-manifestos.

Niehaus, I. 2010. "Witchcraft as Subtext: Deep Knowledge and the South African Public Sphere." *Social Dynamics* 36 (1): 65–77.

PAPLR&A (Presidential Advisory Panel on Land Reform and Agriculture). 2019. *Final Report of the Presidential Advisory Panel on Land Reform and Agriculture.* 4 May. Accessed July 1, 2019. https://www.gov.za/sites/default/files/gcis_document/201907/panelreportlandreform_0.pdf.

Perry, A. 2017. "Building the Homestead: Social Change in the Former Transkei." Unpublished PhD thesis, University of Fort Hare.

Platsky, L., and C. Walker. 1985. *The Surplus People: Forced Removals in South Africa.* Johannesburg: Ravan Press.

Polanyi, K. 2001. *The Great Transformation – The Political and Economic Origins of Our Time.* 2nd ed. Boston: Beacon Press.

Schwikowski, M. 2019. "2019: Africa Heads into an Election Year." *Mail and Guardian*, January 2. Accessed February 28, 2019. https://mg.co.za/article/2019-01-02-2019-africa-heads-into-an-election-year.

Sennett, R. 2018. *Building and Dwelling: Ethics for the City.* Milton Keynes: Penguin.

Shackleton, S., and P. Hebinck. 2018. "Through the 'Thick and Thin' of Farming on the Wild Coast, South Africa." *Journal of Rural Studies* 61: 277–289.

Van Onselen, C. 2005. *The Seed is Mine: The Life of Kas Maine, A South African Share Cropper 1894–1985.* Johannesburg: Jonathan Ball Publishers.

Verdery, K. 1998. "Transnationalism, Nationalism, Citizenship, and Property: Eastern Europe Since 1989." *American Ethnologist* 25 (2): 291–306.

Weidman, M. 2004. "Who Shaped South Africa's Land Reform Policy?" *Politikon* 31 (2): 219–238.

Wilson, M. 1972. *The Interpreters.* Grahamstown: 1820 Settlers National Monument Foundation.

Wolpe, H. 1972. "Capitalism and Cheap Labour-power in South Africa: From Segregation to Apartheid." *Economy and Society* 1 (4): 425–456.

Coexistence as a Strategy for Opposition Parties in Challenging the African National Congress' One-Party Dominance

Isaac Khambule ⓘ, Amarone Nomdo, Babalwa Siswana and Gilbert Fokou

ABSTRACT

Post-apartheid democratic South Africa experienced the pitfalls of one-party dominance when the country's fifth democratically elected parliament (2014–2019) faced growing corruption, state capture, undermining of parliamentary oversight and the abuse of political power and state institutions. These events threatened the country's constitutional democracy and its principles of an accountable government as the ruling party undermined parliamentary oversight structures through majoritarianism to evade accountability by the Legislature and Executive. This led to the growing coexistence and cooperation of opposition parties (despite their ideological differences) in parliamentary oversight as a means of challenging the African National Congress' (ANC) one-party dominance. This process resulted in the establishment of formal and informal coalitions for governing key cities such as Johannesburg, Tshwane and Nelson Mandela Bay. Against this backdrop, and building on a case study of these three metropolitan municipalities, this paper analyses the coexistence of the opposition parties in parliamentary oversight and in the governance of key cities as a means of challenging the ANC's one-party dominance. The analysis delineates the prospects and challenges of using coexistence as a strategy for challenging the ANC's one party-dominance post the 2019 general election.

Introduction

South Africa's post-apartheid political landscape has been defined as a one-party domi-nant political system as the African National Congress (ANC) has won six consecutive national elections with an overwhelming majority of the votes since its ascension to power in 1994 (Butler 2009a; Southall 2014). International literature defines a one-party dominant state as a country where the political landscape is perpetually overshadowed by a single dominant political party that wins consecutive elections and governs for a pro-longed period (Erdmann and Basedau 2013; Ferim 2013). In the South African context, the ANC government has been in power for 25 years, which is largely due to the party's status as a former liberation movement, which resonates with the majority of the voting popu-lation. Other African countries such as Zimbabwe, Mali, Namibia, Botswana, Cameroon and Senegal have also witnessed some form of one-party dominance under the control of former liberation parties and movements (Doorenspleet and Nijzink 2013). Notably, one-party dominant states are not unique to the African context, as South and Central American countries such as Venezuela, Colombia and Costa Rica, as well as European states such as Italy and Sweden, have had similar experiences.

One-party dominant states are often criticised for their degeneration into despotism, patronage networks, destruction of economies and refusal to leave office after losing elections (DasGupta 2015; Magaloni 2006; Scheiner 2006). The veracity of this criticism is evident in the case of Zimbabwe's 2005 elections, where authoritarian tactics and violence were used to silence opposition parties and subvert democratic principles as Zimbabwe African National Union – Patriotic Front (ZANU PF) Mugabe refused to relinquish political power (Moore 2014). Thus, ZANU PF could be characterised as a marginally dominant party because of its use of authoritarian methods. In Cameroon, the Cameroon People's Democratic Movement (CPDM), previously known as the Cameroonian National Union (CNU), has been in power since independence in 1960. Since the spread of multi-party systems around the world in the 1990s, the CPDM has employed tactics ranging from corruption and nepotism to constitutional manipulation and the marginalisation of oppositions to consolidate its dominance in the political space (Ferim 2013; Van de Walle 2003).

In the South African context, the problems caused by one-party dominance were witnessed when the country's constitutional democracy and its principles of an accountable government were threatened by the governing party's parliamentary majoritarianism. The ANC used this majoritarianism to evade horizontal accountability in the legislature, leading to what can be seen as an abuse of the party's majority to protect individual interests over national interests, thereby blurring state and party lines. These events transpired in the midst of what is now termed the 'state capture' debacle, which exposed the country's growing corruption under the Zuma administration (Bhorat et al. 2017). These events, largely under the Zuma administration, were attributed to the dominant position the ANC enjoys, which resulted in minimal accountability and the abuse of state institutions for individualist purposes. Consequently, opposition parties turned to the judiciary to effect accountability and oversight in an effort to facilitate horizontal accountability.

This paper analyses the coexistence of opposition parties to challenge the ANC's one-party dominant position. Coexistence here refers to multiple parties that coexist with the common goal of challenging a dominant party. Coexistence can be defined as a strategic, temporary and informal coalition between two or more political entities to counter a dominant political party. Various scholars have argued that an electorally dominant party may undermine checks and balances, and as such, once dominance is challenged it opens the political space for a multi-party democracy (Hoff, Horowitz, and Milanovic 2005). This paper identifies two examples that demonstrate the coexistence of opposition parties to challenge a dominant ANC: (1) the coexistence of political parties displayed in effecting the parliament to force the executive to account, including the use of the judiciary, and (2) the informal coalitions of opposition parties in the governance of key metropolitan municipalities such as Nelson Mandela Bay, Tshwane and Johannesburg. Local politics in large metropolitan municipalities is important because it highlights the complex and dynamic challenges that inform the dynamics that shape coexistence between opposition parties who may hold very different ideologies.

A Review of one party dominance

A one-party dominant state refers to a country in which one political party dominates the political, electoral and governing landscape by winning overwhelming majorities in at least four consecutive democratic elections and staying in power for a prolonged number of years (Doorenspleet and Nijzink 2013). There is no overarching definition for a one-party dominant state as scholars have proposed different thresholds, ranging from 40% to 70% of parliamentary seats, to meet the criteria of a one-party dominant state (Erdmann and Basedau 2013). In addition to perpetual electoral dominance, broad criteria include a party's ability to dominate state institutions and the public agenda (Southall 2005). Ziegfeld and Tudor (2017) highlight that many democracy scholars hold a belief that alternating political power is a key indicator of the strength of a country's democracy. However, Knutsen and Wig (2015, 882) argue that an 'alternation of power biases against estimated economic benefits of democracy'. They further argued that 'strong economic performance reduces the probability of incumbents losing democratic elections, [as such,] young democracies with high growth may falsely be coded dictatorships' (Knutsen and Wig 2015, 882).

Dominant parties win elections and ultimately gain control of the legislature through parliament and the executive through what is seen as *cadre deployment*. Scheiner (2006) called one-party dominant democratic states 'uncommon democracies', due to the inability of opposition parties to attract enough votes to unseat dominant parties. Ziegfeld and Tudor (2015, 263) argued that 'highly proportional electoral rules accurately translate the party's popular majority into a legislative majority, while disproportional electoral rules tend to award it a seat share much larger than its vote share'. While various reasons cause the emergence of a one-party dominant state, the foremost justifications and motives are as follows:

(1) A party's characteristics and ability to win national legitimacy (Arian and Barnes 1974).
(2) The embodiment of national consensus (Tudor 2013).
(3) The use of patronage, targeted public spending, vote-buying, and neopatrimonialism (Magaloni 2006).
(4) Distinct ideological positions (Greene 2007).
(5) The absence of a strong opposition party (Scheiner 2006; Ziegfeld and Tudor 2017).
(6) The way a party stigmatises its opposition (Ferree 2010).
(7) Sustained economic growth and the effective use of public policy (Kim 2010).

Factors such as a party's characteristics and its ability to build national consciousness play a significant role in ensuring continued electoral success. The capacity for mobilising the political elite through targeted appointments to major government and administrative positions further increases party dominance. As often observed in developing countries, former liberation movements tend to stay in power longer due to their status of bringing democracy or change. This is evident in countries such as South Africa, Namibia and Zimbabwe, where the ANC, the South West African People's Organisation (SWAPO) and the ZANU PF have respectively governed since the dawn of democracy in those countries (Doorenspleet and Nijzink 2013). Common to these dominant parties are their history of being liberation movements and their ability to unite diverse racial and ethnic groups during the transition period and by acting as a 'broad church' for diverse political interests (Doorenspleet and Nijzink 2013; Erdmann and Basedau 2013).

One party dominance may not promote meaningful democratisation when there is an abuse of power. The use of majoritarianism by dominant parties often leads to control regimes, whereby the leading party prioritises tightening political control across every level to ensure effective control over resources. For example, the Liberal Democratic Party (LDP) in Japan managed to instil clientelism through a financially centralised government structure in order to undermine opposition parties' ability to challenge its dominance (Scheiner 2006). In Africa, the ability of dominant parties to control government increases the propensity to buy votes and dedicate public resources in areas where the party is popular to consolidate its support (Erdmann and Engel 2007). In some African countries, the dominant parties use government finances to undermine opposition parties, enhance their fissiparous tendencies, and disincentivise any attempts to form anti-government coalitions (Van de Walle 2003). Dominant parties stay in power due to the use of patronage, targeted public spending, vote-buying, and neopatrimonialism (Magaloni 2006). This leads to the emergence of rent-seeking and uncontrollable corruption that affects not only the party, but also the government and society as a whole. The problems associated with many dominant parties can therefore be traced to the historical weaknesses associated with their inability to manage the infighting for resources as well as emerging factional battles (Erdmann and Engel 2007; Magaloni 2006).

Although there are notable drawbacks of one-party dominant states, such as the rise of rent-seeking, neopatrimonialism and clientism, there are also some positive aspects. For example, the Social Democrats in Sweden during the 1930s and 1980s spearheaded one of the prestigious welfare states in the world. Dominant parties may enjoy different levels of legitimacy, depending on their institutionalisation, capacity to deliver developmental outcomes, sustainable economic growth, in conjunction with radical changes in the country's economy. The ability of states such as China to attain unprecedented and rapid economic growth, ultimately moving millions out of poverty, has strengthened the legitimacy of the Chinese Communist Party, and in turn the political legitimacy of the one-party state system (Kim 2010; Leftwich 2002). The Chinese example highlights a successful case study in a one-party state, and as such it receives less attention from democratic theorists because it is an authoritarian state. Essentially, China does not meet the requirement to be considered a dominant party because there are no general elections as compared to other democratic countries such as Sweden, South Africa and Cameroon (Doorenspleet and Nijzink 2013). This does not mean that the party's ability to sustain unprecedented economic growth should be ignored because dominant parties can learn from some of China's political leadership attributes and characteristics.

The dominance of the ANC, its pitfalls and the coexistence of opposition parties

Since the end of apartheid, South Africa has held six general elections, with the ANC consistently achieving an overwhelming victory. Southall (2005) observes that the dominance the ANC enjoys is complex, over-exaggerated and not static. He also argued that the ANC is a 'weak dominant party' where their power is constrained, which would eventually be 'subjected to considerable challenge over coming years' (Southall 2005, 78). Indeed, the

ANC has, in recent times, faced various challenges in maintaining electoral support result-ing in a rise of coexistence amongst opposition parties. In 2014, the ANC won the election with 62.2% of votes, equating to 249 seats in the National Assembly. By 2019, a mere five years later, the party's electoral support fell to 57.5%; its lowest level since the 1994 found-ing elections, and, for the first time in post-apartheid history, the party could not secure 60% of the vote. Concomitantly, voter turn-out was at 66%, in 2019, the lowest level in post-apartheid history, compared to approximately 74% in 2015. This is a significant decline, especially given an increase in numbers of both registered and eligible voters.

Figure 1 demonstrates that between 1994 and 2019 electoral support for the ANC sur-passed the combined support for the opposition parties. The ability of the ANC to win six consecutive elections is due to its history as the liberation movement, the legacy of Nelson Mandela, and its ability to embody national consensus under the umbrella of the 'rainbow nation' (Maserumule 2016a). Tudor (2013) defined this as the ability to embody national consensus. This consensus was critical given the transition from apartheid and rebuilding an inclusive and democratic society. The ANC thus constructed itself as an inclusive party to gain resonance with the majority of voters.

Under the leadership of Thabo Mbeki, the ANC continued its dominance when it secured its highest election win with 69.7% in 2004; the highest level of electoral support it has secured to date. Butler (2009b) noted that one-party dominance in South Africa worked to create political stability. However, the ANC's dominance under Zuma's tenure undermined good governance and hampered service delivery, as evidenced by the ongoing service delivery protests (Southall 2014). Furthermore, one saw extraordinary cases of corruption, under the Zuma administration. As with most dominant party systems, Zuma drew on patronage to maintain political control.

A key mandate of South Africa's democratic parliament is to ensure the promotion of accountability and the independence of state institutions, particularly those tasked with supporting the country's Constitution.[1] Despite these important institutional norms, there are several examples that show to what degree one-party dominance undermine South Africa's constitutional democracy. Noticeable examples include the abuse of state institutions for political goals, as evidenced in the cases of the State Security Agency and the disbandment of South Africa's anti-corruption unit, the Scorpions.[2] The extent

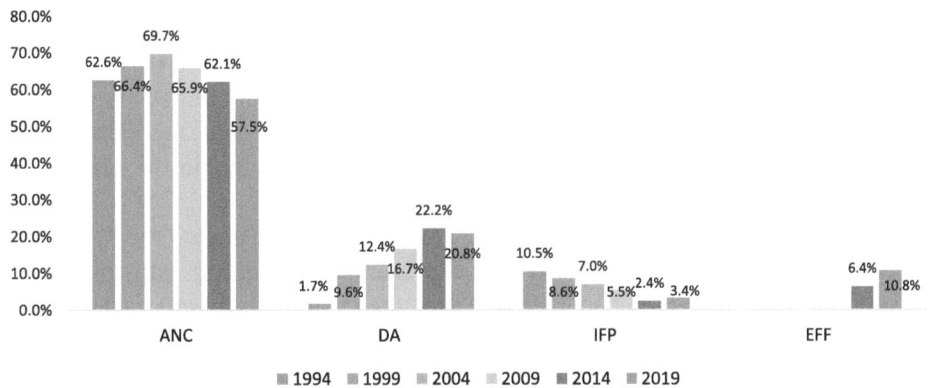

Figure 1. National Assembly Representation (%) from 1994 to 2019 (IEC 2019).

of the abuse of state institutions was detailed in a report entitled *High Level Review Panel Report on the State Security*:

> There has been a serious politicisation and factionalisation of the intelligence community ... based on factions in the ruling party, resulting in an almost complete disregard for the Constitution ... turning our civilian intelligence community into a private resource to serve the political and personal interests of particular individuals. (High Level Panel Report 2018, ii)

Drawing on its hegemonic dominant position in the legislature and executive, the ANC used its majority to disband the Scorpions due to a belief that the anti-corruption unit was abusing its power by prosecuting high-ranking political figures and government officers (Berning and Montesh 2016). According to Schönteich (2014), however, the disbandment was due to infighting within the National Prosecuting Authority (NPA), which was brought about by the political capture of this state institution by prominent figures within the party. Thus, the ANC was able to exert its influence on state institutions, undermining the independence of state institutions, and effectively blurring the line between party and state.

Chapter 13 of the *South African National Development Plan* (NDP) identified parliamentary oversight as a key component to strengthen the country's democracy and achieving its developmental goals (National Development Plan 2012). While this function is recognised as a key priority by the NDP, under the Zuma administration, parliament did not carry out its oversight role to hold the executive to account in the midst of the state capture debacle. Munzhedzi (2016) highlights that accountability measures were undermined through the ANC's majority, which enabled the party to shield members from scrutiny. Consequently, the ANC used its dominance to weaken the ability of parliament to hold the executive to account.

The most notably example of parliament's inability to hold the executive to account is the Nkandla matter, where the parliament failed to hold then President Zuma to account for misusing public funds to upgrade his homestead. Here the ANC drew on its overwhelming majority in parliament, seemingly, to protect former President Jacob Zuma from the political reprecussions of the Nkandla scandal. Despite the Public Protector's '*State of Capture*' report (Public Protector of South Africa 2016) and its binding recommendations, the ANC used its majority to abuse and undermine democratic processes by outvoting opposition parties and disregarding the Public Protector's report. This led to the former President Jacob Zuma being 'exonerated' from any wrongdoing. The ANC achieved this through its dominant status with 62% of parliamentary seats. This case demonstrates the ANC's inability to draw party lines over parliamentary functions as it resulted in a failure to promote accountability and oversight as members of parliament voted along party lines. The case also demonstrates the beginning of the coexistence of opposition parties in challenging the ANC's dominant position in the legislature.

The emergence of the coexistence of opposition parties in challenging the ANC's dominant position is evident in many instances. For example, in dealing with the Nkandla scandal, opposition parties began to coordinate their efforts and work collectively to push the legislature to hold the executive accountable. Opposition parties voted together in subcommittees such as the Nkandla and State Capture committees, and walked out of sittings when the ruling party used its dominant position to evade accountability and shield its members. It is noteworthy that although the opposition parties have very different ideologies, they chose coexistence in an attempt to ensure effective parliamentary oversight.

Southall (2014) asks whether the problems caused by the ANC's one-party dominance are a threat to South Africa's democracy. The blurred line between the political party and the state is marked by the rise of unprecedented corruption in the public sphere, especially under the Zuma administration. Southall rightly observed that the ANC:

> appoints party loyalists to positions of state and wider public office ... party loyalty trumps qualifications, relevant experience, and competence; the constitutionally required independence of various bodies is thereby seriously undermined, and the functionality of numerous institutions (and the commercial health of parastatals) is severely compromised. (Southall 2014, 59)

Nowhere is this more evident than in the growing prevalence of state capture, where state-owned enterprises such as Transnet, PRASA, Eskom and Denel have served rent-seeking interests and party loyalists have channelled lucrative procurement contracts to business interests closely linked to former president Jacob Zuma and his loyalists. Cadre deployment in key state entities impact on the government's ability to effectively deal with corruption, as the deployed cadres may influence decisions to the benefit of individuals rather than common societal good. As such, the blurred line between the state and the party threatens South Africa's democratic principles and norms because it impedes on accountability and transparent governance.

Coexistence between opposition parties in South Africa has also been demonstrated in other instances, both inside and outside parliamentary structures. Outside parliamentary structures, coexistence was seen in two Constitutional Court cases (Economic Freedom Fighters v Speaker of the National Assembly and Others; Democratic Alliance v Speaker of the National Assembly and Others [2016] ZACC 11) when the opposition parties coordinated their efforts and approached the Constitutional Court to assist in ensuring that the parliament held the executive to account in the face of the ANC abusing its majority in parliament for political expediency, most notably to absolve former President Zuma of any wrongdoing in the Nkandla saga. The court judgement ruled that:

> [99] By passing that [to absolve the president of wrongdoing] resolution the National Assembly effectively flouted its obligations ... [105] Neither the President nor the National Assembly was entitled to respond to the binding remedial action taken by the Public Protector as if it is of no force or effect or has been set aside through a proper judicial process. The ineluctable conclusion is therefore, that the National Assembly's resolution based on the Minister's findings exonerating the President from liability is inconsistent with the Constitution and unlawful ... [104] Similarly, the failure by the National Assembly to hold the President accountable by ensuring that he complies with the remedial action taken against him, is inconsistent with its obligations to scrutinise and oversee executive action and to maintain oversight of the exercise of executive powers by the President. (Constitutional Court of South Africa 2016, Cases CCT 143/15 and CCT 171/15)

The failure of parliament to perform its oversight role has led to the courts often having to make decisions entrusted to the legislature. The involvement of the judiciary in parliamentary matters, despite the separation of powers, suggests the pitfalls of one-party dominance in a democratic system. In this particular context, the persistent use of the ANC's dominant position in parliament not only signalled an abuse of democratic processes, but also resulted in undermining parliament to effectively exercise its constitutional mandate of executive oversight. At the heart of this issue is the promotion of party interests over the constitutional duties of parliament and broader South African national interests (Southall 2014). This is also indicative that the ANC may see the state and its constitutional obligations within the *trias politica* as secondary to the party. This is seen in the United Democratic Movement v Speaker of the National Assembly and Others [2017] ZACC 21 judgement.

The coexistence of opposition parties in governing key metros

The coexistence of opposition parties in challenging the ANC's one-party dominance has thus far been covered at a macro scale through reviewing parliamentary oversight. Outside parliamentary structures, coexistence was further seen with opposition parties coordinating court cases against the speaker and the National Assembly to enforce parliamentary oversight and counter the ANC's dominance. One also finds further significant examples of coexistence are demonstrated via informal coalitions at the micro-level in metropolitan municipalities. At a micro level, coexistence is demonstrated through opposition parties forming formal and informal coalitions or partnerships to keep the ANC out of power in several metros after the 2016 local government elections. Figure 2 provides the voting outcomes in South Africa's metropolitan municipalities from the 2011 and 2016 local government elections, which saw opposition parties oust the ANC from power in several metropolitan municipalities.

The 2016 local government elections signified the rise of opposition parties in challenging the electoral dominance of the ANC at the micro-level. Figure 2 demonstrates that the ANC experienced a significant decrease in electoral support in all metropolitan municipalities. The DA and the EFF (which contested its first local government elections) emerged as key players in challenging the ANC's electorally dominant position in the South African political landscape. In comparison with the 2011 Local Government Elections, the 2016 Local Government Elections saw the ANC losing 13% in Ekurhuleni, 11% in Buffalo City,

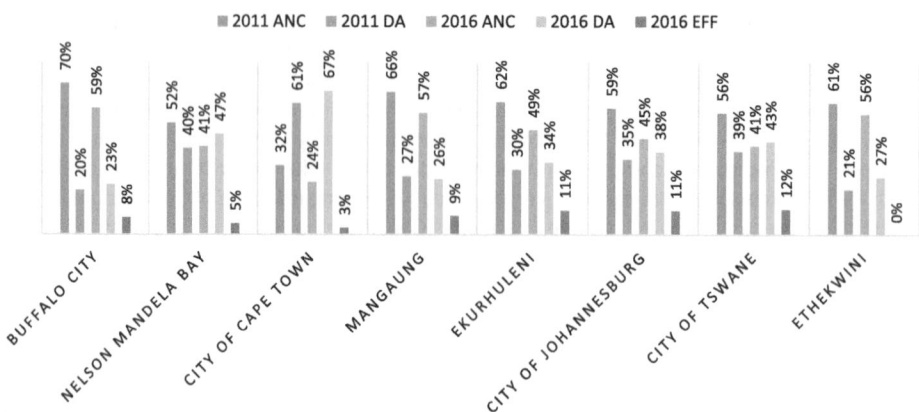

Figure 2. Council Seats in Metropolitan Municipalities (IEC 2011, 2016).

9% in Mangaung and 5% in EThekwini (IEC 2011, 2016). The increasing support for opposition parties such as the DA and the EFF led to coalition governments in three key metros–Tshwane, Johannesburg and Nelson Mandela Bay. However, coexistence as a political strategy produced varied outcomes in different metropolitan municipalities.

City of Johannesburg

An ANC-led government controlled the City of Johannesburg from the first democratic local government elections in 2000 until the 2016 local government elections. Under the ANC-led government, the city experienced rising corruption and a lack of accountability, which led to a loss of trust in the government (Booysen 2016). Within the city, 89% of residents believed that corruption impacts negatively on democracy, while 78% believed that public officials were failing to live up to the *Batho Pele* principles that prioritise the developmental needs of citizens (Gauteng City Region Observatory 2017).

Consequently, the ANC experienced a 15% decline in electoral support in the Johannesburg metro in 2016, with the party's support dropping from 59% to 44%. Booysen (2016) observed that many previous ANC supporters either voted for opposition parties or abstained from voting. While the ANC dropped support, Figure 2 demonstrates that the DA went from 35% in 2011 to 38% in the 2016 local government elections. The EFF, which contested its first local government elections, received 11% of the vote. These results led to the DA and EFF engaging in an informal partnership, which saw the ANC losing political power in this metropolitan municipality. Several reasons led to the EFF working with the DA. This includes the failure of the ANC to effectively deal with corruption, the recall former President Jacob Zuma and a lack of exercising effective oversight (Booysen 2016). While these may be seen as national issues, they had a significant impact on which party ended up governing the City of Johannesburg.

The informal partnership between the DA and the EFF in the City of Johannesburg demonstrates the emergence of coexistence as a political strategy used by the opposition in challenging the ANC's hegemony but also to advance the party agenda. For example, even though the DA is seen as a liberal party (DA 2019) and the EFF (EFF 2019) being a socialist party, the two political parties collaborated to allow the DA to take political power in the City of Johannesburg. This was, however, contingent on the Mayor of Johannesburg tabling a pro-poor budget acceptable to the EFF. Mokgosi, Shai, and Ogunnubi (2017) observed that such a move allowed the EFF to promote their political agenda and exercise political influence in shaping policy directives. For example, the City of Johannesburg insourced all security guards and cleaning staff based on the proposition of the EFF. Through coexistence and coalition, we note that no political party can maintain a policy hegemony, thus promoting collaboration between ideologically diverse parties. Through coexistence, political parties at the micro-level may work to undermine the ANC's dominance in the long term through building grassroot support and dismantling partisan structures that facilitated the ANC's electoral dominance in previous elections.

The City of Tshwane

The ANC was the governing party in the City of Tshwane from 2000 to 2016. Darkey and Visagie (2013) demonstrate that under the ANC-led government, the quality of life in

Tshwane's informal settlements barely changed, with discontent growing amongst the poor about the lack of access to water, jobs, houses and electricity. The underlying issues related to this are poverty, unemployment and inequality. Stats SA (2017) identified unemployment and a lack of basic services such as water, electricity and housing as drivers of multi-dimensional poverty in the country.

The ANC electoral support in the City of Tshwane declined by 11% to 41% in the 2016 Local Government Elections compared to the 56% the party had garnered in the 2011 Local Government Elections (IEC 2011, 2016). The loss of the City of Tshwane signifies the growing anger and loss of trust associated with the ANC-led government at the micro-level due to a lack of adequate service delivery. A contributing factor to the ANC losing the City of Tshwane was the announcement of National Executive Committee (NEC) member, Thoko Didiza, as a mayoral candidate for the city, despite the region having submitted its preferred candidates (Maserumule 2016b). This led to widespread violence and destructive protests from ANC supporters. Kgatle (2017, 1) argued that the Tshwane protests were driven by 'factionalism, tribalism, sexism, economic exclusion and patronage politics'. While the ANC's support declined, the EFF gained 12% of the vote. The DA saw a 4% increase in electoral support from 39% in 2011 to 43% in the 2016.

The coexistence of the DA and the EFF in the City of Tshwane signifies another milestone in the bid to challenge the ANC's political dominance in the South African political landscape. The informal partnership between the DA and the EFF is driven by factors such as the need to address corruption, the promotion of accountability, and the provision of basic services to the most marginalised. As with the case of the Johannesburg metro, the EFF votes with the DA on an issue by issue basis (Essop 2016), particularly on the DA tabling a pro-poor budget that will resonate with the EFF's constituents. The coexistence of these parties was tested when it emerged that the mayor of the City of Tshwane had hired an unqualified Chief of Staff and was accused of corruption in the Glad Africa project (Nicolson 2018). This led to a vote of no confidence that the EFF did not support because it was tabled by the ANC. This seems to demonstrate that the coexistence of these parties is not only dependent on keeping the ANC out of power, but on promoting good governance as evident in Msimang resigning as the Mayor of City of Tshwane. Here the EFF pushed for the resignation of the mayor from his position and the termination of the Glad Africa project.

Nelson Mandela Metropolitan Municipality

Nelson Mandela Bay Metro is a key municipality in the Eastern Cape, which contributes 44% of the province's economy (Socio-Economic Review 2017). The ANC held comfortable majorities in Nelson Mandela Metropolitan Municipality, until the 2006 Local Government Elections. Increasingly one saw allegations and evidence of high rates of corruption that remained unaddressed by the political leadership. In the run up to the 2016 local government elections, the ANC leadership and the Minister of Cooperative Governance and Traditional Affairs deployed prominent figures to head the metro to regain voter confidence. Olver (2017), in his book entitled *How to Steal a City: The Battle for Nelson Mandela Bay*, detailed how this metropolitan municipality was captured by rogue and corrupt elements in partnership with the political leaders. According to Olver (2017), the ANC fired its regional leadership in Nelson Mandela Bay due to the party's decaying local structures, which had created various factions that sought to control the administration's fiscus. Political infighting, factionalism and corruption undermined the ability of the council to deliver basic services to its citizens, promoting widespread protests from disgruntled citizens.

Overall, the ANC's support in the metro dropped by 11% from the 52% it had obtained in 2011 (IEC 2011, 2016); in spite of the moral and leadership regeneration project that the ANC had embarked on in the region. The main opposition party, the DA, managed to increase its support by 7%, as it moved from the 40% it obtained in 2011 to 47% in the 2016 local government elections. The EFF gained 5% of the vote. Other parties such as the United Democratic Movement (UDM) earned 2% of the vote, whereas the remaining parties such as the African Independent Congress (AIC), United Front of the Eastern Cape (UFEC), Congress of the People (Cope) and Patriotic Alliance (PA) gained less than 1%, resulting in each party gaining one seat in the council. The demise of the ANC led government in Nelson Mandela Bay can therefore be attributed to the corrupt elements and activities that undermined the municipality's ability to adequately deliver basic services to the people.

The 2016 local government election results in Nelson Mandela Bay led to a formal coalition of opposition parties to oust the ANC from power. The DA, UDM, Patriotic Front (PA) and other smaller parties forged their coexistence, which resulted in a DA mayor and a UDM deputy mayor, with other several important positions such as Members of the Mayoral Committee (MMC) being spread out across other coexisting partners. This was the first visible coexistence of opposition parties without the EFF playing a central role, and was short-lived due to various internal issues such as corruption, infighting for positions, ideological differences and the land expropriation debate. The breakdown of the relationship between the DA and the UDM (after the ousting of Deputy Mayor Bobani) led to the removal of Trollip, who was later replaced by former deputy mayor, Bobani, of the UDM (Ndletyana 2018). A key issue for the EFF in supporting the recall of Trollip was the inability of the DA to vote for the EFF's motion for land to be expropriated without compensation, as the DA believes that expropriation should be with compensation, illustrating key ideological differences between the the parties. These sets of challenges resulted in small parties withdrawing their formal and informal support for the DA, thereby undermining the ability to challenge the ANC's dominance.

The prospects and challenges of using coexistence to challenge the ANC's dominance

The coexistence of opposition parties in governing key metropolitan municipalities signals a new era in South African politics – an era that demonstrates the depth of opposition parties in challenging the ANC's dominance. Ndletyana (2018) argued that it is misleading to suggest that coalitions are new in South Africa, based on the observation that there were 97 coalition municipalities before the 2016 local government elections. While Ndletyana's (2018) observation is true, coalitions at the metropolitan level represents a new era in South African politics because the country's economic hubs are no longer governed by one party. The changing political landscape in metropolitan areas is due to the ability of opposition parties to appeal and penetrate metropolitan voters and coexist when governing. This is evident in that the EFF has been able to absorb some of the disillusioned ANC voters since 2014, largely due to their unique ideological and radical nature which sets it apart from the ANC and the DA.

The outcome of the 2016 Local Government Elections shows that there is no one rising opposition party, but rather an emergence of the coexistence of better-performing opposition parties and other smaller parties in challenging the ANC's dominance. As observed from the 2014 and 2019 national government elections, the ANC continued to earn the majority of the national votes. The DA experienced a 5% increase from 17% in 2009 to 22% in 2014, before dropping to 20% in 2019, with the EFF managing 6% in 2014 and 10% in 2019. (IEC 2019, 2014, 2009). While opposition parties lack the requisite numbers to challenge the ANC's electoral dominance at the macro level, key trends suggest that opposition parties are challenging the ANC's dominance at the micro-level as seen in the case studies presented in this paper. Here we see opposition parties engaging in both formal coalitions and informal partnerships to ensure that the ANC does not take the reins of political power. The DA and EFF demonstrated coexistence to govern the various metropolitan municipalities despite their ideological differences. The coexistence of these opposition parties is driven by their desire to challenge and undermine the ANC's long-held dominance in the South African political landscape.

The success of coalition governments in Johannesburg and Tshwane demonstrates that the strategy of opposition parties coexisting to challenge the dominance of the ANC is sound. A particularly important phenomenon to note is that the informal partnerships include parties with opposing ideologies, with the DA being proponents of a free market economy and the EFF aspiring to create a state-led economy (DA 2019; EFF 2019). These differing ideologies influence the policy direction of coexisting parties, as evident in that the EFF votes with the DA on an issue by issue basis, signalling the need for consensus on key issues. As observed by Mokgosi, Shai, and Ogunnubi (2017), balancing the expectations of the left-wing EFF constituency and the liberal DA constituency is a key task for mayors in Johannesburg and Tshwane, as it has the potential to weaken both parties' identities. Nowhere is this more evident than in the case of the DA-led government insourcing security guards and stopping the privatisation of PIKITUP, as the EFF advocated for and effected by the DA-led local government.

Balancing the political agendas of ideologically different parties promotes consensus-based governance between the ideologically opposed parties. Consensus-based governance in the context of governing the three metropolitan municipalities is important because it promotes accountability in the absence of one dominant party. The City of Johannesburg and the City of Tshwane showed improved governance due to their enhanced oversight and ability to address corruption in their administrations. Further to this, consensus-based governance also strengthens the coexistence of these parties through the use of consultation, negotiation and joint-decision making processes. In this regard, consensus on policy coordination and compromises between the DA and EFF are fundamental conditions for the success of the coexistence of these parties in not only challenging the ANC's dominance, but also in consolidating their governance of the metros.

The coexistence of the opposition parties at the micro-level cannot be studied in isolation of the macro level, as the loss of the Johannesburg and Tshwane metros was linked to the Nkandla debacle and the ANC's reluctance to recall former President Jacob Zuma. A further link was the failure of the DA to vote with the EFF to expropriate land without compensation, which played a significant role in the ousting of the mayor of the Nelson Mandela Bay metro. This is in addition to the former mayor being accused of protecting corrupt officials and the recall of former deputy mayor without any evidence implicating him in any wrongdoing. These events suggest that national issues also affect the coexistence of the opposition parties in governing key cities and fighting the ANC's dominance. Greene (2007) emphasised that ideological differences play a crucial role in undermining coexistence, resulting in the maintenance of the status quo of single-party dominance. The case of Nelson Mandela Bay, therefore demonstrates how different ideologies and competing interests might undermine the coexistence of opposition parties in challenging the ANC's dominance. In this context, national issues can undermine the coexistence of opposition parties if there is a lack of compromise on immediate socio-economic conditions, such as the land issue in South Africa.

It remains unclear, however, to what extent such coexistence can be sustained, particularly for a country divided along racial and economic fault lines. As is evident in the South African context, the bitter history of disposition under apartheid and colonialism that the EFF is proclaiming to address stands in contrast to the DA's indifference to the country's history. The coexistence of these parties will therefore intensify or attenuate the country's ideological tensions through trade-offs between the parties. The ability of parties to compromise on policy issues is a prerequisite for coexistence to work, especially when it comes to governing metros.

Conclusion

The rise of the ANC in post-apartheid South African politics has been accompanied by rampant corruption and the abuse of state resources, with little to no accountability. While corruption was evident in the later years of Nelson Mandela's and Thabo Mbeki's presidencies, the Zuma years can be regarded as being heightened years of rampant corruption due to the state capture debacle, the Nkandla saga, and the ANC's role in undermining parliamentary oversight and accountability. This article has demonstrated that there is not one single rising opposition party to the ANC, but rather an increase in the number of opposition parties that have chosen to coexist under the banner of informal coalitions to challenge the one-party dominance of the ANC. The extent of coexistence was demonstrated by the opposition parties that came together to challenge the ANC's use of majoritarianism through parliamentary processes and outside parliamentary structures (i.e. the Judiciary). At the subnational or metropolitan level, coexistence has been demonstrated through the informal coalitions of opposition parties in governing the Johannesburg, Tshwane and Nelson Mandela Bay metros.

The overall observation based on recent key developments in the coexistence of opposition parties that are ideologically different suggests that coexistence will only work through consensus-based governance. The ability of the DA, EFF and other smaller parties to govern Tshwane and Johannesburg has ensured continuity in accountability and service delivery, accompanied by the protection of workers through insourcing. Further to this, the coexistence of the opposition parties is evident in their ability to compromise on their ideological differences and ensure enhanced accountability. Accountability is enhanced through the absence of unilateral power of one political party to make or veto decisions. While such coexistence is the cornerstone of these coalitions, underlying issues such as ideological differences may undermine the coexistence of opposition parties, as already seen in the case of Nelson Mandela Metropolitan Municipality. This example demonstrates how national issues are likely to impact on coexistence at the sub-national level if parties fail to compromise on their ideological and policy differences.

Drawing from the three examples, this paper concludes that coexistence is a possible strategy for challenging the ANC's one-party dominance in a South African context. Given the immediate socio-economic challenges facing the country, such as high unemployment, poverty and inequality, coexistence can promote accountability, transparency, good governance, and access to basic social services, as well as minimise corruption. The prospects of using coexistence as a strategy to challenge the ANC's dominance depend on the ability of opposition parties to strengthen their consensus-based governance in metros.

Notes

1. It should be noted that one-party dominant states can also have significant positives as discussed on page 6 which is the case for the ANC as well. However, for the scope of this article, the pitfalls and loss of support are important. For a comprehensive view on OPD in South Africa, see Butler (2009a) and Southall (2005) as referenced below.
2. South Africa has been experiencing a rapid increase in the use of state institutions to fight political battles as evident in the National Prosecuting Authority (NPA), State Security Agency (SSA) and more recently, the Hawks. The High Level Review Panel on SSA report found that that there was a 'parallel intelligence structure serving a faction of the ruling party and, in particular, the personal political interests of the sitting president of the party and country'. Therefore, illustrating a compromise of state institutions and blurring party and state lines.

Disclosure statement

No potential conflict of interest was reported by the authors.

ORCID

Isaac Khambule ⓘ http://orcid.org/0000-0002-4227-6916

References

Arian, A., and Barnes, S. 1974. "The Dominant Party System: A Neglected Model of Democratic Stability." *The Journal of Politics*, 36 (3): 592–614.

Berning, J., and M. Montesh. 2016. "Countering Corruption in South Africa: The Rise and Fall of the Scorpions and Hawks." *SA Crime Quarterly* 39: 3–10.

Bhorat, H., M. Buthelezi, I. Chipkin, S. Duma, L. Mondi, M. Peter, M. Qobo, M. Swilling, and H. Friedenstein. 2017. *Betrayal of the Promise: How the Nation is Being Stolen*. Johannesburg: Public Affairs Research Institute.

Booysen, S. 2016. "Edging Out the African National Congress in the City of Johannesburg: A Case of Collective Punishment." *Journal of Public Administration* 51 (3.1): 532–548.

Butler, A. 2009a. "Considerations on the Erosion of One-Party Dominance." *Representation* 45 (2): 159–171.

Butler, A. 2009b. *The ANC's National Election Campaign of 2009: Siyanqoba!'. Zunami*. Pretoria: Jacana Media.

Constitutional Court of South Africa. 2016. *Economic Freedom Fighters v Speaker of the National Assembly and Others; Democratic Alliance v Speaker of the National Assembly and Others [2016] ZACC 11*. Johannesburg: Constitutional Court.

Darkey, D., and J. Visagie. 2013. "'The More Things Change the More They Remain the Same: A Study on the Quality of Life in an Informal Township in Tshwane'." *Habitat International* 39: 302–309.

DasGupta, A. 2015. "Why Dominant Parties Decline: Evidence from India's Green Revolution." Unpublished manuscript. Harvard University, USA.

Democratic Alliance. 2019. *The Manifesto for Change: One South Africa For All*. Cape Town: DA.

Doorenspleet, R., and L. Nijzink. 2013. *One-Party Dominance in African Democracies*. Boulder: Lynne Rienner Publishers.

EFF. 2019. *Our Land and Our Jobs Now! People's Manifesto and A Plan of Action*. Johannesburg: EFF.

Erdmann, G., and M. Basedau. 2013. "An Overview of African Party Systems." In *One-party Dominance in African Democracies*, edited by R. Doorenspleet, and L. Nijzink, 25–48. Boulder, CO: Lynne Rienner Publishers.

Erdmann, G., and U. Engel. 2007. "Neopatrimonialism Reconsidered: Critical Review and Elaboration of an Elusive Concept." *Commonwealth and Comparative Politics* 45 (1): 1–25.

Essop, R. 2016. "There Will be No Coalition with Any Party." *Eyewitness News*, 17 August.

Ferim, V. 2013. "'One-Party Domination, a Flaw in Africa's Democracy: Comparative Cases from Cameroon and South Africa'." *African Journal of Political Science and International Relations* 7 (7): 304–309.

Ferree, K. E. 2010. *Framing the Race in South Africa: The Political Origins of Racial-census Elections*. New York: Cambridge University Press.

Gauteng City Region Observatory. 2017. *Quality of Life IV Survey (2015/16)*. Johannesburg: GCRO.

Greene, K. F. 2007. *Why Dominant Parties Lose: Mexico's Democratization in Comparative Perspective*. New York: Cambridge University Press.

High Level Review Panel Report. 2018. *High Level Review Panel Report on the State Security Agency*. Pretoria: The Presidency.

Hoff, K., S. Horowitz, and B. Milanovic. 2005. *Political Alternation, Regardless of Ideology, Diminishes Influence: Buying Lessons from Transitions in Former Communist States*. Washington, DC: Carnegie Endowment for International Peace.

IEC. 2009. *Detailed Results Data: 2009 National and Provincial Elections*. Pretoria: IEC.

IEC. 2011. *Detailed Results Data: 2011 Municipal Elections*. Pretoria: IEC.

IEC. 2014. *National and Provincial Elections Report 2014*. Pretoria: IEC.

IEC. 2016. *Local Government Elections 2016*. Pretoria: IEC.

IEC. 2019. *National and Provincial Elections Results*. Pretoria: IEC.

Kgatle, M. S. 2019. "The Causes and Nature of the June 2016 Protests in the City of Tshwane: A Practical Theological Reflection." *HTS Teologiese Studies/Theological Studies* 73 (3): 1–8.

Kim, E. M. 2010. "Limits of the Authoritarian Developmental State of South Korea." In *Constructing a Developmental State in South Africa*, edited by O. Edigheji, 97–125. Cape Town: HSRC Press.

Knutsen, H. K., and T. Wig. 2015. "Government Turnover and the Effects of Regime Type: How Requiring Alternation in Power Biases Against the Estimated Economic Benefits of Democracy." *Comparative Political Studies* 48 (7): 882–914.

Leftwich, A. 2002. "Debate: Democracy and Development. A Contradiction in the Politics of Economics." *New Political Economy* 7 (2): 269–281.

Magaloni, B. 2006. *Voting for Autocracy: Hegemonic Party Survival and its Demise in Mexico*. New York: Cambridge University Press.

Maserumule, M. 2016a. "South Africa's ANC has Remained Dominant Despite Shifts in Support Base." *The Conversation*, Accessed 12 May 2019. http://theconversation.com/south-africas-anc-has-remained-dominant-despite-shifts-in-support-base-63285.

Maserumule, M. H. 2016b. "City on Fire: Pre-Poll Mayhem in Tshwane and the Fate of the African National Congress." *Journal of Public Administration* 5 (3.1): 549–572.

Mokgosi, K., K. Shai, and O. Ogunnubi. 2017. "Local Government Coalition in Gauteng Province of South Africa: Challenges and Opportunities." *Ubuntu: Journal of Conflict and Social Transformation* 6 (1): 37–57.

Moore, D. 2014. "Death or Dearth of Democracy in Zimbabwe?" *Africa Spectrum* 49 (1): 101–114.

Munzhedzi, P. H. 2016. "Fostering Public Accountability in South Africa: A Reflection of Successes and Challenges." *The Journal for Transdisciplinary Research in Southern Africa* 12 (1): 1–7.

National Planning Commission. 2012. *National Development Plan: Vision for 2030*. Pretoria: The Presidency.

Ndletyana, M. 2018. "Coalition Councils: Origin, Composition and Impact on Local Governance." *Journal of Public Administration* 53 (2): 139–141.

Nicolson, G. 2018. "DA Takes Tough Stand Against EFF-led No Confidence Vote in Tshwane." *Daily Marverick*. Accessed 20 August 2019. https://www.dailymaverick.co.za/article/2018-08-29-da-takes-tough-stand-against-eff-led-no-confidence-vote-in-tshwane/.

Olver, C. 2017. *How to Steal a City: The Battle for Nelson Mandela Bay*. Port Elizabeth: Jonathan Ball Publishers.

Public Protector of South Africa. 2016. *State of Capture: A Report of the Public Protector*. Johannesburg: Public Protector of South Africa.

Schönteich, M. 2014. "The National Prosecuting Authority, 1998–2014." SA Crime Quarterly 50: 5–15.

Scheiner, E. 2006. *Democracy Without Competition in Japan: Opposition Failure in a One-party Dominant State*. New York: Cambridge University Press.

Socio-Economic Review. 2017. *The Eastern Cape Socio-Economic Review and Outlook 2017*. East London: Department of Economic Development, Environmental Affairs and Tourism.

Southall, R. 2005. "The 'Dominant Party Debate' in South Africa." *Africa Spectrum* 40 (1): 61–82.

Southall, R. 2014. "Democracy at Risk? Politics and Governance Under the ANC." *The Annals of the American Academy of Political and Social Science* 652 (1): 48–69.

Tudor, M. 2013. *The Promise of Power: The Origins of Democracy in India and Autocracy in Pakistan*. Cambridge: Cambridge University Press.

Van de Walle, N. 2003. "Presidentialism and Clientelism in Africa's Emerging Party Systems." *Journal of African Studies* 41 (2): 97–321.

Ziegfeld, A., and M. Tudor. 2017. "How Opposition Parties Sustain Single-Party Dominance: Lessons From India." *Party Politics* 23 (3): 262–273.

Election of the National President: South Africa's Approach and Its Implications for Presidentialism

Dirk Kotze ⓘD

ABSTRACT
Political Science research on the President's role in South African politics has been limited and therefore poses a research challenge. In this article, the President's election by the National Assembly is linked to a number of factors. The legislative electoral system has a direct impact on it; also, South Africa's government is a hybrid, presidential/parliamentary system; and political party electoral procedures are followed to elect party leaders. The presidential electoral system has several implications for legislative-executive relations, including presidential accountability, approval of the Presidency's budget by Parliament, and Parliament's power to remove the President from office. Special attention is paid to the 2019 party campaigns, to the extent of their co-existence with presidential campaigns, and to the parliamentary electoral procedure. Conclusions identify the implications of the fact that the President's election is primarily determined by the power balance between the main political parties. Especially since 2007, it is also determined by internal party dynamics.

Introduction

The President is arguably the most influential actor in South African politics, though many South African voters are unaware of how she/he is elected or appointed. During the 2019 election campaign, most of the bigger parties portrayed their national leader as their main branding symbol – some of them were presented as standing 'for President'.

In a search of the literature on South African elections, it has been impossible to find any publication specifically focused on the President's election. The absence of significant research should not imply that it does not pose a research problem of relevance for us. The prominence of the president's office is so overwhelming that it deserves much more focused attention.

Section 86 (1) in the South African Constitution determines that Parliament's National Assembly must elect the President in its first sitting after every national election. Though the South African president is responsible for the Executive (s.85 (1)), the office-bearer is elected in neither the same manner as most other executive presidents nor in a manner similar to a prime minister's appointment typical of a parliamentary system. An additional motivation for this research is the electoral nature of the President's status. South African general elections are only about legislative elections and executive elections are not part of it – which presents, therefore, the question: How can an executive president (who is also not a prime minister) claim to have received an electoral mandate? This article focuses on most of the dimensions of the President's election and their possible implications. It does not address therefore all the aspects of the South African President, or how the incumbents over time have used the office in their own way. Richard Calland (2006, 2013) and others have done that.

The electoral lens through which this research is approached is informed by theories about constitutionalism (including the separation of powers and the executive's account-ability to the legislature), theories about public representation within broader democratic theories, and theories about presidentialism and parliamentarianism. New Institutionalism, as a theoretical framework, could also be included, because Guy Peters (2016), like others, draws a link between the structural and individual elements in institutions: 'The emphasis [in this theoretical framework] is clearly on the role of structure, but at the same time indi-viduals influence the behaviour and very nature of institutions, and institutions may shape individuals' (Guy Peters 2016). An analysis of the South African President could certainly benefit from such an approach, because of a focus on the individuality of a president and not only the president as an institution. At the same time, presidents, in particular, are often studied more in terms of their personalities or personal styles and less as the incumbent of an institution. New Institutionalism tries to find a theoretical balance between the two, though in this discussion the institutional focus will be more prominent.

In the absence of extensive research literature on this matter, the literature used for this article is more in the form of 2019 election media reports, as well as parliamentary and elec-toral documents. Fieldwork in the form of personal interviews by the author and the author's observations during the 2019 election campaign forms part of the research methodology. The methodology, therefore, emphasises a qualitative interpretation of the available information, based mainly on primary sources and supported by media reports.

The article is structured in four parts. The first identifies the aspects in the South African electoral system which relate to the presidential election. The second part is about the implications of the electoral system for the relationship between Parliament and the Pre-sident. In the third part, the focus moves to the 2019 election. It concentrates on the phenomenon of presidential candidates and presidential campaigns. The final section is about the parliamentary election of the current President on 22 May 2019.

The South African electoral system and the President

Section 46 (1) (d) in the Constitution stipulates that the electoral system for the National Assembly must in general produce results that amount to proportional representation. The details of the National Assembly's electoral system are set out in the Electoral Act, 1998. This system has direct relevance for the President's election. It is a combination of a party list and proportional representation system in terms of which South Africa is divided into nine constituencies (or provinces). Each party's candidates for the National Assembly's 400 seats are presented to the voters in the form of two fixed party lists: a national-to-national list of 200 candidates and a provincial-to-national list, also of 200 candidates. When the elec-tion results become available, a rather technical procedure (but not relevant for the presiden-tial election) is followed for the proportional allocation of seats to each party.

Once the National Assembly has been constituted in this manner, the national Presi-dent can be elected. It is worth noting that the nine provincial executive heads or premiers are elected in a similar manner. At the local level, executive mayors are also elected in a similar fashion. The electoral systems for all three spheres of government and the legisla-tures, therefore, follow similar principles.

The electoral system and government system

What type of government system is produced by these elections: a presidential, semi-presidential, parliamentary or hybrid system? The first point to note is that in the context of the president as head of state, South Africa follows a republican model. The post is therefore not a ceremonial state president or a constitutional monarchy (such as Commonwealth states like Australia or Canada). Notwithstanding this constitutional principle, the Constitution also recognises several traditional monarchs and other traditional leaders in South Africa, but their political roles do not influence the status of the head of state. Secondly, this discussion intends to establish the type of presidentialism that is applicable in South Africa.

A first type of presidential system is a 'pure' presidential system, which usually refers to a directly elected president, who is not a member of parliament / the legislature. In this type of system, the executive, including members of the cabinet, are also not parliamentarians. Usually, in such a pure presidential system, the executive has various forms of accountability to the legislature, but they cannot be removed from office by a parliamentary motion of no confidence or by other means. Only the President can remove them. A directly elected president is normally assisted by a vice- or deputy president. It will be seen later that the South African President is not directly elected and most of the executive have to be members of parliament. They can be removed collectively by no-confidence motions and the President also by impeachment. Presidentialism in its pure form is therefore not applicable in the South African context.

The second possibility is a semi-presidential system (such as in France or several African states), with a directly elected president assisted by a prime minister, who is normally the leader of the parliamentary majority party but appointed by the President. Executive or government powers are divided between the two posts. By contrast, presidential powers in South Africa are centralised and not shared with government leaders in parliament. Semi-presidentialism is therefore also not applicable in South Africa.

In a parliamentary system, as the third possibility, the head of state is a ceremonial position while the Prime Minister is the head of government or the executive. The latter is the leader of the majority party or coalition of parties and is neither directly elected by the voters nor by the members of parliament. The position of Prime Minister depends on internal party electoral processes, while the general public has no say in it (Siaroff 2003, 288–295). South African presidents are almost in the same position, except that they are not members of parliament. In both cases, they can be removed by no-confidence motions, but the South African President can also be removed by impeachment, while prime ministers normally cannot.

It means that the South African position of president and the executive system fits none of the three well-known systems perfectly. Differently stated, Romano Orrù (2014, 29) concluded in his own constitutional analysis that the system is *'quasi-parliamentary* in formal or static terms and as *basically presidential with parliamentary aspects* in dynamic terms'.

The electoral system in comparative terms

Is this presidential electoral system a uniquely South African invention? No, Angola and Botswana use variations of it. In several other states, their executive president is also not directly elected but elected by a parliament. They include Micronesia, Kiribati, the Marshall Islands, Myanmar, Nauru, San Marino, Suriname, Vietnam, Albania, Lebanon, Serbia &

Montenegro, Guyana and Switzerland (Presidential Power, n.d.). With a few exceptions, most of them are small states, and quite a number of them are Pacific islands. In addition to Angola and Botswana, other examples that attract attention are Lebanon, Switzerland, and Serbia and Montenegro. All of them have diverse populations and have adopted a consociational, collective presidential system in which there is no 'winner who takes all'.

The examples of Angola and Botswana can be used to illustrate systems comparable with the South African one. The Angolan constitution of January 2010 determines in Article 109 the presidential election process as follows (Angolan Constitution 2010, 38):

> The individual heading the national list of the political party or coalition of political parties which receives the most votes in general elections … shall be elected President of the Republic and the Head of the Executive.

It implies that an election by Parliament is not required. In its place, a general, or parliamentary election serves two purposes: it elects the majority party as government and, secondly, that party's top parliamentary candidate is automatically elected as president.

In the case of Botswana, a more complex procedure is followed: s.32 of its Constitution (1966) determines that, prior to the election day, each parliamentary candidate has to indicate on their nomination form their presidential preference. The preference indicated on the nomination form of each elected parliamentary member serves automatically as a vote for the next president. A majority of 50%+1 of the total number of National Assembly members is required for a president to be elected. In the absence of this majority, 'the returning officer shall declare that no candidate has been elected' (s.32(3)(d)). Under these circumstances, the National Assembly will have to be convened within 14 days and elect the President. Section 32(8) of the Constitution provides an exceptional arrangement for the President's removal from office: a parliamentary motion of no confidence supported by a 'majority of elected members of the Assembly' would be sufficient to for it. No reference is made to an impeachment option.

Both the Angolan and Botswanan systems created a direct link between the outcome of parliamentary elections and identifying the new President. It is not an indirect form of election either in the form of a parliamentary election such as in South Africa or by an electoral college as in the USA. In both cases, the presidential nominations are already known *before* election day and the parliamentary election results directly determine the presidential outcome. It will be seen later that the South African case differs, in that formal nomination and election of presidential candidates take place only *after* the general election.

Choice of a presidential dispensation in South Africa

No official record or publication is available that presents a justification of the choice made at the constitutional negotiations during 1993–1996 of the presidential system to be used in South Africa. The National Party chief negotiator at the time, Roelf Meyer (personal interview, 17 April 2018) indicated that it was not one of the contentious matters and the negotiators soon reached a consensus that the President should not become involved in populist campaigning that focuses mainly on the individual candidates. At an early stage in the negotiations and for this reason, the American model was already disqualified as an option. According to Meyer, the negotiators shared the view that the system of executive power they had to agree to, should respect their understanding of the separation of powers principle. Moreover, Meyer referred to the electoral system of pro-portional representation as an additional factor that influenced them to find an executive system in which the political parties will be the main agents in determining the presiden-tial candidates, and not the individuals themselves. It did not involve a broader debate about the political role of presidentialism or its relationship with the legislature authority.

The national electoral system and internal party systems

One of the implications of opting for a parliamentary electoral approach is that the deci-sive moment about who the next president will be is to be found within internal, party political processes, and not in Constitution or the parliamentary election of the President. In the South African case, internal party processes are not similar in all the parties. The ANC's process differs in most respects from those of the DA, and they, again, differ from those in the other parties.

Since 1994, only the ANC has been in the position that its candidates have been elected as national President. For that reason, only the ANC's internal electoral system is briefly discussed here.

The term of office of all the ANC's office-bearers, including the President, is five years and they are elected by the ANC's National Conference (ANC 2019, Constitution of the ANC). Their current five-year term is from December 2017 to December 2022. Compare it with the current parliamentary and presidential five-year term from May 2019 to May 2024. A gap (or overlap) of about 15 months between the ANC's and the national elections, therefore, exists every five years but is more pronounced every ten years, when the national President's two terms expire. In theory, it means that after every two terms the outgoing ANC President can continue for another 15 months as national President in the presence of the newly elected ANC President. It is one of the manifestations of the ANC's notion of 'two centers of power' (*Mail & Guardian* 2007).

While the national Constitution puts a limit of two terms on the national President (s.88 (2)), the ANC's Constitution does not do the same with its President. So far, in practice, the two sets of terms have been aligned to one another in the sense that no ANC President has held that office for more than two terms. Moreover, the practice is that the ANC's Deputy President is also the national Deputy President and that the ANC's Deputy President suc-ceeds the ANC President. Two partial or potential exceptions to this practice were in 2007 when President Mbeki stood for a third term as ANC presidential candidate, but failed against Jacob Zuma, and in 2012 when Deputy President Kgalema Motlanthe stood against President Zuma (and also failed).

The ANC has its own Electoral Commission which receives the nominations from the ANC's provincial councils and then finalises the list of candidates for each vacancy. The del-egates from the ANC branches constitute 90% of all the elective conference delegates. The remaining 10% are the top six executives, the outgoing NEC, provincial delegates and representatives from the three ANC leagues (i.e. women, youth and veterans). Elections are concluded by first-past-the-post majorities and not by absolute (50%+1) majorities. About 15 months later, at the time of national elections, these processes culminate in the decision that the ANC President is nominated as candidate number 1 on the party's national-to-national list. The deterministic nature of an internal party process in the elec-tion of the national President should be clear from this description. At the same time, the limited representative nature of this procedure becomes more apparent when one notes that the number of voters at the ANC's 2017 National Conference where the ANC's President was elected, had been less than 5000, while in the 2019 national election the ANC received about 10 million votes.

In the next section, the implications of this presidential electoral system are contemplated, in particular, the relationship between Parliament and the President. This discussion is not confined to the 2019 general election but applies to national elections in general.

Presidential election and the relationship between Parliament and the President

This section discusses three points on the relationship between Parliament and the President. The first is the President's accountability to Parliament. The next point is how the position of Deputy President differs from the President's in the context of legislative-executive relations. Finally, Parliament's role in the removal of the President from office is considered.

The President's accountability to Parliament

Accountability is an essential component of most democratic theories. It is in the first instance associated with those elected to a public office. In the case of the South African President and as a consequence of the national electoral system, for the purpose of this discussion, it is presumed that presidential accountability is due to both the electorate or public, and Parliament. Parliamentary accountability is included despite the fact that a new president has to resign as member of Parliament immediately after his/her election as President. It is therefore argued that parliamentary membership is not the decisive determinant of accountability but rather the fact that the democratically elected Parliament elected the President. Presidential accountability to Parliament might also be derived from the fact that the office of President is able to claim its electoral mandate only from the electoral mandate given to the parliamentary representatives.

The Constitution, especially in s.92, expects the President to maintain a close relationship with Parliament. In this respect, three practices could be listed which are direct manifestations of presidential accountability. The first is that the President has to present a state of the nation address (SONA) at the beginning of the year to Parliament. In the years when a general election is held, a second SONA is delivered soon after the new President's inauguration. This address is delivered in the President's capacity as both head of state and head of government (South African Government 2019). It resembles, on the one hand, a ceremonial opening of Parliament by the head of state and, on the other hand, the annual State of the Union address by the American President. The SONA is expected to articulate the Executive's plan of action for the coming year. It is followed by parliamentary debate and concluded by the President's response to the debate. No parliamentary vote is taken on the SONA and therefore it represents more a form of executive accountability than a decision-making process. In that sense it differs from the national budget, for example, which is presented by the Executive to Parliament for consideration, debate and approval or amendment. The theoretical or philosophical foundations of presidential accountability to Parliament in South Africa are therefore intricate and deserving of a study of its own.

The second practice of presidential-parliamentary accountability is in the form of four scheduled sessions of parliamentary questions posed by MPs to the President every year. The same process applies also to the Deputy President and is repeated in both houses of parliament. The relevance of this form of accountability is demonstrated by the Public Protector's report in July 2019 dealing with the President's response on 6 November 2019 to a parliamentary question posed to him about his alleged relationship with the private company BOSASA.

The third practice is that the President has to discuss and justify in the National Assembly his Office's annual budget, as part of the national budget. This budget vote debate in Parliament's opportunity to demand accountability from the President's office about its line-function activities in exchange for approving the Office's operational budget.

It should be noted that none of the three accountability practices mentioned here is typical of a presidential system. The relationship between the President and Parliament in South Africa is therefore much more direct and intimate than in typical presidential systems.

Position of the Deputy President

The national Deputy President is appointed and can be dismissed, by the President (s.91 (2)). The Deputy must be a member of the National Assembly. It is significant that the post does not have original constitutional powers, like most vice-presidents, or prime ministers in a semi-presidential dispensation, but according to s.91 (5), has to assist the President in his/her functions.

The most controversial occurrence so far that involved the Deputy President, was when President Thabo Mbeki dismissed his then-Deputy, Jacob Zuma in 2005. It was in response to Schabir Shaik's conviction on corruption charges in a criminal trial in which Zuma featured prominently. After his dismissal, Zuma continued as the ANC Deputy President while Mbeki appointed Phumzile Mlambo-Ngcuka as the new national Deputy. After Mbeki's forced resignation as national President following his 'recall' as party president by the ANC's National Executive Committee and about eight months before the 2009 general election, the new ANC Deputy President, Kgalema Motlanthe, was elected by Parliament as a care-taker national President, and he appointed the ANC National Chairperson, Baleka Mbete, as his national Deputy. This was the only period between 1994 and 2019 that the ANC's President and Deputy President did not occupy the same positions in the national Executive.

The Constitution provides also for the position of Leader of Government Business in the National Assembly (s.91 (4)), which might resemble the position of prime minister in a semi-presidential system. This position is, however, not necessarily attached to the Deputy President, but can be any Cabinet minister. In practice, however, it has always been the responsibility of the Deputy President. The Leader of Government Business is hence not the leader of the majority party. Arguably, in terms of parliamentary status, the Deputy President can be described as, at least amongst Cabinet members, the 'first amongst equals'.

A parliamentary advisor of the current Deputy President DD Mabuza, Ebrahim Ebrahim (personal interview, September 27, 2018) interpreted the function of this post as mainly to coordinate and monitor the role played by Cabinet ministers in Parliament, such as attending portfolio committee meetings steering legislation through the legislature. Parliament's official website also states that the position requires of the incumbent to introducing measures to monitor and improve the quality of legislation and implementation of the Government's programme (Parliament 2019 – Leader of Government Business).

In general elections, the ANC's Deputy President is normally not presented as the President's running mate. They don't appear together on campaign posters and that applies not only to the ANC but also to all the parties which campaigned with presidential candidates. Arguably, in the case of the ANC, it is explained by the fact that the position of national Deputy President is finalised only when the Cabinet is appointed after a general election. Two instances that demonstrated this point were in 2009 and 2019. After the 2009 election, ANC President Jacob Zuma was elected by Parliament to the position of national President. Former President Motlanthe's deputy, Baleka Mbete, made it known that she wanted to continue in the Deputy position but Zuma appointed Motlanthe instead (*Mail & Guardian* 2009). In 2019, uncertainty about DD Mabuza's ethical clearance by the ANC's Integrity Committee leads to speculation that other senior ANC leaders could be considered for the post of Deputy President. In the end, Mabuza intervened and made himself available for appointment (Hunter 2019).

From this discussion, it should be evident that the position of Deputy President does not fit any of the mentioned presidential or parliamentary systems. The post is also not a mirror image of the President's, though at a lower level, and therefore it reinforces the argument that the South African Constitution has produced a hybrid executive system, especially in its relationship with Parliament. This is further illustrated by Parliament's powers to remove the President from office.

Parliament's removal of the President

The Constitution provides for two mechanisms by which Parliament can remove the President from office. Both of them are standard mechanisms in their own right but a combination of the two is relatively unique. A parliamentary motion of no confidence is typically used in parliamentary systems to remove a prime minister or cabinet member from office. Botswana is one of the exceptions where it can be used to remove the President (S.32(8), Constitution of Botswana 1966). Impeachment, on the other hand, is typical of presidential systems. It has a quasi-judicial nature and often depends on official charges and incriminating evidence against a president for violating the constitution or for gross misconduct.

In the South African case, a parliamentary motion of no confidence is provided for in the Constitution's s.102. Such a motion does not require any supporting, objective evidence but is in essence a political judgement about the level of support for the government. Theoretically, it is the reverse of an election, because it can result in one government being replaced by another without an election. Such a judgement depends on the ability of parliamentarians to diagnose a change in public support for the executive, and a willingness by these public representatives to defy party caucus discipline for strategic political/democratic or self-interested reasons. This is the reason why, until the Jacob Zuma years, adoption of a motion of no confidence against the South African President was unimaginable.

Section 102 of the South African Constitution determines that such a motion can be tabled only in the National Assembly and not in the National Council of Provinces

(NCOP). It requires support by an absolute majority of members, i.e. 201 votes, even if fewer than 400 members are present. If a no-confidence motion in the Cabinet (without the President) is accepted, then the President has to reconstitute it. If the motion against the President is accepted, then President and all the other members of the Cabinet, as well as the Deputy Ministers, have to resign.

In practical terms, the Speaker plays a critical role in deciding whether the motion would be tabled in Parliament and what the voting procedure would be. However, party caucuses are the fora where parties decide how they will approach such a motion. The closed party-list proportional representation electoral system provides so much power to political parties that deviation by any party member from the caucus decision constitutes a high risk for their continued individual political future as a public representative, especially in cases when the vote on the motion is not secret. One exception was as a result of the Constitutional Court's judgement in the United Democratic Movement v Speaker of the National Assembly and Others (2017), when the Court ordered 'that the Speaker of the National Assembly has the constitutional power to prescribe that voting in a motion of no confidence in the President of the Republic of South Africa be conducted by secret ballot' (*UDM* case 2017). In response, the Speaker, Baleka Mbete, decided that a secret ballot would be held to determine support for the motion against President Zuma (Whittles 2017). Because of this secrecy, it was impossible to make an exact determination but about 30 ANC MPs voted against Zuma – a first-ever occurrence in the ANC's parliamentary caucus. As a consequence of party discipline arising from the closed party list system, in the first 25 years since 1994, no president had been removed by such a motion.

Impeachment ('removal', according to the Constitution) of the President is authorised in s.89. It stipulates that it can happen only with support by two-thirds (i.e. 267) of the members of the National Assembly. It can be justified by three reasons only: serious violation of the Constitution or the law, or serious misconduct, or inability to perform the functions of the President. In recent times, impeachment processes have been successful in South Korea and Brazil but not in Madagascar, and earlier also not against American President Clinton. President Zuma could be added to this list as an unsuccessful example.

In December 2017, the Constitutional Court concluded in the case of *Economic Freedom Fighters v The Speaker and Others (CCT76/17)* that s.89 required detailed, written procedures before it can be implemented. The Rules Committee of Parliament convened and tabled a report to the National Assembly that was accepted at the end of August 2018. The detailed impeachment procedure can be summarised as follows:

Any member of the National Assembly may initiate the impeachment proceedings by way of a substantive notice of motion. It differs from a no-confidence motion in terms of the substantive requirements: it has to be a 'clearly formulated and substantiated charge' in terms of one or more of the three abovementioned reasons for impeachment. The charge must relate to an action or conduct performed by the President in person, and therefore not indirect responsibility. The motion has to be supported by reliable evidence attached to it. Impeachment, therefore, assumes a quasi-judicial nature. It is significant to note that impeachment, as in other countries, presumes that elected parliamentarians can play the quasi-judicial role and that it does not justify referral to a court of law for adjudication. Presumably, in the South African case, the philosophical justification for it could be that Parliament has embraced a person as president and in the process provides him/her with democratic legitimacy. Parliament is, therefore, the only institution that can withdraw that legitimacy from the President. Legitimacy, in the context of impeachment, appears to be more closely associated with legality and determined less by popular support or political confidence in the President. Having said that, the final decision in the impeachment procedure is a vote by politicians in the National Assembly. That is why impeachment can, at best, be described as a quasi-judicial process.

The judicial dimension receives similar prominence in the Rules Committee's Procedures' (2018) second step, when the Speaker has to refer the member's motion and supporting documentation to an independent panel of three legal experts to conduct a preliminary inquiry. This step was the outcome of debates in the parliamentary Rules Committee, which focused on two options about who should determine the President's fate: an independent panel of experts or the National Assembly itself. In the end, a compromise was reached, because s.89(1) prescribes that 'a resolution adopted with a supporting vote of at least two-thirds of its members, may remove the President'. The final decision was a compromise in that, on the one hand, the panel has to be responsible for a preliminary inquiry and, on the other hand, the National Assembly for the final decision.

The National Assembly's decision consists of two stages: the first is to consider the panel's recommendation. If it presents sufficient evidence against the President, the matter has to be referred to the Assembly's multiparty Impeachment Committee. The Committee has to determine the 'veracity and seriousness' of the charges. In that process, the Procedures determine that the President has the right to present his/her case, with the assistance of legal representation, to the Committee. After concluding its hearing, the Committee reports its findings and recommendations to the National Assembly. The Assembly debates the report and takes the final vote that requirements affirmation by a two-thirds majority. Neither the Constitution nor the new Procedures state whether that vote has to be by secret ballot. (A suggestion could be that because the President's election by the National Assembly has to be by secret ballot [Constitution Schedule 3, Part B, s.6(a)], there is reason to argue that the impeachment vote should also be done in secret [Report of the National Assembly Rules Committee 2018, 1–5; *Politicsweb 2018*, 1–2]).

In conclusion, the relationship between the President and Parliament is predetermined by the prominence of the main political parties in the electoral system and, therefore, in parliamentary processes. It is apparent that the President, though in a powerful political position and with extensive executive powers, cannot act completely independently of Parliament. Generally speaking, the political persona of presidents and the power they exercise in their own parties determine the latitude they enjoy in relation to Parliament. It is generally assumed that in South Africa the Executive dominate Parliament, because of the ANC President's dominance in his/her party (arising from the party's constitution) and the strict, hierarchical tradition of discipline amongst ANC members in the party and in Parliament. However, the controversial nature of the Zuma years has changed this tradition and strengthened Parliament in relation to the Executive. The fact that five motions of no confidence and one impeachment motion were prepared against Zuma, reflects a more assertive stance (Wilkinson 2017). Several sessions by portfolio committees to investigate state-owned enterprises managed by Zuma supporters, also increased pressure on the Executive. President Cyril Ramaphosa's relationship early in his presidential term with Parliament has been in stark contrast to Zuma's. Opposition parties' assertiveness after the 2019 elections and the ANC's decline in electoral support have made Parliament an ideal terrain of the contest between them and the ANC.

Having dealt with most of the salient aspects of the President's post and the presidential election, the discussion shifts now to the 2019 general elections.

The 2019 general elections and the presidential campaigns

The nature of national and provincial election campaigns in South Africa has changed in some respects over time but in many other ways, it has remained quite old-fashioned. The first consideration is the question about what has been presented by the parties to the electorate in 2019. In earlier years, the focus of parties' campaigns used to be on their election manifestos. But that focus faded away quite soon. Election manifestos do not refer to candidates but deal mainly with policy proposals and how parties present to the public their record of government at different levels. No presidential manifesto is therefore found in the election manifestos. What the voters vote for is determined by how each of the election campaigns unfolds.

The 2019 campaign

The ANC launched their election campaign with the slogan 'Let's grow South Africa together'. It reflected some of Cyril Ramaphosa's main values: to unite, firstly, the ANC, by using the election as a common and unifying goal; secondly, to unite South Africa as a country in response to political polarisation and social disharmony; thirdly, it focuses on Ramaphosa's emphasis on economic growth, and his insistence on a social compact as a mechanism of commitment to cooperation – between the private and public sectors, between business and labour, and between different groups in society. The DA launched their campaign with the slogan 'One South Africa for All'. At their last Federal Congress in Tshwane in 2018 they adopted the principle of diversity as the fourth pillar of their Constitution (Herman 2018). The DA in the months before the election had been inundated by issues related to race and redress, such as land expropriation without compensation, employment equity and earlier also black economic empowerment. Symptomatic of these policy contestations and uncertainties had been Gwen Ngwenya's resignation as the DA's head of policy (Ngwenya 2019). Ironically, the ANC started to use the same slogan as the DA, and a public contestation developed about who has the most genuine claim to it.

The EFF concentrated on one slogan: 'Our land and jobs', while other posters depicted the leader Julius Malema under the caption: 'Son of the Soil'. Since the period of Malema's presidency in the ANC Youth League, the EFF's formation in 2013 and the recent land expropriation debate, the land issue is for them a primary policy matter. The EFF is also the main driving force for the Constitution to be amended so that land expropriation without compensation could be used. In the same social analysis, the land has been identified as the main driver of poverty, and therefore job creation is regarded as the main panacea for South Africa's social problems (Polity 2019).

The Freedom Front Plus (FF[+]) is one of the smallest parties in Parliament, but in the 2019 election they increased their number of parliamentary seats by almost three times. Their slogan was 'Fight back' and 'Slaan terug' in Afrikaans. The FF[+] occupies the conservative end of the political spectrum, concentrates on Afrikaans as a public language and are sup-ported predominantly by white persons. In this context, they are opposed to expropriation without compensation and employment equity as it is implemented at the moment, and the party favours a decentralised government system in which cultural communities have more power to govern themselves. The FF$^+$ is a party to the DA's coalition agreement at the local government level (Freedom Front Plus 2019). The 'fight back' sentiment should be understood in the context of the land and employment equity policies and their criti-cism of government corruption (known as 'state capture').

A newcomer to this election was the Black First Land First (BLF) party led by Andile Mngxitama, founded in 2015 after his expulsion from the EFF. The BLF is also in favour of expropriation of land without compensation and accused the ANC of being too close to (white) business interests, or 'white monopoly capital'. The BLF is supportive of ex-Pre-sident Zuma and in the past also of the Gupta family. After the election, the BLF was dereg-istered by the Electoral Commission of South Africa (IEC) because its membership was limited only to black persons, which was considered inconsistent with the nonracial pro-visions of s.16(1)(c)(ii) in the Electoral Commission Act (Mailovich 2019). During their elec-tion campaign, they used the slogan 'Land or Death'. Two days before the election, the Equality Court concluded that it constituted hate speech and that the slogan had to be removed from their regalia, social media accounts and website (*News24* 2019).

The presidential campaign

Is it possible to identify a presidential campaign within the 2019 election campaigns? It has been established already that the general electoral system does not incorporate a vote for the President. However, several parties used election posters to present their leaders 'for President'. In other instances, provincial election posters promoted candidates 'for Premier'; also, in the absence of a direct vote for that post.

Parties have adopted different strategies in the case of the posts of President and provincial Premiers. The ANC, African Transformation Movement (ATM) and the Azanian People's Organisation (Azapo), for example, promoted their leaders as presidential candi-dates. The DA, FF$^+$ and Patricia de Lille's GOOD party campaigned for their Premier candi-dates but did not identify presidential candidates. Therefore, DA leader, Mmusi Maimane, was therefore not presented in the campaign as a contender for Ramaphosa's post (Figure 1).

The ANC did not campaign for Premiers and announced their candidates for election by provincial legislatures only after the election. A number of parties did not campaign for either the President or Premiers, notably the EFF, Inkatha Freedom Party (IFP) and the UDM. Julius Malema (EFF), for example, was promoted simply as the 'Son of the Soil', which not only was an identity denotation of African indigenous origin but served also as a suggestion to the EFF's emphasis of the land issue (Figure 2).

Ramaphosa followed a long tradition of presidential candidates with the 2019 poster of 'Ramaphosa for President: The People's Choice', which was identical to Nelson Mandela's in 1994. In the 1999 election, the ANC poster simply stated: 'Mbeki for President' (Figure 3).

It is relevant to raise the question why parties include a presidential (or premiership) campaign in their general campaigns, when the voters would not have an opportunity to vote for them? This question has not been addressed by any of the parties. Some

Figure 1. Difference in approach between the ANC and DA: presidential versus premier candidates (Photo taken by the author).

might argue that a distinct profile for presidential candidates could provide a 'presidential' allure to party leaders so that they are not entirely overshadowed by the ANC President's prominence. In two significant cases in the past, opposition candidates enjoyed prominence. The first case was in the 2009 General Election campaign, when the Congress of the People (COPE) identified Rev. Mvume Dandala as their presidential candidate separate from the COPE President, Mosiuoa Lekota. It was not simply a political decision, but the outcome of a formal selection process chaired by Dr Barney Pityana (Lobe 2009).

The second case was in the 2014 General Election campaign, when Dr Mamphela Ramphele was announced as the DA's presidential candidate. At the same time, she was the leader of Agang SA, a party which she formed a year before (Gundan 2014). The controversy that followed about her conflicts of interest soon brought the Ramphele experiment to an end and she was not replaced by anyone else.

Figure 2. Difference in how party leaders were presented by their parties. (Photo taken by the author).

Ironically, President Ramaphosa's popularity and contribution to the ANC's election victory in 2019 emerged as a bone of contention within the ANC. In February 2019 – slightly more than two months before the election – the media reported on an ANC survey that recorded Ramaphosa's approval rating amongst the voters to be at 73%, while the approval rating for the ANC as a party was 60%. Referring to Ramaphosa's impact, the party's head of elections, Fikile Mbalula, said: 'When he acts in government and does good things, people see Ramaphosa, not the ANC, but that is so because of where we come from with an ANC that was associated with badness because of the head of state', meaning Jacob Zuma (Mvumvu 2019, 4).

Arguably, Ramaphosa's popularity and perceptions about his contribution to the ANC's victory follow the ANC's factional fault-lines. The party's Secretary General and leader of the Zuma faction, Ace Magashule, challenged the value attached to Ramaphosa's contribution. In his view, the ANC's collective leadership should receive the credit. Magashule

Figure 3. Ramaphosa's and Mandela's election posters in 2019 and 1994 (Photo taken by the author).

said: 'He is not candidate premier (sic), it's not about [the] individual, it's about the ANC' (Citizen Reporter 2019). Mbalula, on the other side of the factional divide, compared Ramaphosa with the Zuma government, and how much it has improved after Zuma's departure (Manyathela 2019; Citizen Reporter 2019).

Observation of the campaign, in general, leads to a construction that the 2019 presidential campaign was dominated by Ramaphosa's persona. There were no other candidates of any significance. The 15 months after his election as ANC President and before the election, during which he concluded the Zuma term of office, gave him the opportunity to make already important changes in government and the public sector, and to work on an economic stimulus plan. Ramaphosa presented it in the context of a 'new dawn' after the 'nine wasted years' of the Zuma era. In summary, Magashule insisted on an institutional and pluralist or even Schumpeterian interpretation of elections in which political parties, as institutions, are the primary focus; on the other hand, the support for Ramaphosa could be interpreted in a new institutional theoretical manner (Guy Peters 2016), in terms of the influence of individuals on institutions and how personalities can use the same institution with very different effects. The final step in the 2019 elections was the President's formal election. It is discussed next.

The parliamentary election of the President

The parliamentary electoral procedure is based on three sources: s.86 in the Constitution, which provides the constitutional authority for the election; Schedule 3 Part A in the Constitution ('Election procedures for constitutional office-bearers'), and the 'Rules for the Election of the President of the Republic' (and several other offices).

In summary, the procedure is the following: All the presidential candidates have to be members of the National Assembly and the Chief Justice, or a judge identified by him/her, acts as the presiding officer. Each candidate has to be nominated by two members of the

National Assembly. If only one candidate is nominated, that person is declared elected. If more than one candidate has been nominated, a secret ballot vote must be taken by the members of the National Assembly. If no candidate receives a majority of 50%+1, consecutive run-off rounds of voting must be held until one candidate has secured a majority (Rules for the Election of the President 2019, 1–11).

The parliamentary election in 2019 has been the eighth election of a South African president. Two of them were conducted after President Mbeki's resignation in 2008 and when President Zuma did the same in 2018. The other six presidential elections were held after general elections.

Presidents Mandela and Mbeki were elected unopposed in 1994, 1999 and 2004. President Kgalema Motlanthe was also elected unopposed in 2008. The only contested presidential election had been in 2009 when the ANC's candidate, Jacob Zuma, stood against COPE's candidate, Rev. Mvume Dandala. Why did it happen then? 2009 was a changing political environment. It was less than a year after President Mbeki's recall as president by the ANC, which resulted in the formation of COPE as a break-away party. It was therefore understandable that COPE believed it had to oppose the ANC on all fronts. The choice of Rev. Dandala as a national religious leader was a deliberate decision to challenge Zuma also on a moral level, given the fact that a few months prior to the election he was charged with corruption. At the same time, it is significant that the DA, again elected with the second-largest number of votes, enabling its recognition as the Official Opposition, did not nominate its own candidate. The elections results were: Zuma 277, Dandala 47, while the DA's 67 members abstained from voting (*People's Assembly* 2009; Mbola 2009).

In 2014, Zuma was re-elected unopposed as President. Early in the national election campaign, Mamphela Ramphele's appearance as the DA's presidential candidate presented a possible contestation with Zuma, but her continued leadership of her own party torpedoed the initiative. It is significant that the DA use ostensibly different considerations for the different senior positions and therefore, by contrast, the position of Speaker (but not Deputy Speaker) was contested. Baleka Mbete (ANC) received 260 votes and the DA's Nosimo Balindlela (a former ANC Eastern Cape Premier) 88 votes, while 18 votes were invalid (South African History Online 2014).

In the 2019 election, Ramaphosa was elected unopposed as President – as in 2018. In a similar vein to 2014, the position of Speaker was again contested by the DA. The results were: Thandi Modise (ANC) 250, Richard Majola (DA) 83, 17 spoilt ballots and the EFF abstained from voting (Chantall Presence 2019). Given the ANC's small provincial majority in Gauteng, election of the Gauteng provincial Premier became a hotly contested election. The ANC received an electoral majority of only one seat in the Provincial Legislature, but in the Premier's election the results were: David Makhura (ANC) 38 and Solly Msimanga (DA) 32 (eNCA 2019).

Though not in the form of a formal election, the appointment of DD Mabuza as the national Deputy President deserves some attention, because of its unusual dynamics. Mabuza is the ANC's Deputy President and was, after President Ramaphosa replaced Jacob Zuma in early 2018 and until the 2019 election, also the national Deputy President. In line with ANC tradition, he was expected to continue in that position after 2019. The complicating factor was that 22 of the ANC's parliamentary candidates, including Mabuza, were mentioned in revelations at commissions of inquiry and email leaks about government corruption during the Zuma era. Their names were sent to the ANC's Integrity Committee for investigation. By the time of Ramaphosa's presidential inauguration, the Committee had not yet finalised their work. Ramaphosa, therefore, could not immediately after his inauguration announce his Cabinet and Deputy President and, for four days, there was no cabinet in South Africa. The matter reached an end when, unilaterally and without a formal announcement of any findings by the Integrity Committee, Mabuza announced that he was ready to assume his office and Ramaphosa proceeded to make his appointments, including Mabuza (Hunter 2019).

Conclusion

The first important conclusion of this article is that the South African electoral system is one of the most relevant factors in determining the legislative-executive relationship. It arranges a relationship of direct presidential accountability to Parliament and gives an unusually strong combination of powers to Parliament to remove the President from office. A second conclusion is that during the past 25 years, a pattern has emerged of presidential elections not being contested by the main opposition parties. The post of Speaker has become much more targeted for contestation. A possible explanation is that in the case of the President and Deputy President, a symbiotic relationship exists between their party positions and government positions, but the same does not apply to the Speaker. The DA, as official opposition, therefore, targets it. The discussion showed that the EFF, as a small but growing opposition party, has not been interested in contesting any of these positions, arguably because of their still small support base and their limited electoral power in Parliament.

In the past, the opinion has often been expressed that the South African President should be directly elected in order to constitute more of a conventional presidential system. Under the current political conditions, it would, however, be detrimental to Parliament's oversight role of the Executive, thereby making the President less accountable and too powerful. It would also change the prominence of political parties in dictating the political system. Finally, this article identified an ostensible contradiction as a conclusion: that the President is arguably the most important institution in South African politics, but that his/her election by Parliament is almost a non-event because it has become so predictable. A very important related conclusion is that the determining moment is, instead, at party conferences when parties elect their leaders. This closes the narrative circle in the sense that it returns to the initial discussion of the parties' prominence in the PR electoral system as an explanation for why it is the decisive moment for the choice of leader of the nation.

Disclosure statement

No potential conflict of interest was reported by the author.

ORCID

Dirk Kotze ⓘ http://orcid.org/0000-0003-4327-6616

References

ANC. 2019. "Constitution of the ANC." Accessed September 30, 2019. https://www.anc1912.org.za/constitution-anc

Calland, R. 2006. *Anatomy of South Africa: Who Holds the Power?* Cape Town: Zebra Press.

Calland, R. 2013. *The Zuma Years: South Africa's Changing Face of Power.* Cape Town: Zebra Press.

Chantall Presence. 2019. "Thandi Modise Elected National Assembly Speaker." *IOL News*, May 22. Accessed May 22, 2019. https://www.iol.co.za/news/politics/thandi-modise-elected-national-assembly-speaker-23759676

Citizen Reporter. 2019. "ANC's Election Win Is 'not about' Ramaphosa – Magashule." *The Citizen*, May 10. Accessed May 31, 2019. https://citizen.co.za/news/south-africa/elections/2129198/ancs-election-win-is-not-about-ramaphosa-magashule/

Ebrahim, E. 2018. *Personal interview by the author.* September 27, 2018.

Economic Freedom Fighters and Others v Speaker of the National Assembly and Another (CCT76/17). 2017. ZACC 47; 2018 (3) BCLR 259 (CC); 2018 (2) SA 571 (CC), December 29, 2017.

eNCA. 2019. "ANC's David Makhura Re-Elected as Gauteng Premier." May 22. Accessed May 30, 2019. https://www.enca.com/news/ancs-david-makhura-re-elected-gauteng-premier

Freedom Front Plus. 2019. "2019 Election Manifesto." Accessed May 17, 2019. https://www.vfplus.org.za/2019-election-manifesto

Government of Angola. 2010. "Constitution of the Republic of Angola." Accessed April 1, 2019. http://extwprlegs1.fao.org/docs/pdf/ang72591ENG.pdf

Government of Botswana. 1966. "Constitution of Botswana 1966." Accessed April 1, 2019. http://www.commonlii.org/bw/legis/const/1966/

Government of South Africa. 2019. "State of the Nation Address 2019." June 20. Accessed June 21, 2019. https://www.gov.za/sona2019

Gundan, F. 2014. "One of South Africa's Richest Women, Dr. Mamphela Ramphele Announces Run for President." *Forbes*, January 29. Accessed April 4, 2019. https://www.forbes.com/sites/faraigundan/2014/01/29/one-of-south-africas-richest-women-dr-mamphela-ramphele-announces-run-for-president/#768ae184604b

Guy Peters, B. 2016. "The New Institutionalism Revisited." *Oxford Bibliographies.* Accessed May 10, 2019. https://www.oxfordbibliographies.com/view/document/obo-9780199756223/obo-9780199756223-0149.xmland

Herman, P. 2018. "DA Adopts Diversity Clause, But Rejects Quotas, at Congress." *News24*, April 7. Accessed April 15, 2019. https://www.news24.com/SouthAfrica/News/da-adopts-diversity-clause-but-rejects-quotas-at-congress-20180407

Hunter, Q. 2019. "MUST READ: A History of the David Mabuza Debacle and the ANC Integrity Committee." *Times Live*, May 28. Accessed May 29, 2019 https://www.timeslive.co.za/politics/2019-05-28-must-read-a-history-of-the-david-mabuza-debacle-with-the-anc-integrity-committee

Lobe, C. 2009. "Mvume Dandala COPE's Presidential Candidate." *Politicsweb*, February 20. Accessed April 10, 2019. https://www.politicsweb.co.za/documents/mvume-dandala-copes-presidential-candidate.

Mail & Guardian. 2007. "ANC Debates Two Centres of Power." Accessed April 15, 2019. https://mg.co.za/article/2007-06-27-anc-debates-two-centres-of-power.

Mail & Guardian. 2009. "Mbete Denies She Was Chasing Deputy President Post." Accessed April 13, 2019. https://mg.co.za/article/2009-05-12-mbete-denies-she-was-chasing-deputy-president-post

Mailovich, C. 2019. "BLF Registration as Political Party Is Unlawful, IEC Rules." *Business Day*, July 15. Accessed September 30, 2019. https://www.businesslive.co.za/bd/politics/2019-07-15-blf-registration-as-political-party-is-unlawful-iec-rules/

Manyathela, C. 2019. "Magashule Stands by Comment on Ramaphosa Election Success." *EWN*, May 14. Accessed May 15, 2019. https://ewn.co.za/2019/05/14/magashule-stands-by-comment-on-ramaphosa-election-success

Mbola, B. 2009. "Voting Completed to Elected New President." *SAnews.gov.za*, May 6. Accessed April 11, 2019. https://www.sanews.gov.za/south-africa/voting-completed-elect-new-president

Meyer, R. 2018. *Personal Interview by the Author.* April 17.

Mvumvu, Z. 2019. "Cyril More Popular than ANC – Poll." *Sunday Times*, February 24. Accessed April 20, 2019. https://www.timeslive.co.za/sunday-times/news/2019-02-24-cyril-ramaphosa-more-popular-than-the-anc-poll/

News24. 2019. "Equity Court Finds BLF's 'Land or Death' Slogan Is Hate Speech." May 6. Accessed May 8, 2019. https://www.news24.com/SouthAfrica/News/equality-court-finds-blfs-land-or-death-slogan-is-hate-speech-20190506

Ngwenya, G. 2019. "How Race Poisoned the DA." *Politicsweb*, July 17. Accessed July 17, 2019https://www.politicsweb.co.za/opinion/how-race-poisoned-the-da.

Orrù, R. 2014. "South African 'Quasi-Parliamentarianism'." In *The Quest for Constitutionalism: South Africa Since 1994*, edited by H. Corder, V. Federico, and R. Orrù, 27–38. Surrey: Ashgate.

Parliament. 2019. "Leader of Government Business." Accessed April 1, 2019. https://www.parliament.gov.za/leader-of-government-business

People's Assembly. 2009. "Election of President of The Republic." May 6. Accessed April 18, 2019. https://www.pa.org.za/hansard/2009/may/06/proceedings-of-the-national-assembly-wednesday-06-/election-of-president-of-the-republic

Politicsweb. 2018. "Parliament Adopts New Rules to Remove President." August 30. Accessed August 31, 2018. http://www.politicsweb.co.za/news-and-analysis/parliament-adopts-new-rules-to-remove-a-president.

Polity. 2019. "EFF 2019 Election Manifesto." February 4. Accessed May 4, 2019. https://www.polity.org.za/article/eff-election-manifesto-2019-2019-02-04.

Presidential Power. n.d. "List of Presidential, Semi-Presidential, and Parliamentary Countries." Accessed May 18, 2019. https://presidential-power.com/?p=1740.

Report of the National Assembly Rules Committee. 2018. "Procedures to Give Effect to Section 89 of the Constitution." August 28 (mimeo.).

Rules for the Election of the President of the Republic of South Africa, Speaker and Deputy Speaker of the National Assembly, Chairperson and Deputy Chairperson of the NCOP, Premier of a Province, Speaker and Deputy Speaker of a Provincial Legislature, Parliament, April 2019. Accessed May 5, 2019. https://www.parliament.gov.za/storage/app/media/misc/2019/may/rules-of-election-of-president-and-pos-002.pdf.

Siaroff, A. 2003. "'Comparative Presidencies: The Inadequacy of the Presidential, Semi-Presidential and Parliamentary Distinction." *European Journal of Political Research* 42 (3): 287–312. doi:10.1111/1475-6765.00084

South African History Online. 2014. "The 2014 National and Provincial Election Results." May 29. Accessed June 5, 2019. https://www.sahistory.org.za/article/2014-national-and-provincial-election-results

United Democratic Movement v Speaker of the National Assembly and Others. 2017. ZACC 21.

Whittles, G. 2017. "Baleka Says Yes, No Confidence Vote in Zuma Will Be Secret." *Mail & Guardian*, August 7. Accessed May 8, 2019. https://mg.co.za/article/2017-08-07-zuma-no-confidence-vote-to-be-held-by-secret-ballot.

Wilkinson, K. 2017. "Fact Sheet: How Many Motions of No Confidence Has Zuma Faced?" *EWN*, June 29. Accessed September 30, 2019. https://ewn.co.za/2017/06/29/fact-sheet-how-many-motions-of-no-confidence-has-zuma-faced

The Decline of Partisan Voting and the Rise in Electoral Uncertainty in South Africa's 2019 General Elections

Collette Schulz-Herzenberg

ABSTRACT

South Africa's democratic elections have produced highly stable and predictable outcomes, largely as a result of the slow pace of change in partisanship. However, a sudden decline in partisanship in the years before the 2019 General Elections was likely to have obvious and predictable effects on electoral behaviour. This article contends that the shrinkage in partisan loyalties manifested in a number of ways, notably through the poor performances of the two largest parties, higher abstentions, individual level vote shifts, vote splitting, and later-than-usual vote decisions. The decline in partisan loyalties also prompted a shift in the voter calculus, with many more voters preoccupied with the campaign and short-term party performance, issue and candidate evaluations, and far fewer with long-standing, traditional party loyalties. The overall effect of weakening partisanship increased the fluidity of voting behaviour and, in turn, increased the unpredictability of the 2019 electoral outcome.

Introduction

South Africa's sixth general elections saw the African National Congress (ANC) returned to power with a reduced national vote share of 58%, and continued control of eight of the nine provinces. The ANC won despite its negative performance in the years preceding the election, while the opposition parties' electoral performance remained subdued. The results, to a large extent, reflected the predictable nature of electoral politics of the previous twenty-five years, characterised by the continuation of a dominant albeit declining party and relatively weak opposition.

Predictable election outcomes can often be explained by the slow pace of change in voter behaviour. People hold party attachments that endure over time, and these individual level loyalties structure the vote and produce stable aggregate electoral outcomes (Dalton 2014, 187). As Dalton (2014, 194) explains, 'party identification stabilises voting patterns for the individual and the party system'. South Africa's six democratic elections have produced highly stable and predictable outcomes, returning large majority vote shares for the governing African National Congress (ANC) precisely because the distribution of partisan attachments have remained fairly stable over time, with the majority of voters declaring partisan loyalties towards this party, and many choosing to vote in the same direction.

But are today's South African voters as loyal as they once were? Compared to previous elections, when the largest political parties could comfortably rely on their partisan support bases to turn out at the polls and cast a vote in their favour, evidence from the

2019 General Elections suggested this was no longer the case. While the standard measure of partisanship in South Africa had remained fairly stable over the years of democracy, data shows a sudden decline in the years before the 2019 General Elections, suggesting that party identification had begun to respond to more immediate environmental factors. The erosion of party ties has obvious and predictable effects on electoral behaviour (Dalton 2014, 197). This article contends the shrinkage in partisanship in the years before the 2019 General Elections manifested in a number of ways, notably through the poor performances of the two largest parties, higher abstentions, individual level vote shifts, vote splitting, and later-than-usual vote decisions. The decline in partisan loyalties also prompted a shift in the voter calculus, with many more voters preoccupied with the campaign and short-term party performance, issue and candidate evaluations, and far fewer with long-standing, traditional party loyalties. The overall effect of weakening partisanship increased the fluidity of voting behaviour, and in turn, increased the unpredictability of the 2019 electoral outcomes.

Electoral stability across South Africa's elections

Since the founding 1994 democratic elections scholars have expressed serious concerns about the quality and stability of South African democracy. In particular, they question the extent of multi-party competition due the electoral imbalances in the political party system and the static nature of voting outcomes that have characterised elections since 1994. Doubts have been raised about the existence of genuine multi-party competition due to the politicisation of numerically imbalanced racial cleavages, the weakness of opposition parties, and the associated electoral dominance of the governing ANC (Southall 1998; Friedman 1999; Mattes and Gyimah-Boadi 2005). Seeing South Africa through the prism of a highly divided society, scholars writing during the early years of democracy warned that the legacies of colonialism and apartheid would encourage enduring and inflexible racial and ethnic cleavages that would continue to inform electoral behaviour into the future (Lijphart 1991). The 1994 founding elections were widely described as a racial or ethnic census, since the electoral outcome seemed to reflect a link between the voter and race or ethnicity. In the years since, partisan support appeared racially aligned or, at least, motivated by notions of group politics.

The central concern among scholars is the need for electoral competition, understood as the quantity of mobile voting or electoral availability (Bartolini and Mair 1990, 286). A truly competitive political party system demands a degree of uncertainty about the outcomes of political competition to ensure accountable and responsive government. If voting behaviour is motivated by fixed sociological and cultural factors such as race and ethnicity, there are no incentives for political uncertainty. When voters are constrained by strong cleavage identities they are unavailable to respond to the political market created by political parties. Parties have little reason to try and persuade new voters and governments have little reason to consider voter reactions to public policy in terms of its impact on electoral prospects. This impacts the quality of a democracy by undermining essential components such as competitiveness, accountability, responsiveness and equality (Lipset 1983; Horowitz 1985; Dahl 1989). When a dominant party, such as the ANC, is able to take the citizenry's vote for granted it ceases to 'fear the ballot box' because it is not seriously threatened at the polls. If there is no threat to prospects for

Table 1. Aggregate electoral results 1994–2019 (%).

	1994	1999	2004	2009	2014	2019
ANC	62.7	66.4	69.7	65.9	62.2	57.5
Opposition parties[a]	37.3	33.6	30.3	34.1	37.8	42.5
Total	100	100	100	100	100	100

Source: Independent Electoral Commission. [a]Calculations are authors own.

re-election the value of elections as a means to discipline elite behaviour is eroded (Riker 1982). Overall, these circumstances diminish competition for political leadership and opportunities for elite rotation or government turnover (Schumpeter 1962, 269). Political certainty about electoral outcomes and the prospects of re-election invites predictable politics, which in turn, signals the deterioration of responsive and accountable government to citizens (Schedler 2001, 19). A lack of electoral uncertainty is therefore still widely regarded as a key challenge to South African democracy, with these inevitably negative implications for the quality and stability of democracy.

Over 25 years, the ANC's vote share has been reasonably stable, increasing from 63% in 1994 to 70% by 2004, declining thereafter to 62% in 2014, but then sharply to its lowest percentage of support at 58% in 2019. The opposition, as a bloc, saw its vote share decline and fragment in the years between 1994 and 2009. The opposition bloc then recovered slightly in 2009, halting the opposition-related de-alignment trend, when they collectively received 34% of the overall vote share. In 2014 this rose to 38% and again in the 2019 General Elections to 43%. Table 1 presents these aggregate election results over six national elections showing similar outcomes with consistent proportions of votes obtained by the governing party and opposition parties respectively until 2019 when the opposition collectively makes a significant recovery, while the ANC, in a corresponding fashion, declines sharply. At first glance therefore, voting patterns in South Africa appeared fairly stable for the governing party with vote shares in the 60 percentage range, until the most recent 2019 General Elections, marking it as the first election where the ANC achieved a vote share in the fifties.

As mentioned above, predictable election outcomes result, in part, from the slow pace of change in aggregate electoral behaviour (Dalton 2014, 187). People harbour party attachments that endure over time, and these individual level affiliations structure the vote and give the appearance of stable aggregate electoral outcomes. In other words, South Africa's democratic elections produced highly predictable outcomes because the distribution of partisan attachments in the electorate remained fairly stable over time, with the majority of voters declaring a party loyalty towards the governing ANC and choosing to vote in the same direction.

However, levels of partisanship have declined in recent years. This raises the question about the extent to which partisan attachments can still be regarded as a lingering reflection of old political sentiments from the founding 1994 election when political parties and South African citizens were seen as 'captives' of a historical moment with the demise of apartheid and the significant electoral victory of the ANC as a struggle movement.

The decline in partisanship

Partisanship, also known as party identification, is a long-term, affective, psychological attachment with one' preferred party that guides electoral behaviour (Campbell et al.

1960, 24). Many voters go into an election campaign with their partisan predispositions already set. People use their partisanship as a 'standing decision' to negotiate the array of choices and complexities in politics (Dalton 2014, 186). Partisanship also serves as an organising device for the voter's political evaluations and judgments by providing a clear and low-cost information cue. Partisans are more likely to vote and very likely to vote for their preferred party. It is an enduring, highly stable political attitude and changes very slowly.

However, party loyalties can weaken and diminish over time. Party loyalties have weakened in recent decades across many advanced industrial societies where increasing levels of education and non-partisan news media have eroded long standing party ties in these countries, leading to a process of 'partisan dealignment', as more people increasingly fail to feel close to any particular political party (Dalton 2014, 194).

South Africa has also witnessed a recent decline in levels of party identification. Numerous surveys indicate that a growing segment of the South African electorate are non-partisans. In other words, a growing proportion of eligible voters lack a party affiliation or attachment. As Figure 1 shows, in September 2018, less than a year before the 2019 General Elections, Afrobarometer found that party identification had declined from 73% in 2015 to 45% (Felton 2018). Around the same time, in the last quarter of 2018, the South African Citizen Survey (SACS) poll also found that that 53% of eligible voters felt close to a political party but by March 2019 this had declined to 50% (SACS report, 22).[1] The overall message was clear. The proportion of non-partisan voters had increased in recent years and would make up a significant portion, or roughly half, of the electorate in the 2019 elections.

The distribution of partisan support across political parties indicated that the ANC still enjoyed the lion's share. Afrobarometer data from September 2018 showed that of the 45% who declared that they felt close to a political party, 29% felt close to the ANC. However, the governing party had lost partisan supporters during the years of the Zuma presidency and entered the election campaign unable to count on its previous partisan base. Afrobarometer shows that ANC partisan affiliations had declined since 2009 from 51% to 29% in 2019. This corresponds well with the SACS data which also showed a decline in the proportion of eligible voters who reported a party loyalty towards the ANC from 39% in early 2018 to 35% in early 2019 (SACS report, 22).

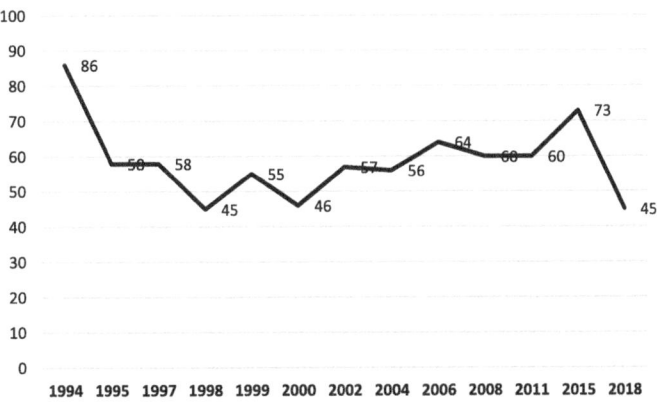

Figure 1. Party identifiers, 1994–2018. Source: Afrobarometer www.afrobarometer.org

Party identification for the largest opposition party, the Democratic Alliance (DA), had not necessarily declined in the years prior to the 2019 General Elections, but neither had it increased; a surprising outcome given that the party should have benefitted from negative voter sentiments towards the ANC, fuelled by media exposure of the party's transgressions. SACS found that only 7% of all respondents reported 'feeling close' to the DA in early 2019 (SACS report, 22). A few months prior, in late 2018, Afrobarometer survey had estimated a slightly smaller partisan figure of 4% for the DA (Felton 2018).

On other affinity indicators, the DA had actually declined during the three years prior to the 2019 General Elections. SACS respondents who declared that they both 'liked and preferred' the DA declined from 18% in late 2015 to 14% by March 2019 (SACS report, 22). This was a likely consequence of messy internal party issues, and the de Lille debacle in the Western Cape government which deterred voters. Thus, from a partisan perspective, the main opposition party posed little threat to the ANC in 2019.

By comparison, the EFF grew its popularity ratings and in March 2019 almost matched the DA with 6% reporting political loyalties to the EFF (SACS report, 22). Yet, a 10% popularity rating, which included respondents who reported both 'liking and preferring' the party above all others (SACS report, 22), also suggested that the EFF would struggle to gain traction in South Africa's divided society despite the use of populist, radical and racial appeals.

Therefore, the three largest parties entered the final months of the 2019 election campaign with the ANC relying on core partisan support from far less than 50% of the electorate, while the DA and EFF had much smaller and similarly sized partisan support bases.

Causes of partisan decline

The overall decline in party identification begs some theoretical explanation. Early research on party identification viewed it as an enduring loyalty that acts as a perceptual screen, filtering out perceived negativities that might affect the social bonds that link citizens to partisan groups and thereby ensuring its stability and relationship to the vote (Campbell et al. 1960). This view of party identification suggests that these enduring loyalties should withstand periods of poor performance by one's preferred party, thereby remaining stable. Yet, partisan dealignment has occurred in almost all democracies as voters move away from feeling close to political parties (Dalton 2014, 196).

One explanation for dealignment breaks with the traditional view above by arguing that partisans do eventually respond to the poor performance of political parties. Scandals, poor incumbency records and unfulfilled voter expectations have perpetuated dealignment trends globally, especially among young people (Dalton 2014, 198). This revisionist view stresses a more rational view of party identification, arguing that voters adjust their attachments based on ongoing retrospective and prospective evaluations of how parties perform in office. From this point of view, Fiorina (1981, 84) describes party identification as a 'running tally of retrospective evaluations of party promises and performance'. Green, Palmquist, and Schickler (2004) contend that while party identification is typically stable, it is also responsive to environmental forces. As they state (2004, 111): 'Partisans neither shed their attachments when their party performs poorly nor maintain their attachments by shutting out bad news. On the contrary, the public does take notice of political events ... '. Thus, this scholarly research suggests that partisans do update their party identification as new information becomes available.

As mentioned above, performance evaluations of political parties particularly affect young people. As a result, partisanship is widely found to be noticeably weaker among young people (Campbell et al. 1960, 161–165; Abramson 1976; Shively 1979), although there is disagreement about whether young people will develop strong party attachments through life-cycle effects on the basis of earlier political socialisation, or whether generational effects have simply weakened partisan feelings among recent generations (Abramson 1976, 472).

In addition, negative performance evaluations have led to declining levels of trust in political parties. South African studies appear to confirm all these observations. First, there is scholarly evidence to suggest that South African party identification is affected by performance evaluations. Mattes (2014, 181) demonstrated the performance bases of ANC party identification over the years, rising and falling with voters' assessments of government performance and economic trends. In addition, Schulz-Herzenberg found that multiple factors impact on party identification as new information about political and economic developments combines with assessments of party images, sociological cues and cognitive skills (Schulz-Herzenberg 2009, 248). As she concludes (2009, 262): 'There is strong evidence to suggest South African voters are not as idiosyncratic as often thought. South African voters much like voters elsewhere, respond to a multitude of short and long terms factors'.

Second, regarding young people, another study found partisanship was significantly weaker among 18–24 year old voters, with a related negative impact on their likelihood of voting (Schulz-Herzenberg 2019a). This presents an important part of the explanation for the decline in aggregate levels of partisanship. The national population has expanded rapidly in recent decades effectively transforming the age distribution of the eligible electorate. A bulging youthful population has produced a significant proportion of young voters in recent elections. Their increasing size as an electoral cohort together with their relatively weaker, nor non-partisanship has contributed to the decline in aggregate partisanship levels.

Finally, studies also show that trust levels in South African political parties have plummeted in recent years (Gouws and Schulz-Herzenberg 2016, 19). Recent Afrobarometer data also confirms that a mounting trust deficit among South Africans has affected most state institutions, but specifically the ruling party. Trust in the ANC declined over the years from 62% in 2006 to 38% in 2018.

It is not coincidental therefore that levels of party identification have declined for the two largest parties at a time when both endured some of their greatest public challenges. An underlying concern at the 2019 General Elections was that 25 years after the passing of apartheid, South African democracy was in trouble and in danger of 'democratic backsliding' and joining a global resurgence of authoritarianism (Southall 2019, 13). The ANC entered the 2019 electoral campaign having presided over nine wasted years and revelations of pervasive corruption and state capture which had plunged the economy, already characterised by massive structural injustices left over from apartheid, into an extended crisis (Southall 2019, 14). Against this backdrop, Cyril Ramaphosa was elected at the ANC elective conference to replace former president Jacob Zuma who was considered a central figure in the demise of the party and the state of the country. As Butler (2019, 66) explains,

> The ANC approached the 2019 national and provincial elections in a parlous condition. Opposition parties could point to its remarkably poor performance in government over the previous five years. The ANC could not credibly campaign for office based on its immediate record.

By comparison, the largest opposition party, the DA had enjoyed growing popular support during the Zuma administration by demanding more accountability using parliament and the courts. However, as the election approached the party suffered a series of setbacks that had negative consequences for its electoral fortunes, including messy internal ideological party battles, incoherence over key policy positions and the 'race and redress' question, poor management of the Western Cape water crisis, ill-fated experiences in municipal coalition politics which culminated in the loss of the Nelson Mandela Bay metro, the De Lille debacle in the Western Cape government which especially deterred provincial voters, and the resignation of the party's policy chief just before the elections (Jolobe 2019). These events ensured that the 2019 campaign was especially difficult for the DA.

If South Africans update their party identification over time – and as Fiorina (1981) argues, it acts as a 'running tally' of current events and developments – these dire developments should have served to weaken voters' party loyalties towards these two parties in particular in the years and months preceding the election. Moreover, existing partisans should also have become more responsive to the immediate political environment, contributing to the rise in unpredictable behaviour. Although partisanship and the vote choice of an individual are closely correlated, because the first informs the latter, voters occasionally, under unusual circumstances, defect from long-standing partisanship and vote for another party or candidate (Weisberg 1999).

Thus, the second interpretation which regards partisanship as an enduring but changeable attitude or orientation better explains the decline in partisanship and illuminates the losses witnessed for the ANC and DA in the 2019 General Elections.

The decline in 2019 party performance

The decline in the partisan bases of the two largest parties appeared to affect their electoral performances. Thus, an early indication that the 2019 elections was not overly determined by strong partisan loyalties was found in the ANC and DA's actual election results. The two largest parties did not increase, or even maintain, their previous support but instead lost votes, a surprising fact given that both parties lay claim to the largest partisan bases in the country, and that the registered voter population had also increased by 5% in 2019, thereby providing both parties with a larger pool of potentially active voters to mobilise.

Although the ANC mustered a majority the party performed dismally. The ANC won the 2019 elections with a reduced majority national vote share of 58% down from 62% in the previous election. The national vote for the ANC by province also highlighted significant regional losses in actual votes cast for the party. In contrast to the 2014 elections, the ANC's vote count dropped in every province. The party's largest provincial decline was in KZN where the vote share dropped by 10% (Table 2).

Table 2. National vote for ANC and DA by province: 2014 and 2019 national elections.

Provinces	2014					2019				
	All votes	ANC votes	ANC %	DA votes	DA %	All votes	ANC votes	ANC %	DA votes	DA %
Eastern Cape	2,243,497	1,587,338	70.8	356,050	15.9	2,052,818	1,399,455	69.3	303,309	15.0
Free State	1,034,337	721,126	69.7	167,972	16.2	918,313	570,980	63.0	153,450	16.9
Gauteng	4,592,219	2,552,012	54.9	1,309,862	28.5	4,580,286	2,413,979	53.2	1,112,883	24.5
KwaZulu-Natal	3,874,833	2,530,827	65.3	517,461	13.4	3,715,985	2,026,069	55.5	520,169	14.2
Limpopo	1,523,169	1,202,905	79.0	100,562	6.6	1,530,837	1,163,091	77.0	81,066	5.4
Mpumalanga	1,385,407	1,091,642	78.8	139,158	10.0	1,290,908	918,756	72.2	116,050	9.1
North West	1,126,691	763,804	67.8	141,902	12.6	1,012,250	633,223	63.7	112,417	11.3
Northern Cape	436,065	278,540	63.9	101,882	23.4	417,248	239,221	58.2	99,977	24.3
Western Cape	2,168,147	737,219	34.0	1,241,424	57.3	2,133,062	659,548	31.2	1,107,065	52.4
Out of country	18,132	1,508	8.3	15,311	84.4	19,909	2,153	10.8	14,802	74.4
Total Votes	18,402,497	11,436,921	62.2	4,091,584	22.2	17,671,616	10,026,475	57.5	3,621,188	20.8

Source: Data from IEC website.

Table 3. Comparison in party support for three largest parties across elections.

Comparisons	2004	2009	2014	2019	% change: 2004–2009	% change: 2009–2014	% change: 2014–2019
Registered voters	20,674,926	23,181,997	25,390,150	26,756,649	12.1	9.5	5.4
Actual votes cast (incl. spoilt ballots)	15,863,554	17,919,966	18,654,771	17,671,616	13.0	4.1	−5.3
ANC	10,880,915	11,650,748	11,436,921	10,026,475	7.1	−1.8	−12.3
DA	1,931,201	2,945,829	4,091,584	3,621,188	52.5	38.9	−11.5
EFF			1,169,259	1,881,521			60.9

Source: Schulz-Herzenberg (2019b, 173). Source: Data from IEC website. Calculations are author's own.

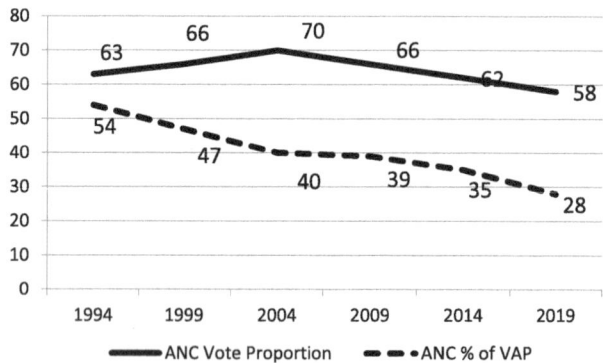

Figure 2. ANC electoral support, 1994–2019, as percentages. Source: Schulz-Herzenberg (2019b, 173). Data from Statistics South and IEC website. Calculations are author's own.

Table 3 shows that the ANC attracted 1,5 million fewer voters than in the previous elections. These were also the second consecutive elections where the party experienced significant percentage change losses. In 2014 the party shrunk by a percentage loss of 2% from the previous 2009 General Elections (Schulz-Herzenberg 2014, 31). In 2019, as Table 3 shows, the percentage loss increased by a far larger margin to −12%. Moreover, as Figure 2 shows, the portion of eligible voters casting a vote for the ANC declined yet again to 28% from 35% in 2014, and far below its highest point of 54% in 1994. These losses meant that the ANC returned to national parliament with a reduced number of 230 seats from the 249 secured in 2014.

The DA also performed poorly. As the largest opposition party, the DA should have benefitted enormously from the ANC's weakened position. Yet it attracted half a million fewer votes than it did in 2014, which also resulted in a −12% loss for the party (Table 3). Moreover, the party's share of support from the eligible voting age population dipped for the first time since 1994, retreating back to its 2009 figure of 10% (Figure 3). Table 2 shows the DA also attracted fewer votes and lost vote share generally across provinces, only increasing its vote shares marginally in the Free State, Northern Cape and KZN.

The decline in voter participation

Party identification binds people to a preferred party and mobilises them to turn out to cast a vote (Dalton 2014, 192–197). When these ties weaken so does partisan-centered voting. Non-partisans are therefore less likely to vote than partisans. With fewer people

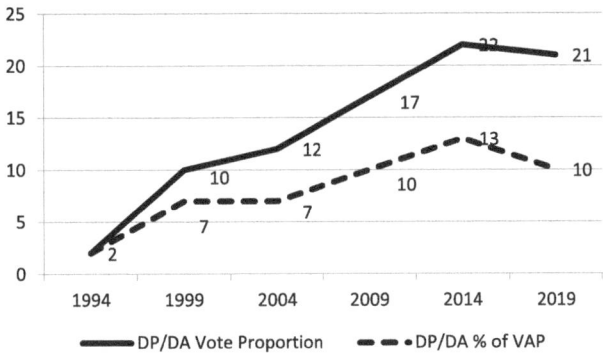

Figure 3. DA/DP electoral support, 1994–2019, as percentages. Source: Schulz-Herzenberg (2019b, 175). Data from Statistics South and IEC website. Calculations are author's own.

identifying with a party and thus less motivation to cast a ballot, the large and increasing numbers of non-partisans in the South African electorate may well have caused turnout to decline. As Dalton (2014, 197) states of dealignment globally, 'it is no surprise that dealignment is paralleled by declining turnout in elections. Nonpartisans are less likely to vote, and if there are more nonpartisans overall, then turnout decreases'.

Afrobarometer self-reported turnout data suggests that this theoretical logic holds in South Africa. Non-partisans are always far less likely than ANC or opposition partisans to turn out to cast a vote. Moreover, self-reported turnout among non-partisans declined steadily between 1994 and 2018 from 79% to 50%. By contrast, self-reported turnout among ANC partisans in 2018 was far higher at 72%, although it had also declined over time. Using the most recently available post-election data from the SACS survey, fielded shortly following the May 2019 elections, a simple crosstabulation of party identification and voter turnout appears to substantiate the trends shown in Figure 4. While 75% of ANC partisans and 64% of opposition partisans reported having voted in 2019, a lesser 63% of non-partisans said that they cast a vote.[2]

In the event, voter turnout among registered voters declined more dramatically than expected in May 2019, from 73% in 2014 to 66%. The sudden decline was the steepest since the 2004 elections. Moreover, turnout as a proportion of the eligible voting age population (VAP), a standard and more accurate measure for voter turnout in cross-national research (Norris 2002, 41; Franklin 2004, 86), was much less impressive and confirmed overall declines in participation seen in previous elections, from 86% in 1994, to 72% in 1999, to 58% in 2004, rising to 60% in 2009, then dropping again to 57% in the 2014 elections, and then again to 49% in 2019 (Figure 5).[3] Figure 5 also clearly demonstrates that abstainers, the percentage of eligible voters who do not vote at elections, continue to grow in South Africa. While abstainers constituted 43% of the eligible electorate in 2014, their proportion rose to 51% in 2019. This meant that less than half of all eligible South Africans cast a vote in 2019. Moreover, voter turnout has dropped no less than 37 percentage points between 1994 and 2019.

While the increase in non-partisans, with their relatively lower turnout rates than ANC partisans, had a negative effect on overall turnout as Figure 4 suggests, the relatively higher likelihood of turnout among ANC partisans helped the party win the elections. In other words, although the proportion of ANC partisans had declined over the years they were still more likely to turn out than the increasing numbers of non-partisans in the electorate, or indeed opposition supporters, and the disproportionately higher turnout rate among ANC partisans assisted with clinching a victory.

At the same time, however, many non-partisans were likely to be former ANC partisans that had become increasingly disillusioned. As noted above, while party identification is a stable attitude it can erode over time due to growing negativity towards one's preferred party. This should have left many more voters able and willing move their support across to other opposition parties. However, a substantial portion of South Africans do not regard opposition parties as viable alternatives to the ANC.

> Where the political choices on offer are not convincing in themselves and voters are unable to identify a 'credible' party, they cannot move their support, nor, ultimately, cast a vote. If an ANC voter grows disillusioned and distances himself from his previous political home, distrust or disaffection with an incumbent or opposition party does not necessarily translate into a vote against them' (Schulz-Herzenberg 2014, 36).

Thus, many former traditional ANC supporters probably abstained on election day, which served to depress the aggregate turnout rate even further.

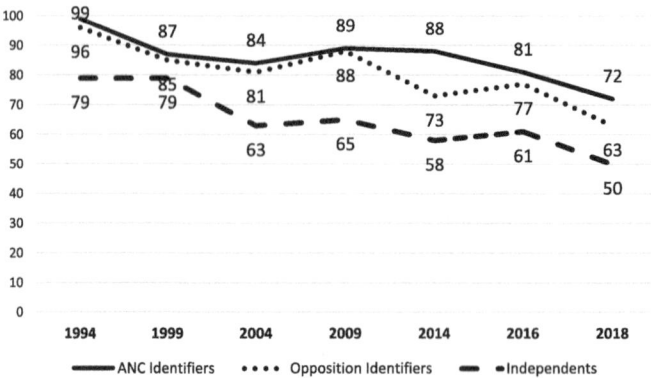

Figure 4. Self-reported turnout, as percentages. Source: Afrobarometer and the South African National Election Studies (SANES).

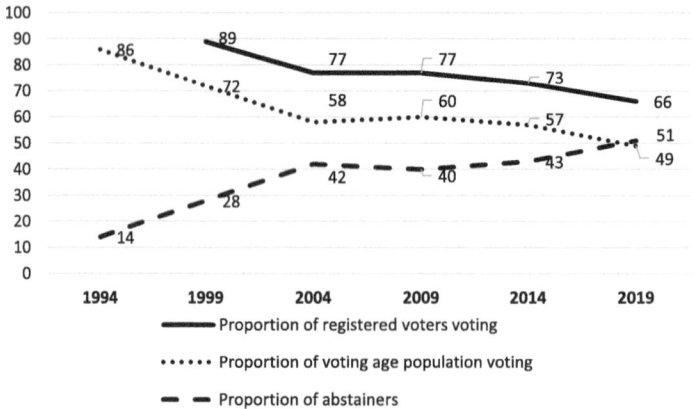

Figure 5. National voter turnout and abstentions, 1994–2019, in percentages. Source: Data from Statistics South and IEC website. Calculations are author's own.

Vote shifts

Although many disgruntled ANC partisans probably declined to vote for any other party, changes in the aggregate vote shares for political parties across the provinces suggest that some in fact did. The changes in the aggregate vote shares for parties suggest individual level vote shifting occurred among traditional ANC and DA partisans, some of whom may have defected from their long-standing party loyalties by deciding to vote for another party. Vote shifts across political parties between consecutive elections is cited as evidence of weakening partisan ties. As Dalton (2014, 197) explains, 'partisanship binds people to a preferred party. As these ties weaken … people should become more likely to shift their party support between elections as they react to the flow of events rather than choose based on habitual party loyalties'. So, although non-partisans are harder to mobilise at elections, they are more open to persuasion and shifting their vote across parties. Their increased numbers should have therefore increased the numbers of abstainers, as discussed in the previous section, but also the likelihood of vote shifting.

System level party realignment occurs when the party balance of the electorate shifts in an enduring way, either as the result of conversion, when voters on a large scale switch their political allegiance to a new party, or as the result of mobilisation which is when large-scale voting occurs for one or two parties by people who were previously non-voters (Weisberg 1999, 682). Party switchers fall into the first category by changing their vote choice (choice of political party) across two consecutive elections.

There is mounting evidence to suggest that South Africans do shift their votes across parties. The globally established Comparative National Elections Project (CNEP) post-election surveys, held in South Africa after the 2004, 2009 and 2014 General Elections, found an increasing percentage of respondents who declared that they supported a different political party across elections: 8% reported switching their vote choice between the 1999 and 2004 General Elections, 12% between 2004 and 2009, and 15% between 2009 and the 2014 General Elections.[4]

In the absence of individual level post-election survey data for the 2019 General Elections, one can merely speculate as to the extent of conversion or mobilisation as explanations for the shifts in party support. To infer individual level behaviour from aggregate figures is to commit what behavioural scientists call an ecological fallacy. However, we can make some intuitive speculations based on the available data. The losses experienced by the two largest parties and the gains of their respective competitors are uncannily similar and require some reflection. On the one hand, there is an aggregate vote share shift from the ANC to the EFF in a number of provinces. The populist appeals of anti-system or ethno-nationalist parties have found traction in electorates with declining partisanship, and this may have favoured the EFF. In Limpopo, the ANC and EFF lost and gained 3% respectively. In Mpumalanga, the ANC and EFF lost and gained 7% respectively. In the North West, the ANC lost 5% from its vote share while the EFF gained 6%, and in the Northern Cape the ANC lost 6% while the EFF gained 5%. In the Free State, the ANC's provincial vote share dropped by 9% while the EFF increased its share by 5%. In other words, ANC losses were most pronounced in provinces that showed measurable increases for the EFF rather than any other realistic contender to the ANC. However, vote shifting was likely to be far more complicated in provinces like KZN where multiple partisan bases probably experienced movements in numerous directions.

While the EFF probably reduced ANC strongholds, the DA appeared to experience losses to the conservative Freedom Front Plus (FF+). After achieving less than 1% at each election since 1999 the FF+ won over 2% nationally in 2019, assumed to be at the expense of the DA in the North West, Northern Cape and Gauteng. With equivocal positions on key issues like land reform and redistribution, property rights and employment equity, conservative voters whom the DA had attracted from right-wing parties in previous elections left the DA in 2019 (Schulz-Herzenberg 2019c, 174).

As one of the most electorally competitive provinces, Gauteng represented the most obvious terrain for vote shifting. The ANC would barely retain its hold over the country's economic hub. In the event, the ANC secured its majority in Gauteng by less than one percentage point, settling at 50.2% down from 54% in 2014. The Gauteng City Region Observatory (GCRO) findings lend support to the vote shifting argument. The GCRO released a series of 'dot-density' maps that plotted the spatial distribution of votes in the 2014 and 2019 provincial elections (Götz, Katumba, and Maree 2019). The maps show votes for each of the top five parties per voting district, with one dot representing 20 votes, and votes for each party represented by a different colour. Looking across voting districts it becomes possible to see clear geographic concentrations of support for particular parties in certain areas. The most visible change between the 2014 and 2019 maps is the increase in support for the EFF and FF+ in areas previously dominated almost exclusively by the ANC and the DA. The maps show a significant increase in black dots, representing the FF+, particularly in DA strongholds (blue dots) in northern Pretoria, western parts of Johannesburg, and around Vereeniging, and there are significantly more red dots, representing the EFF, especially but not only in township areas dominated by the ANC such as Mamelodi, Daveyton and KwaThema, and Orange Farm, Evaton, Sebokeng and Sharpeville (Götz, Katumba, and Maree 2019).

Vote splitting

Split ticket voting occurs when voters choose to support different parties across different levels of government. Reasons for split ticket voting are highly debated in the literature with no one mechanism offered as a definitive answer (Burden and Helmke 2009). While the different scholarly explanations are too numerous and too complex to elaborate here, many scholars agree that split-ticket voting is a by-product of diminishing partisanship (Fiorina 1996; Green, Palmquist, and Schickler 2002, 17; Dalton 2014, 197). Some scholars argue that as the influence of partisanship has waned voters increasingly use split ticket voting to express their desirability for a particular candidate over a party (Wattenberg 1991, 39). Spilt ticket voting in the absence of partisan loyalty may also express voter disenchantment and cynicism with political parties as voters seek to dissipate their overall control and influence (Fiorina 1996, 403). Another generalisation in the comparative literature recognises split ticket voting as a product of short-term forces intervening and disturbing the usual pattern of voting, such as campaign effects, incumbency, candidate popularity and voter uncertainty (Burden and Helmke 2009, 3). Split ticket voting is also likely to occur when there are visible cleavages within a particular party, particularly when a party's issues and policies at different levels of government are not strictly comparable (Burden and Helmke 2009, 3).

South African voters choose a political party on separate national and provincial ballots concurrently. Generally, most voters tend to support the same party at both levels of government. However, in 2019, it appears that many more voters than usual chose to split their support across different parties for national and provincial government. Again, without individual level data, it is unreasonable to speculate about the reasons for vote splitting. However, the various theoretical explanations provided above offer plausible explanations for the South African case. A desire to secure a popular presidential candidate, namely Cyril Ramaphosa, to support a reformist agenda and reduce the increasing political uncertainty in the national domain, coupled with a conflicting desire to diminish the ANC's political dominance over governance, based on its visibly poor performance, likely motived both ANC and opposition supporters to split their vote. Ramaphosa enjoyed high approval ratings before the elections (Schulz-Herzenberg 2019c, 182). The electorate had extended him substantial goodwill coupled with the expectation that he would tackle the many difficult and controversial problems that faced the country, but also within his divided party. The political elite transmitted similarly favourable reports, which citizens were exposed to. In the weeks before the election Ramaphosa received resounding endorsements from the *Economist* magazine, and well-known commentator and former *Business Day* editor, Peter Bruce (The Economist 2019; Bruce 2019). The ANC's main election draw card was therefore Ramaphosa himself, rather than the party brand which had worked wonders in previous elections, and certainly not the party's recent paltry performance in office. In other words, the widely cited 'Ramaphosa effect' which was unique to the 2019 General Elections probably motivated many South Africans to split their national and provincial votes. Opposition supporters wanted to ensure provincial governance remained out of ANC reach, but simultaneously wished to extend Ramaphosa a personal mandate to secure his presidency and seniority in the party. Disgruntled ANC supporters may have acted to punish the party by voting for the opposition at the provincial level but, for the same reasons, extended national support to Ramaphosa's reformist programme.

Table 4 compares national and provincial vote shares for the ANC and for the DA. It shows that Gauteng voters gave the ANC 53% on their national ballot but only 50% on their provincial ballot, opting rather to support one of the opposition parties for provincial government. In fact, across every province the ANC did better on the national ballot.

Table 4. Vote splitting: comparison of national and provincial vote shares for ANC and DA.

Provinces	ANC		DA	
	National	Provincial	National	Provincial
Eastern Cape	69.3	68.7	15.0	15.7
Free State	63.0	61.1	16.9	17.6
Gauteng	53.2	50.2	24.5	27.5
KwaZulu-Natal	55.5	54.2	14.2	13.9
Limpopo	77.0	75.5	5.4	5.4
Mpumalanga	72.2	70.6	9.1	9.8
North West	63.7	61.9	11.3	11.2
Northern Cape	58.2	57.5	24.3	25.5
Western Cape	31.2	28.6	52.4	55.5
Total National	57.5	55.7	20.8	21.9

Source: Data from IEC website.

Western Cape voters show a similar pattern. Although the DA dominates Western Cape politics, on the national ballot the DA obtained 52% while the provincial ballot shows 56% – a clear indication that DA voters in the Western Cape opted instead to support another party at national level. The Western Cape's national ballot for the ANC was higher than its provincial ballot lending further support to the argument that voters in this province also provided an endorsement of Cyril Ramaphosa's ANC at the national level whilst preferring to secure the DA's rule provincially. The ANC collected 645,537 more votes on the national ballot compared to the total of all provincial ballots. These figures can be interpreted as indications of a conscious effort by voters to support a specific candidate, Ramaphosa, whilst balancing provincial priorities. Green et al argue that proincumbent voting tends to occur when voters are left to choose between a popular, well known incumbent and obscure challengers (Green, Palmquist, and Schickler 2004, 19). Schulz-Herzenberg has made the argument elsewhere that, given the dearth of clear policy options between the main parties in the 2019 campaign, voters were forced to rely on their comparative assessments of the main leadership candidate qualities when deciding which party to vote for; 'a contest that President Ramaphosa was always likely to win' (Schulz-Herzenberg 2019c, 171).

A vote for Ramaphosa was not to be understood as a vote for the ANC but rather as an important investment in the future. It would provide him with a sufficiently large presidential mandate to reform state institutions and his own party, revive the economy, force contentious criminal prosecutions and entrench his presidential claims in an adversarial political environment. Reports suggested that Ramaphosa might even attract support from non-traditional constituencies, including white South Africans, because his appeal was cross partisan, symbolising what most South Africans yearned for: an effective state, accountable government and a more secure future (De Klerk 2019). After the elections, as the results emerged, evidence of vote splitting suggested that voters had in fact opted for a strategic approach: to return Cyril Ramaphosa as president, while choosing to punish his party at the provincial level.

Issue voting and late deciders

Finally, the decline in partisanship also changes how the public reaches its voting choices (Dalton 2014, 198). As the importance of party cues dissipate within the South African electorate so many more voters should be influenced by more temporal issues, such as the tone of the campaign, and the issues that feature in the campaign, including the state of the economy and corruption. Similarly, short term evaluations of parties, their leaders and incumbent job approval should become increasingly important to non-partisan voters (Green, Palmquist, and Schickler 2004, 19; Dalton 2014, 198). As mentioned above, leadership and candidate evaluations appeared to be pivotal to the 2019 vote decision (Schulz-Herzenberg 2019c). In this regard, the ANC had the winning card. Cyril Ramaphosa was an asset, providing a buffer against negative voter sentiment towards the ANC as a party. Moreover, opposition leaders struggled to dent his credibility. The vote-splitting trends also point to the importance of Ramaphosa as a national figure and a cross-partisan draw card for the party. Ironically, the increasingly importance of short-term evaluations may have actually helped the ANC cling to power. The party won the 2019 General Elections despite its dismal performance record precisely

Table 5. When did you decide to vote for that party?

	Percentage of respondents
On election day	25
In the last week before election day	8
A few weeks before election day	6
At least a month before election day	5
Before the election campaign started	17
Always intended voting for this party	31
Cannot remember / Don't know	8
Total	100

Source: SACS survey, May 2019

because positive evaluations of President Cyril Ramaphosa were widespread among voters and compensated for the decline in ANC partisanship, and for the party's increasing trust deficit (Schulz-Herzenberg 2019c, 171).

It follows that a sign of issue voting and partisan decline is the tendency for voters to make their decisions later in the campaign (Dalton 2014, 198). While partisans go into an election campaign with their minds already make up, non-partisans are likely be late deciders, making their decisions about which party to vote later in the election campaign (Green, Palmquist, and Schickler 2004, 216). The data suggests a hesitant and unattached electorate. When respondents were asked in the SACS post-election survey when they decided to vote for their chosen party, only 31% indicated that they had always intended voting for their chosen party, while almost half, or 44%, decided in the month before election day. In fact, a quarter, or 25%, only decided which party to support on election day (Table 5).

Conclusion

This paper argues that while party identification was an important attitudinal component of voter behaviour for roughly half of the South African electorate at the 2019 General Elections, the other half were not guided by party loyalties. The consequences of party dealignment for electoral behaviour were evident. The performance of the two largest parties fell short of previous achievements, suggesting a change in their active partisan support bases. The sudden increase in voting abstention and associated decline in aggregate voter participation suggests that party identification no longer guaranteed that the electorate would turn out 'en masse' for political parties. The system level party realignments that occurred in numerous provinces also suggest that some voters abandoned their previous political homes. Split ticket voting (or vote splitting) featured prominently in key provinces, which signalled a breakdown in partisan loyalty, and a rise in strategic, performance-centred voting. And finally, the decline of partisan-centred voting meant that a significant proportion of the electorate decided which party to support only on the eve of the election, producing further evidence to suggest that voters relied less on party identification and more on short-term evaluations to make their decision about which party to support. Without a ready partisan guide, millions turned to the rhetoric and style of the election campaigns, the quality of party leadership, and evaluations of ANC performance to inform their vote. As such, the behaviour of the electorate was more fluid and less predictable than in previous elections.

This paper offers several reasons to be optimistic that electoral fluidity might increase among South African voters. The general dealignment trend suggests that voters are not unwilling to distance themselves from their traditional political homes, even if they return to it in later years. If party ties are not inflexible, it suggests that more voters are free to move their partisan support to new parties at elections. Together, these factors are capable of producing partisan change or fluidity within the electorate. South African voters should become electorally volatile or mobile as they begin to respond to a multitude of factors. This should improve the quality of democracy in the long term as voter behaviour becomes less predictable and incumbents are forced to consider popular opinion.

However, several findings hold negative implications. A partisan dealignment process that produces high levels of abstentions, as an increasing amount of people decline to cast their ballots for any party whatsoever, can spell disaster for electoral politics. Far from freeing more voters to shift their party support, dealignment ensures that participation at elections simply declines. This decreases the chances for electoral competition and consolidates the support given to existing parties.

Ideally South African politics matures with some degree of electoral stability, where the electoral strength of the major parties remains reasonably stable. Extreme levels of volatility in the party system is detrimental to conflict management and democratic institutionalisation. On the other hand, whilst ANC majorities have lent a degree of stability and provided a crucial backdrop for democratic consolidation, most would agree that dominant party systems lack a level of electoral uncertainty that are crucial to ensure responsive and accountable government. There is a need for some degree of electoral competitiveness within the system to allow for the creation of potentially winning alternatives. The argument here is that the 2019 General Elections provided perhaps the first occasion where the effect of weakened partisanship produced this much-needed fluidity and uncertainty in South African voter behaviour.

Notes

1. The author sincerely thanks Citizen Surveys for the use of the South African Citizen Survey (SACS) dataset and report, and especially to Reza Omar for his assistance with the data. The SACS has been carried out since 2015. Face-to-face interviews are conducted with a nationally representative, multi-stage, stratified probability sample of 3,900 adult South African respondents on a quarterly basis. See South African Citizens Survey: Core Report, Quarter 1, 2019.
2. The correlation has a significant and moderate effect. Cramer's V: .127***
3. The VAP data used in this study can also be understood as the voting eligible population (or VEP) because all non-citizens and foreign nationals were removed from the data by Statistics South Africa.
4. The Comparative National Elections Project (CNEP) is a multi-national project that studies political communication and social structure within the context of election campaigns using compatible research designs and a common core of survey questions. See https://u.osu.edu/cnep/. The South African surveys were conducted nationally following the 2004, 09, and 14 elections and includes 1,300 personal interviews. The samples were drawn using multi-stage, stratified, area cluster, probability sampling.

Disclosure statement

No potential conflict of interest was reported by the author.

ORCID

Collette Schulz-Herzenberg ⓘ http://orcid.org/0000-0002-6039-801X

References

Abramson, P. R. 1976. "Generational Change and the Decline of Party Identification in America: 1952–1974." *American Political Science Review* 70 (2): 469–478.

Bartolini, S., and P. Mair. 1990. *Identity, Competition, and Electoral Availability: The Stabilisation of European Electorates 1885-1985*. Cambridge: Cambridge University Press.

Bruce, P. "Who Else but Cyril?" *Business Day*, April 11. Accessed 12 April 2019. https://www.businesslive.co.za/fm/features/cover-story/2019-04-11-peter-bruce-who-else-but-cyril/

Burden, B. C., and G. Helmke. 2009. "The Comparative Study of Split-Ticket Voting." *Electoral Studies* 28 (1): 1–7.

Butler, A. 2019. "A Campaign Born of Desperation: The "Good ANC" Battles the "bad ANC" in the Electoral Last Chance Saloon." In *Election 2019: Change and Stability in South Africa's Democracy*, edited by C. Schulz-Herzenberg, and R. Southall, 66–82. Auckland Park: Jacana Media.

Campbell, A., P. Converse, W. Miller, and D. Stokes. 1960. *The American Voter*. New York: John Wiley & Sons.

Dahl, R. 1989. *Democracy and its Critics*. New Haven: Yale University Press.

Dalton, R. J. 2014. *Citizen Politics: Public Opinion and Political Parties in Advanced Industrial Democracies*. Thousand Oaks: CQ Press.

De Klerk, A. 2019. 'White Voters May Rescue the ANC', *Business Day*, March 10. Accessed 11 March 2019. https://www.businesslive.co.za/bd/politics/2019-03-10-white-voters-may-rescue-the-anc/.

Felton, J. 'As Non-partisanship Grows, Majority of South Africans Willing to Trade Elections for Services'. *Afrobarometer Dispatch* No. 48. October 30. Accessed 10 February 2019. https://afrobarometer.org/sites/default/files/publications/Dispatches/ab_r7_dispatchno248_south_africa_elections1.pdf.

Fiorina, M. 1981. *Retrospective Voting in American National Elections*. New Haven: Yale University Press.

Fiorina, Morris. 1996. *Divided Government*. 2nd ed. Boston: Allyn and Bacon.

Franklin, M. N. 2004. *Voter Turnout and the Dynamics of Electoral Competition in Established Democracies Since 1945*. New York: Cambridge University Press.

Friedman, S. 1999. "No Easy Stroll to Dominance: Party Dominance, Opposition and Civil Society in South Africa"." In *The Awkward Embrace: One-Party Domination and Democracy*, edited by H. Giliomee, and C. Simkins, 97–126. Cape Town: Tafelberg Publishers.

Gouws, A., and C. Schulz-Herzenberg. 2016. "What's Trust Got to do with it? Measuring Levels of Political Trust in South Africa 20 Years After Democratic Transition." *Politikon* 43 (1): 7–29.

Götz, G., S. Katumba, and G. Maree. 2019. 'Gauteng Provincial Election Results'. *Gauteng City-Region Observatory (GCRO)* May 31. Accessed 16 June 2019. http://www.gcro.ac.za/outputs/map-of-the-month/detail/2019-gauteng-provincial-election-results/.

Green, D., B. Palmquist, and E. Schickler. 2004. *Partisan Hearts and Minds: Political Parties and the Social Identities of Voters*. New Haven: Yale University Press.

Horowitz, D. 1985. *Ethnic Groups in Conflict*. Berkeley: University of California Press.

Jolobe, Z. 2019. "The Democratic Alliance at a Crossroads: The Quest for Afro-Liberalism." In *Election 2019: Change and Stability in South Africa's Democracy*, edited by C. Schulz-Herzenberg, and R. Southall, 83–96. Auckland Park: Jacana Media.

Lijphart, A. 1994. *Electoral Systems and Party Systems*. New York: Oxford University Press.

Lipset, S. 1983. *Political Man: The Social Bases of Politics*. London: Heinemann.

Mattes, R. 2014. "The 2014 Election and South African Democracy." In *Election 2014: South Africa: The Campaigns, Results and Future Prospects*, edited by C. Schulz-Herzenberg, and R. Southall, 169–187. Auckland Park: Jacana Media.

Mattes, R., and E. Gyimah-Boadi. 2005. "The Quality of Two African Democracies." In *Assessing the Quality of Democracy*, edited by L. Diamond, and L. Morlino, 238–273. Baltimore: Johns Hopkins University Press.

Norris, P. 2002. *The Democratic Phoenix: Reinventing Political Activism*. Cambridge: Cambridge University Press.

Riker, W. 1982. *Liberalism Against Populism: A Confrontation Between the Theory of Democracy and the Theory of Social Choice*. San Francisco: W.H Freeman and Company.

Schedler, A. 2001. "Taking Uncertainty Seriously: The Blurred Boundaries of Democratic Transition and Consolidation." *Democratization* 8 (4): 1–22.

Schulz-Herzenberg, C. 2009. "Towards a Silent Revolution? South African Voters During the First Years of Democracy: 1994–2006." Unpublished Doctoral Thesis, University of Cape Town.

Schulz-Herzenberg, C. 2014. "Trends in Electoral Participation: 1994–2014." In *Election 2014: South Africa: The Campaigns, Results and Future Prospects*, edited by C. Schulz-Herzenberg, and R. Southall, 20–41. Auckland Park: Jacana Media.

Schulz-Herzenberg, C. 2019a. "The New Electoral Power Brokers: Macro and Micro Level Effects of 'Born-Free' South Africans on Voter Turnout." *Commonwealth & Comparative Politics* 57 (3): 363–389.

Schulz-Herzenberg, C. 2019b. "Trends in Voter Participation: Registration, Turnout and the Disengaging Electorate." In *Election 2019: Change and Stability in South Africa's Democracy*, edited by C. Schulz-Herzenberg, and R. Southall, 44–65. Auckland Park: Jacana Media.

Schulz-Herzenberg, C. 2019c. "The 2019 National Election Results." In *Election 2019: Change and Stability in South Africa's Democracy*, edited by C. Schulz-Herzenberg, and R. Southall, 170–189. Auckland Park: Jacana Media.

Schumpeter, J. 1962. *Capitalism, Socialism and Democracy*. New York: Harper.

Shively, W. P. 1979. "The Development of Party Identification among Adults: Exploration of a Functional Model." *American Political Science Review* 73 (4): 1039–1054.

South African Citizens Survey (SACS) Core Report, Quarter 1, 2019.

Southall, R. 1998. 'The Centralisation and Fragmentation of South Africa's Dominant Party System. African Affairs 97: 443-469.

Southall, R. 2019. "South African Democracy at Risk? The Troubled Context of the 2019 General Elections." In *Election 2019: Change and Stability in South Africa's Democracy*, edited by C. Schulz-Herzenberg, and R. Southall, 12–31. Auckland Park: Jacana Media.

The Economist. 2019. *Good Man, Bad Party*. Accessed 15 June 2019. https://www.economist.com/leaders/2019/04/25/to-stop-the-rot-in-south-africa-back-cyril-ramaphosa.

Wattenberg, M. 1991. *The Rise of Candidate-Centered Politics: Presidential Elections of the 1980s*. Cambridge, MA: Harvard University Press.

Weisberg, H. 1999. "Political Partisanship." In *Measures of Political Attitudes*, edited by J. Robinson, P. Shaver, and L. Wrightsman, 681–736. New York: Academic Press.

The Unconvinced Vote: The Nature and Determinants of Voting Intentions and the Changing Character of South African Electoral Politics

Benjamin J. Roberts ⓘ, Jarè Struwig ⓘ, Steven L. Gordon ⓘ and Yul Derek Davids ⓘ

ABSTRACT
In the lead up to South Africa's sixth National and Provincial Elections in May 2019, the recent performance and leadership dynamics within the country's major political parties raised fundamental concerns about the potential impact on voter turnout. These concerns were not unfounded, given that the 2019 General Elections recorded the lowest voter turnout since 1994, with only 49% of the voting age public participating. Despite this, relatively little remains known about the factors that differentiate decided voters from abstainers, undecided voters and undisclosed voters. To contribute further to the understanding of the determinants of planned electoral participation in the country, this article tests several dominant theoretical accounts of turnout using cumulative data from sixteen annual rounds of the South African Social Attitudes (SASAS) series conducted between 2003 and 2018. Specifically, the relative influence of key socio-demographic attributes, psychological engagement and regime evaluations is examined. The results point to psychological engagement variables playing a decisive role in separating different categories of voter, with age and education also exerting an influence. The article concludes by reflecting on the role of the unconvinced vote in the 2019 Elections, teasing out the implications for future elections in the country.

Introduction and background

This article explores the question of what drives voting intentions in South African elections, using data covering the period between 2003 and 2018, and reflects on the changing nature of the electorate in the country. Despite a national voter outreach campaign organised by the Electoral Commission of South Africa, the country's sixth General Elections had the lowest voter turnout of any national and provisional election since 1994. In addition, there is mounting concern over a growing disinclination to register among younger members of the electorate. The 2019 General Elections represented a pivotal point in the history of electoral democracy in the country. After all, the election came after a decade of increased intra-party factionalism, a diminishing margin of victory for the ruling African National Congress (ANC) in local government elections, high-profile corruption scandals as well as growing discontent with the quality of governance and pace of socio-economic change. Against this background, understanding voter behaviour has become critically important. However, relatively little is currently known about the factors that differentiate decided voters from abstainers, undecided voters and undisclosed voters.

The key narrative of Election 2019 arguably relates to declining participation and it is important to consider this decline in more detail. Despite concerted efforts, voter turnout in the 2019 General Elections was considerably lower than in previous national and provincial elections. Electoral participation among registered voters was 66% in 2019, signifying a drop of seven percentage points relative to the 2014 NPE results (see Table 1). Moreover, turnout as a share of the voting age population (VAP) fell from 57% in 2014 to 47% in 2019. Many young people did not even register to vote ahead of the 2019 NPE. Voter registration among 18–29 year-olds declined from 58% to 49% between the 2014 and 2019 elections, while among 18–19 year-olds the reduction fell more precipitously from 33% to a mere 19%, which translates into a 42% decline (Schulz-Herzenberg 2019b). Despite lower turnout, the ANC secured an electoral victory with 58% of the vote. This represented a decline from the 62% achieved in 2014 and is the third successive drop in a NPE contest since the high of 70% recorded for the party in 2004.

Since the late 2000s scholars expressed concern over this pattern of declining public participation in South African elections (Kersting 2007; Schulz-Herzenberg 2007; Kimmie, Greben, and Booysen 2010), and the aforementioned 2019 statistics are likely to be the source of substantive focus as the country moves to future elections. In many respects, this parallels the growing acknowledgment of, and disquiet over, declining turnout rates in democracies worldwide (Hooghe and Kern 2017). Turnout as a percentage of VAP in South Africa is lower than many advanced industrial countries, though the country still fares better than democracies such as France and Switzerland (International Institute for Democracy and Electoral Assistance 2019). The diminishing voting rate raises critical questions about what social and political mechanisms might be influencing voting intentions in South African elections. In this article, we examine the impact of both socio-demographic attributes and attitudinal factors on individual predispositions towards electoral participation in South Africa, drawing in particular on select theoretical accounts advanced in international turnout literature. It should be stated that quantitative (multivariate) examinations of electoral behaviour in the country remain surprisingly rare, although there is a burgeoning body of evidence on both turnout and voting choice (Roberts, Struwig, and Grossberg 2012; Struwig, Roberts, and Gordon 2016; Schulz-Herzenberg 2019a). The present study differs firstly by focusing on voter turnout decisions ahead of the 2019 General Elections, not only as a binary choice between participation and abstention, but also accommodating voter indecision and undisclosed preferences and

Table 1. Electoral participation in South Africa during national and provincial elections, 1999–2019 (Count '000 and % of the eligible voting age population).

	Voting age population (VAP)	Registered population (RP)		Total votes cast			Spoilt votes			Total valid votes		
	Count	Count	% VAP	Count	% VAP	% RP	Count	% VAP	% RP	Count	% VAP	% RP
1999	22,589	18,173	80	16,480	73	91	251	1	1	16,228	72	89
2004	27,437	20,675	75	16,114	59	78	251	1	1	15,864	58	77
2009	29,957	23,182	77	18,159	61	78	239	1	1	17,920	60	77
2014	32,688	25,388	78	18,907	58	78	252	1	1	18,655	57	73
2019	35,868	26,757	75	17,924	50	67	252	1	1	17,672	49	66

Source: Electoral Commission of South Africa (IEC); Schulz-Herzenberg 2019b.

how these constituencies vary in profile. It also looks at the recent election against a broader period of time, by relying on data covering late 2003 to late 2018, as a means of locating current tendencies against emerging dynamics in political culture. In so doing, the study aims to extend certain aspects of the modelling undertaken by Schulz-Herzenberg (2019a) based on data relating to turnout in the 2014 General Elections.

Classic studies of electoral participation suggest that certain socio-economic character-istics are associated with electoral participation (see, for instance, Campbell et al. 1960; Lipset 1960; Parry, Moyser, and Day 1992; Verba, Schlozman, and Brady 1995). The socio-economic status (SES), material wealth and educational attainment of individuals is said to shape the level of resources (time, money and civic skills) available to facilitate participation in political activities, such as voting (Brady, Verba, and Schlozman 1995). Evi-dence on the predictive power of SES variables associated with the resources model remains weak. Education is nonetheless a stronger predictor of turnout decisions, while age, and gender to a lesser degree, are other significant socio-economic factors informing individual differences in turnout (Blais 2000; Blais, Massicotte, and Dobrzynska 2003; Blais, Gidengil, and Nevitte 2004; Nevitte et al. 2009). Specifically, the weight of evidence suggests that electoral participation increases with age and higher levels of education, and is more common among men than women.

One of the most widely recognised determinants of electoral participation is psycho-logical engagement with politics. Democracy theorists consider low levels of engagement to be damaging to voter turnout. In the seminal study by Almond and Verba (1963), *Civic Culture*, it is maintained that one of the central features of a model citizen in normative democratic theory is engagement in politics (see also Campbell et al. 1960; Verba, Schloz-man, and Brady 1995; Carpini and Keeter 1996). In most empirical research, such engage-ment has been characterised by the degree to which individuals think and talk about politics. Political interest is consequently considered a good measure of how much politi-cal information and knowledge an individual possesses (Norris 2000; Inglehart and Welzel 2005; Dalton 2006). A sense of duty to vote and belief in the efficacy of voting is also seen to play a role (e.g. Blais 2000; Blais, Massicotte, and Dobrzynska 2003; Blais, Gidengil, and Nevitte 2004; Blais and Achen 2019). Research in South Africa shows that an individual's voting efficacy is, to a degree, a product of being on the winning political side (Gordon, Struwig, and Roberts 2018). This finding demonstrates the influence that political partisan-ship has on an individual's beliefs about the political world. The results suggest further questions on how partisanship may drive political attitudes in the country.

Apart from psychological engagement, Almond and Verba (1963) contended that certain civic attitudes might further motivate political participation, identifying evaluative orientations as important. The associated valence politics or regime evaluations model centres on the idea that 'citizen involvement will vary according to levels of (dis)satisfac-tion with the performance of political leaders, the incumbent government and the wider political system' (Clarke et al. 2009, 244–245). For Almond and Verba, citizens' negative attitudes towards the political system could result in alienation, which erodes their willing-ness to participate in the system. In a comprehensive analysis of public opinion trends in South Africa, Struwig, Roberts, and Gordon (2016) found that a considerable segment of the public lost faith in the political class. Satisfaction with democracy and political insti-tutions was low, and public trust in key political institutions (such as national government) had significantly eroded. Such discontent, particularly among the poor, seems to be linked in large part to widespread public dissatisfaction with government's efforts to create jobs and keep people safe (also see Gouws and Schulz-Herzenberg 2016). Disillusionment with politicians and political parties may lead citizens to embrace what some have termed 'anti-politics' or 'anti-formal politics', involving a rejection of conventional forms of political participation and a turn towards alternative forms of political action, such as protest action (Dalton 2006). Concomitantly, a number of studies have been quite critical of the supposed relationship between disillusionment and political behaviour (for, example, Saunders 2014). The question therefore remains whether such discontentment with aspects of regime performance in the country ultimately sways decisions regarding electoral participation.

While a sizeable number of other factors have been proposed as potential influences on turnout, such as mobilising agencies and networks, as well as social context (see Schulz-Herzenberg 2019a), this article focuses on testing of the individual resources, psychological engagement and regime evaluations hypotheses. Following an outline of the data and methods employed for the study, we systematically examine the role of these socio-demographic and attitudinal correlates on planned electoral participation using multivariate modelling. This leads into a concluding discussion that teases out the implications for successive elections in the country.

Methodology

The data used to examine the patterns and determinants of electoral participation derives from the South African Social Attitudes Survey (SASAS), a repeat cross-sectional survey series conducted by the Human Sciences Research Council on an annual basis since 2003. The series was designed to be nationally representative of the adult population aged 16 years or older living in private residence. The sample for each round of surveying consisted of 500 Population Census Small Area Layers (SALs) as primary sampling units, stratified by province, geographical sub-type and majority population group. In each of the sampled localities, seven visiting points were randomly selected for interviewing, followed by the random selection of a single, age-eligible member in each household using a Kish grid. Questionnaires were administered using face-to-face interviewing in the respondent's language of choice. The realised sample size was for each survey round ranges between 2500 and 3300. Data for this study is available for the period 2008–2014. The research instruments and protocols were approved by the HSRC Research Ethics Committee.

For the present study, the main measure used to examine electoral predispositions is a constructed categorical variable deriving from a question on the planned intention to vote. Each SASAS round since 2003 has asked respondents the following: 'If there were an election tomorrow, for which party would you vote?' Those specifying that they would vote for a specific political party were coded as 'decided voters', while those indicating that they would not vote were classified as 'abstainers'. Two additional categories were identified based on the pattern of responses, namely 'undecided voters' who were uncertain of their electoral choice, and 'undisclosed voters' who refused to voice a clear preference when asked the voting intention question. Data from the sixteen survey rounds conducted between 2003 and 2018/19 were combined into a cumulative file, permitting an examination of trends over time and the conducting of multivariate analysis that covers all years of data while controlling for year effects. The study is confined to those age-eligible to vote in each survey round, irrespective of registration status. Trends in electoral intentions and select relevant independent variables are presented over the full period from 2003 onwards, while the modelling is restricted to the 11 rounds conducted between 2008 and 2018/19 due to certain key variables not being fielded during the first five rounds of the SASAS series. The sample size for the combined 2003–2018 data is 47,882, while the 2008–2018 modelling is based on a sample of 33,648 cases. A description of the coding of the independent variables used to test the resources, psychological engagement and regime evaluations hypotheses is presented in an Addendum to the article.

Trends in electoral intentions since the early 2000s

Figure 1 presents trends in relation to responses to the intention to vote question over sixteen rounds of annual SASAS surveying between 2003 and 2018/19. For ease of interpretation, the pattern for the four category of responses – decided voters (those who will vote), abstaining voters, undecided voters and undisclosed voters – are presented on separate line graphs. Firstly, in relation to decided voters, who unequivocally declare an intention to vote for a particular political party if there were to be an election tomorrow,

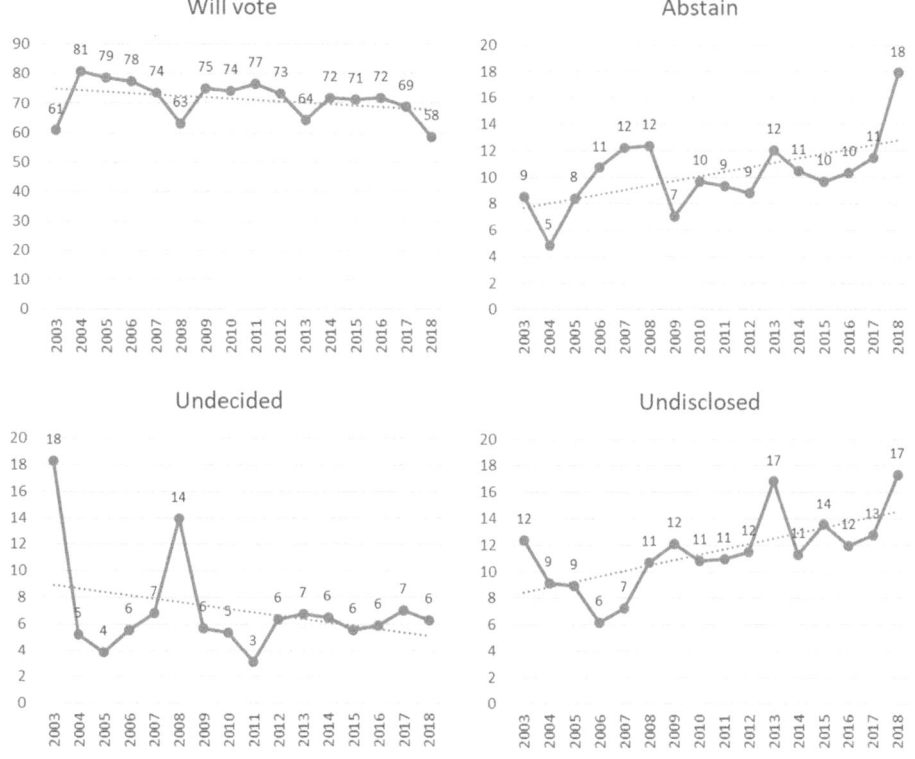

Figure 1. Trends in electoral intention among the voting age public, 2003–2018/19 (%). Source: HSRC SASAS 2003–2018.

Notes: (1) Data is weighted to be nationally representative of the voting age population (18 years and older) living in South Africa, (2) the vertical axis scale in the decided voters ('will vote') graph differs from the other three graphs, with the latter on a finer grained scale in order to better depict dynamics for these unconvinced voters.

there have been fluctuations over time, with a generally declining trend. In the survey rounds conducted approximately six months prior to General Elections (the 2003, 2008, 2013 and 2018 rounds), there are discernible dips in the share of the voting age public openly declaring an intention to vote. Downturns of this type in the pre-election cycle ranged from 10 to 20 percentage points, and are likely to reflect a combination of influences. This may include growing introspection about electoral choice in the build-up to a specific electoral contest as well as a heightened sensitivity to disclosing electoral participation preferences during such periods. The share reporting an intention to vote in the lead-up to the 2019 General Elections (58%) was the lowest recorded over the examined period.

In contrast with decided voters, the tendency to report planned abstention has been increasing on aggregate over time. A careful examination of the year-on-year patterns, shows that there have been ebbs and flows that correspond with political terms of office and contextual events. During former President Thabo Mbeki's second term of office, from 2004 until his 'resignation' in September 2008, there is an observable surge in reported abstention, rising from 5% in late 2004 to 12% in late 2008. This declined again to 7% in the aftermath of the 2009 General Elections, and during the first term and most of the second term of the Zuma administration, this fluctuated within a 7–12% range, with a slight inclining pattern. The results of the 2018 survey, conducted between November 2018 and February 2019, show a rapid upswing in planned abstention, from 11% in late 2017 to 18%. This is the highest recorded share indicating that they would not vote if an election were held tomorrow. This corroborates official registration and turnout statistics, which also displayed a notable downturn, especially among younger age cohorts (Schulz-Herzenberg 2019b). The decline in the share of decided voters and a corresponding upswing in planned abstention remains a defining factor of the 2019 General Elections. Growing absenteeism raises fundamental questions about the underlying determinants and future trajectory of this emerging pattern of behaviour.

Beyond the behavioural extremes of confirmed participation and abstention lie the other two categories of voters presented in Figure 1, namely undecided and undisclosed voters. Expressions of electoral indecision we especially high in the lead-up to the 2004 and 2009 general elections, accounting for 18% and 14% of the voting age population (18 years and older) respectively. The 2004 General Elections posed the electorate with the difficult choice of a second term under the leadership of President Mbeki in the context of growing discontent about the pace and nature of post-apartheid reconstruction and development. The 2009 General Elections, however, occurred barely six months after the recalling of President Mbeki, the rise in electoral fortunes of President Zuma, the outbreak of widespread xenophobic riots and an intensification of protest events around the country. The run up to the 2009 General Elections was also the period of the global financial crises and often considered by many economists as the most serious financial crises since the Great Depression of the 1930s. In a context of complex electoral and broader political dynamics, the observable spikes in voter indecision is perhaps somewhat unsurprising. These spikes did not recur in the context of the 2014 and 2019 General Elections, and with the exception of the 2003 and 2008 survey rounds, the share of undecided voters has remained relatively unchanged, ranging narrowly between 3% and 7% in the other 14 years of observation.

The undisclosed vote is the most difficult group among the electorate to profile. Do these adults with clear party allegiances but a reticence to openly discuss such identification with interviewers? Are they voters with weak levels of partisanship, or even voters with no particular sense of party attachment at all? Could they even be discerning swing voters who decide on their electoral choices following campaigning or on voting day itself based on a careful weighing-up of different factors? It could also be they are a group encompassing a blend of all the above. What is again apparent is that there are upswings in the share of undisclosed voters in each of the survey years prior to general elections falling within the period under examination (the 2003, 2009, 2013 and 2018 survey rounds). Furthermore, like abstention, the share of undisclosed voters shows a upward trend over time, with the highest reported shares falling into this category in both 2013 and 2018/19 (17%). Exploring the factors informing lack of disclosure of electoral intentions, and the manner in which this group differs or approximates decided and abstaining voters would also help to enrich our understanding of the South African voter.

Testing the relative influence of different theoretical models

Using pooled, annual data from the SASAS survey series covering the period from late 2008 through to early 2019, we tested the theoretical assumptions underlying the individual resource, psychological engagement and regime evaluation models. Given the nature of our categorical dependent variable measuring voting intention, we used a multinomial regression approach to mode voting intention. The base category for analysis are decided voters, meaning that the models essentially test for the similarities and variances in the predictors of planned electoral turnout relative to the categories of abstaining, undecided and undeclared voters. The approach employed is similar to that adopted by Schulz-Herzenberg (2019a) in her examination of the determinants of turnout in the context of the 2014 General Elections. Specifically, we begin by independently testing the predictive effect of the three theoretical explanations. This is followed by a fully specified model that includes all clusters of indicators as a means of ascertaining which factors and specific indicators predominate when entered simultaneously. Since the modelling is based on combined data from eleven consecutive annual SASAS rounds, we include a control in the models for year of surveying, in order to account for year effects. This is important given the swings in the relative electoral predispositions of the adult public observed over this period of time.

Individual resources (socio-demographic traits)

The results of the initial testing of the individual resources hypothesis are presented in Table 2. Compared to voters that express a clear intention to vote, abstaining voters are more inclined to be younger on average, Indian or coloured adults, and tend to reside in formal urban areas rather than in rural, former homeland areas. No gender or strong educational effects are apparent. Similarly, the main discernible differences between decided and undecided voters is that the latter are slightly more likely to younger, and Indian or coloured adults rather than black African adults. Again, no statistically significant difference is evident in relation to gender or educational attainment, and there is only a

Table 2. Multinomial logistic regression results testing the impact of individual resources on voter predispositions in South Africa, pooled 2008–2018/19 data.

Individual resources model	Abstainer		Undecided voter		Undisclosed voter	
	Coef.	Sig.	Coef.	Sig.	Coef.	Sig.
Female (ref. male)	−0.088	n.s.	0.119	n.s.	−0.168	**
Age (in years)	−0.024	***	−0.015	***	0.001	n.s.
Population group (ref. Black African)						
Coloured	0.426	***	0.651	***	0.364	***
Indian/Asian	1.178	***	1.215	***	0.739	***
White	−0.014	n.s.	0.135	n.s.	0.317	***
Type of geographic location (ref. Urban formal)						
Urban informal	−0.136	n.s.	0.070	n.s.	−0.200	n.s.
Rural traditional authority areas	−0.273	**	−0.132	n.s.	−0.306	***
Rural farms	−0.200	n.s.	−0.275	*	−0.325	**
Educational attainment (ref. Post-secondary)						
Junior primary schooling or less	0.319	*	−0.046	n.s.	−0.343	*
Senior primary schooling	0.222	n.s.	−0.011	n.s.	−0.416	***
Incomplete secondary schooling	0.199	n.s.	0.024	n.s.	−0.375	***
Complete secondary schooling	0.146	n.s.	0.033	n.s.	−0.200	*
Year of survey	0.056	***	−0.025	*	0.040	***
Constant	−113.429	***	48.013	*	−81.475	***

Notes: (1) Data is weighted to be nationally representative of the voting age population (18 years and older) living in South Africa, (2) the base outcome is 'Decided voters' and (3) the regression model controlled for an individual's province of residence. ***$p < .001$. **$p < .01$. *$p < .05$. n.s. = not significant.

marginal effect on type of geographic location. Finally, the undisclosed voter displays a greater tendency to be male, a coloured, Indian or white adult, and more likely to have a tertiary education than a completed secondary or lower level of educational attainment.

These findings therefore suggest that, in terms of socio-demographic attributes, the factors differentiating decided voters from both undecided and abstaining voters are broadly equivalent. Age and race are the main determinants, coupled with a modest locational influence. Younger Indian and coloured voters are accordingly more likely than to voice a preference for abstention or uncertainty about electoral participation. By contrast, in profile the undisclosed voter seems characteristically better educated, more decidedly urban-based, and has a greater chance of being male than the decided voter. Whether these patterns remain, modify or fall away altogether once other attitudinal factors are taken into account for will be determined a little later on, under the discussion of the fully specified model presented in Table 5.

Psychological engagement

The psychological mood of the voting age public ahead of the 2019 General Elections could be regarded as rather sombre in character, especially in perspective of the trends observed over more than a decade (Figure 2). Levels of political interest have remained fairly stable at a relatively low level, with those declaring that they are 'very' or 'quite' interested in politics varying between a modest 28% and 38% over the 2008–2018 period. In late 2018, the figure stood at 30%, which is below the all-year average of 34%, and in a similar range to that observed over the 2016–2018 period (28–30%). By contrast, the sense of political efficacy expressed by the electorate has shown an appreciable decline since the early 2000s, with 2018 representing a pre-electoral low-point. The political efficacy index represents a combination of internal and external efficacy measures,

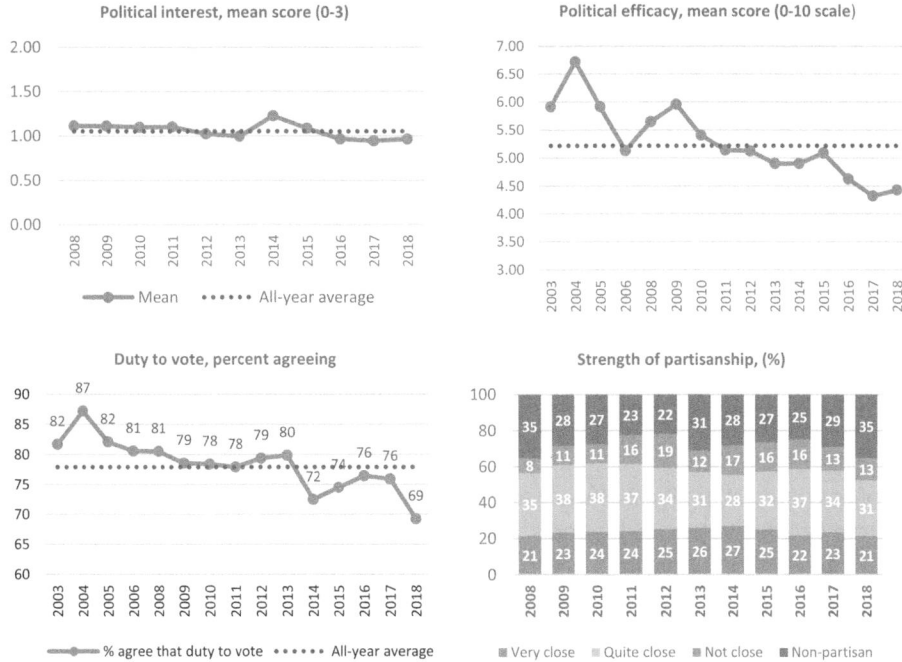

Figure 2. Trends in psychological engagement variables among the voting age public, 2003–2018/19 (%). Source: HSRC SASAS 2003–2018.

suggesting that the public is losing faith in the power of their vote and the accountability of elected officials.

South Africans have tended to display a resolute sense of the duty to vote, a trait that is a likely reflection of the hard-won struggle for the franchise, which was secured for the first time in the country's history in 1994. While this remains true for a clear majority of the voting age population, there has nonetheless been a clear downward trend in this belief, falling from a highpoint of 87% in 2004 to a low of 69% in 2018. Strength of partisanship shows a less distinctive pattern over time, with the share declaring non-partisanship fluctuating between 22% and 35% since 2008, with 2018 falling at the upper limit of this range. Taken together with the other indicator trends, it suggests that entering into the 2019 electoral context, not only was the electorate expressing a lower degree of partisanship than in preceding years, but there was also an unprecedented low level of political efficacy and sense of duty to vote, coupled with a low general level of political interest. The question remains what bearing this has on electoral behavioural intentions, and what it might mean for future electoral contests if the observed patterns continue along the current trajectory.

The multivariate analysis presented in Table 3 tests the combined effect of the psychological engagement factors on the voting age public. The results suggest that political interest, political efficacy and party closeness all yield a significant effect to some degree. In contrast with decided voters, abstaining voters possess significantly lower political interest, political efficacy and duty to vote. They are also less likely than decided voters to have stronger party ties, and instead display a tendency towards non-partisanship. Like abstainers, undecided voters also demonstrate weak partisanship, but fundamentally differ in

Table 3. Multinomial logistic regression results testing the impact of psychological engagement factors on voter predispositions in South Africa, pooled 2008–2018/19 data.

Psychological engagement model	Abstainer		Undecided voter		Undisclosed voter	
	Coef.	Sig.	Coef.	Sig.	Coef.	Sig.
Political interest	−0.161	***	−0.021	n.s.	0.112	*
Political efficacy	−0.171	***	−0.024	n.s.	0.019	n.s.
Duty to vote	−0.199	***	0.028	n.s.	0.031	n.s.
Party closeness (ref. Non-partisan)						
Very close	−4.277	***	−4.633	***	−5.444	***
Quite close	−3.842	***	−3.881	***	−5.490	***
Not close	−3.608	***	−3.654	***	−5.129	***
Year of survey	0.066	n.s.	0.008	n.s.	0.081	***
Constant	−131.439	n.s.	−16.532	n.s.	−162.929	***

Notes: (1) Data is weighted to be nationally representative of the voting age population (18 years and older) living in South Africa, (2) the base outcome is 'Decided voters' and (3) the regression model controlled for an individual's province of residence (not shown) and year of survey. ***$p < .001$. **$p < .01$. *$p < .05$. n.s. = not significant.

that political interest, political efficacy and duty to vote have no bearing in differentiating them from decided voters. As for undisclosed voters, they tend to exhibit marginally higher political interest than undecided voters but there is no distinguishing political efficacy or duty to vote effect. Most notably, undisclosed voters demonstrate a weaker degree of partisanship than abstainers and undecided voters.

Regime evaluations

Moving from psychological engagement to confidence in the democratic regime, we examine three factors of performance and trust. Before moving to the predictive power of such variables among voting-age citizens, we again examine the general trends for the select indicators used in the multivariate analysis (Figure 3). Despite fluctuations over time, satisfaction with the functioning of democracy in the country has displayed a general downward tendency. Although there was a slight recovery in the transition from the Zuma to Ramaphosa administrations between late 2017 and 2018, barely a third (34%) of the electorate was satisfied with democracy ahead of the 2019 election. Evaluations of specific areas of government performance have not demonstrated the same degree of downturn across the 2003–2018 period. Nonetheless based on a composite index of performance in six areas of government service delivery performance (water and sanitation, electricity, low-cost housing, access to health care, crime reduction and job creation), it is evident that satisfaction with service delivery has fallen sharply since 2016 to an all-period low in 2018, slightly below that recorded in 2003. Trust in core political institutions (national and local government, as well as Parliament) has not been immune to the critical evaluations provided for other political support measures. The mean political trust index score fell from a high of 3.47 (on the 1–5 scale) in 2004 to a low of 2.60 in 2018, with scores below the scalar midpoint (of 3.0) evident every year since 2012. There has again been a modest increase in trust between 2017 and 2018, though the level of expressed confidence remains worryingly low.

From this review of trends, it is evident that the 2019 electoral context was one in which greater psychological disengagement among the voting-age public was accompanied by decidedly harsher views on the supply of democracy, the basic performance of the democratic regime, and the level of confidence vested in political institutions. Yet, do these

Figure 3. Trends in regime evaluations variables among the voting age public, 2003–2018/19 (%). Source: HSRC SASAS 2003–2018.

critical voices matter for planned electoral behaviour? We find that these regime evaluations measures exert an influence on the electoral inclinations of the voting age public, though arguably to a lesser extent than psychological engagement variables (Table 4). Views on the functioning of democracy in South Africa, evaluations of service delivery performance, and confidence in political institutions are significant factors that distinguish decided voters from other voters. Those more satisfied with overall democratic functioning and voicing more confidence in key political institutions display a greater likelihood of being a decided voter than an abstaining, undecided or undisclosed voter. By contrast, decided voters are less likely to be content with government's performance in delivering select basic services on average than undecided and undisclosed voters, though no significant effect is present in the case of abstaining voters.

Table 4. Multinomial logistic regression results testing the impact of psychological engagement factors on voter predispositions in South Africa, pooled 2008–2018/19 data.

Regime evaluations model	Abstainer		Undecided voter		Undisclosed voter	
	Coef.	Sig.	Coef.	Sig.	Coef.	Sig.
Satisfaction with democracy	−0.115	***	−0.122	***	−0.130	***
Service delivery index	0.020	n.s.	0.133	**	0.112	**
Political trust index	−0.251	***	−0.158	***	−0.130	***
Year of survey	0.036	***	−0.034	**	0.033	***
Constant	−72.859	***	66.415	**	−66.798	***

Notes: (1) Data is weighted to be nationally representative of the voting age population (18 years and older) living in South Africa, (2) the base outcome is 'Decided voters' and (3) the regression model controlled for an individual's province of residence. ***$p < .001$. **$p < .01$. *$p < .05$. n.s. = not significant.

It is worth mentioning that when the three regime evaluations measures are modelled individually rather than jointly, the pattern of results remains unchanged in relation to satisfaction with democratic functioning and political trust, but there are slight differences in relation to service delivery evaluations. We find firstly that the coefficient on this measure for abstainers is statistically significant ($p < 0.001$) and negative. This implies that abstainers are less satisfied with government's service delivery performance than decided voters on average. Secondly, we find an absence of service delivery performance effect for undecided and undisclosed voters. However, when the three measures are included jointly in a single multinomial regression model, the service delivery effect for abstainers cancels out, while this variable becomes significant ($p < 0.01$) for undecided and undisclosed voters.

Full model

The results of the full model, which jointly includes all sets of measures corresponding to the different theoretical hypotheses explaining electoral intentions, are presented in Table 5. In this final analysis, we find that abstainers differ from decided voters in that

Table 5. Fully specified multinomial logistic regression results testing the impact of individual resources, psychological engagement and regime evaluations factors on voter predispositions in South Africa, pooled 2008–2018/19 data.

	Abstainer		Undecided voter		Undisclosed voter	
	Coef.	Sig.	Coef.	Sig.	Coef.	Sig.
Individual resources						
Female (ref. male)	−0.071	n.s.	0.072	n.s.	−0.166	*
Age (in years)	−0.020	***	−0.011	**	0.005	n.s.
Population group (ref. Black African)						
Coloured	0.334	**	0.560	***	0.298	*
Indian/Asian	0.576	***	0.698	***	0.121	n.s.
White	−0.335	*	−0.150	n.s.	0.033	n.s.
Type of geographic location (ref. Urban formal)						
Urban informal	−0.103	n.s.	0.274	n.s.	0.050	n.s.
Rural traditional authority areas	−0.101	n.s.	0.007	n.s.	−0.148	n.s.
Rural farms	−0.201	n.s.	−0.320	n.s.	−0.415	**
Educational attainment (ref. Tertiary)						
Junior primary schooling or less	0.020	n.s.	−0.255	n.s.	−0.796	***
Senior primary schooling	0.028	n.s.	−0.025	n.s.	−0.475	**
Incomplete secondary schooling	0.074	n.s.	−0.014	n.s.	−0.459	**
Complete secondary schooling	0.013	n.s.	−0.040	n.s.	−0.284	*
Psychological engagement						
Political interest	−0.136	**	−0.004	n.s.	0.095	*
Political efficacy	−0.167	***	−0.010	n.s.	0.020	n.s.
Duty to vote	−0.167	***	0.037	n.s.	0.032	n.s.
Party closeness (ref. Non-partisan)						
Very close	−4.473	***	−4.660	***	−5.445	***
Quite close	−3.927	***	−3.867	***	−5.508	***
Not close	−3.651	***	−3.625	***	−5.125	***
Regime evaluations						
Political trust index	−0.090	*	−0.033	n.s.	0.025	n.s.
Satisfaction with democracy	−0.020	n.s.	−0.077	n.s.	−0.061	n.s.
Service delivery index	0.063	n.s.	0.087	n.s.	0.009	n.s.
Year of survey	0.055	***	0.002	n.s.	0.089	***
Constant	−108.392	***	−4.008	n.s.	−177.394	***

Notes: (1) Data is weighted to be nationally representative of the voting age population (18 years and older) living in South Africa, (2) the base outcome is 'Decided voters' and (3) the regression model controlled for an individual's province of residence. ***$p < .001$. **$p < .01$. *$p < .05$. n.s. = not significant.

they are younger, more likely to be a coloured or Indian adult than a black African adult. Select psychological engagement factors continue to separate abstainers from decided voters, with the former more inclined to exhibit lower levels of political interest, political efficacy and a belief in the civic duty to vote than the latter, together with much lower levels party closeness. The only regime evaluations effect that can be observed in the full model is in relation to political trust, with abstainers generally displaying slightly lower confidence in core political institutions than decided voters.

In the case of undecided voters, in common with abstainers they tend to be younger and more likely to be a coloured or Indian adult than a black African adult than decided voters. The predominant basis of variation is party closeness, with undecided voters less likely to display a stronger degree of partisanship than decided voters. The other psychological engagement factors remain statistically insignificant, and continue to be the traits that differentiate abstainers from the electorally undecided. None of the regime evaluations measures retain statistical significance once the individual resources and psychological engagement measures are controlled for.

Lastly, in comparison to decided voters, undisclosed voters tend to be to be better educated, while also displaying a modest tendency towards being male, coloured, and based in a formal urban area. As with undecided voters, the main psychological engagement attribute that is statistically significant is party closeness. However, in this instance, undisclosed voters demonstrate a lower strength of partisanship than undecided voters and abstainers. Undisclosed voters also tend to be marginally more politically interested than decided voters. The lack of observable effect on regime evaluations measures repeats for undisclosed voters.

Concluding discussion

The analysis presented in this paper comes at a time of earnest reflection about Election 2019 and the state of South Africa's electoral democracy, the changing patterns of registration, turnout and abstention, and what this might presage for future electoral contests (Schulz-Herzenberg and Southall 2019). It has drawn on nationally representative, survey-based data covering a fuller sweep of recent history in an attempt to provide deeper insight into the changing persuasions of the South African electorate leading up to the 2019 General Elections, and test the extent to which three distinct theoretical constructs inform planned electoral behaviour. The results suggest that these theoretical models have a significant though differential degree of influence over electoral intentions.

Psychological engagement

Psychological engagement with politics clearly plays a dominant motivating role in determining whether South Africans turn out to vote, stay away from the ballot box, display electoral indecision or refuse to disclose their preferences. The extent and strength of partisanship is a common factor that separates decided voters from abstainers, undecided voters and undisclosed voters alike. An increasing sense of party closeness therefore serves to raise the likelihood of reporting an intention to vote, whereas weaker party attachment or non-partisanship conversely sways individuals towards uncertainty or a disinclination to vote. The survey series points to party non-identifiers accounting for approximately a third of the voting age population by early 2019. As Schulz-Herzenberg (2019a, 15) maintains, this represents a 'large potential pool of (swing) voters' that political parties should try and persuade to vote, though convincing them to do so is inevitably going to be an exceptionally challenging undertaking.

Apart from party closeness, other psychological orientations to politics variables, such as political interest, sense of efficacy and belief in the civic duty to vote, have a strong bearing in differentiating abstaining from decided voters specifically. Compared to decided voters, abstainers are less interested in politics, less convinced that their vote makes a difference or that the elected are responsive to their needs, and possess a weaker sense of moral obligation to vote. This is perhaps one of the most disconcerting findings from the study, considering the reduced turnout recorded in the 2019 General Elections, as well as the declining trends in political efficacy and duty to vote observed since the early 2000s. Compounding this picture is the effect of age, with abstainers generally presenting as younger on average than decided voters. It should also be mentioned that psychological engagement is the main factor that distinguishes abstainers from undecided voters. On face value, voter indecision emerges as a seemingly unimportant aspect of electoral participation dynamics in the country, reported by a fairly stable 3%–7% of the electorate in general over time. Nonetheless, as the multivariate results signal, if indecision combines with a mounting sense of psychological disengagement, there remains a real possibility that this could fuel the rising tendency towards electoral abstention in future elections.

Regime evaluations

In contrast with psychological engagement in politics, the study findings indicate that regime evaluations do not appear to have a particularly decisive role in motivating electoral intentions in the country. Admittedly, abstainers, undecided voters and undisclosed voters voice less confidence in core political institutions and more general discontent with the functioning of democracy than decided voters. Yet, apart from a modest inverse effect on satisfaction with democracy among abstainers, these influences fell away in the full multinomial logistic regression model, especially following the addition of psychological engagement factors. This is likely due to the fact that those with lower political interest, efficacy, duty and partisanship are also likely to express more critical views on the performance of the democratic regime and institutions post-1994.

Socio-demographic factors

As for the socio-demographic traits that remain salient from the modelling, age, race and education to a lesser degree seem to play a role. Age has already been mentioned as a factor differentiating decided from abstaining voters. Similarly, undecided voters are younger on average than decided voters. The fact that abstention and voter indecision is more likely among younger age eligible adults is worrying given the demographic composition of the electorate. As of 2019, 18–29 year-olds represented approximately a third (33%) of all eligible voters, with a further quarter (25%) in their thirties (Schulz-Herzenberg 2019b). Although a majority of youth still vote, an emerging pattern of lower registration and turnout rates among youth, coupled with generational replacement over time, is likely to have a bearing on the level of participation in future elections.

It is interesting that race remains a significant factor underlying electoral intentions in the country, even after controlling for all the other socio-demographic, attitudinal and evaluative variables in the modelling. The results suggest that black adults are more likely to be decided voters, and less likely than coloured and Indian adults to be abstainers or undecided voters. While controlling for psychological engagement and regime evaluation factors has largely removed the significance of race in separating decided from undisclosed voters, the same is not true for abstainers and undecided voters. The implies that there remain explanatory factors that have not as yet been accounted for that differentiate black adults from other South Africans in motivating electoral participation.

Educational attainment was only significant in explaining differences between decided and undisclosed voters, with the latter tending to be better educated in general. This, taken together with a greater propensity than decided voters towards being urban-based, displaying slightly higher political interest and being appreciably lower levels of partisanship suggests that undisclosed voters might possibly be opposition supporters reluctant to openly state their affiliation with a particular opposition party, or even strategic voters that postpone their vote decision until well into the campaigning period in the lead-up to Election Day.

Limitations and future areas of research

The article examined the relative influence of two of the three core components of the civic voluntarism model of political participation (Verba and Nie 1972; Verba, Schlozman, and Brady 1995) in the South African context, namely individual resources and psychological engagement with politics. It has not tested the role of recruitment networks that bring people to vote, including social networks and news media. Recently, Schulz-Herzenberg (2019a) showed that this might be a particularly salient explanation of turnout in the country, based on data from 2014. Moreover, recent quantitative election research has also point to the existence of a culture of voting, with past electoral participation emerging as a strong determinant of voting intention (Roberts, Struwig, and Grossberg 2012, Struwig, Roberts, and Gordon 2016). Future South African electoral research should continue to monitor the salience of these and other emerging theoretical explanations for electoral behaviour.

Implications for electoral democracy in South Africa

From a broader electoral democracy perspective, how distinctive are the conclusions about the character of the South African voter (and non-voter) described above? In many respects, the decline in electoral turnout, the changing civic norms away from electoral participation among youth, and the rise of critical citizens who are discontent with politics and democratic performance are broadly observed trends in many established liberal democracies (Dalton 2008; Hooghe and Kern 2017). This has given rise to discussions of a global democratic recession or retreat (Schenkkan and Repucci 2019). We would contend that, despite the parallels, these democratic reversals matter more fundamentally in the context of young democracies such as South Africa. In such instances, continued patterns of political disengagement and electoral abstention have the potential to undermine democratic legitimacy and frustrate ongoing efforts at democratic consolidation. In addition, the youthful population structure of the country is a key element that has to be considered. Accordingly, any tendency towards abstention and declining psychological engagement in politics among younger members of the electorate may mean that the process of electoral non-participation and democratic retreat is likely to occur at a faster pace than has been recorded in other more established democracies, which are generally typified by older or ageing electorates.

Further research is needed to disentangle the relative contribution of generational and life-cycle effects underlying changes in electoral attitudes and behaviour in the local context. The South African electorate has clearly become more critical over time, disillusioned with the quality of governance and party politics, and questioning the efficacy of electoral participation. It may however be premature to state that democracy is in crisis. Instead, the findings could be interpreted as an appeal for viable party alternatives and greater representation, as well as a demand for greater accountability and integrity in inter-election periods. The degree to which elected representatives heed this appeal will be decisive in shaping the evolving character of South African political culture.

Disclosure statement

No potential conflict of interest was reported by the authors.

ORCID

Benjamin J. Roberts ⓘ http://orcid.org/0000-0002-0607-5447
Jarè Struwig ⓘ http://orcid.org/0000-0003-2410-654X
Steven L. Gordon ⓘ http://orcid.org/0000-0002-6393-2118
Yul Derek Davids ⓘ http://orcid.org/0000-0002-8226-8937

References

Almond, G. A., and S. Verba. 1963. *The Civic Culture: Political Attitudes and Democracy in Five Nations.* New York: SAGE Publications.

Blais, A. 2000. *To Vote or Not to Vote? The Merits and Limits of Rational Choice Theory.* Pittsburgh, PA: University of Pittsburgh Press.

Blais, A., and C. H. Achen. 2019. "Civic Duty and Voter Turnout." *Political Behavior* 41 (2): 473–497.

Blais, A., E. Gidengil, and N. Nevitte. 2004. "Where Does Turnout Decline Come from?" *European Journal of Political Research* 43 (2): 221–236.

Blais, A., L. Massicotte, and A. Dobrzynska. 2003. *Why Is Turnout Higher in Some Countries Than in Others?* Montreal: Environment Canada.

Brady, H. E., S. Verba, and K. L. Schlozman. 1995. "Beyond SES: A Resource Model of Political Participation." *American Political Science Review* 89 (2): 271–294.

Campbell, A., P. E. Converse, W. E. Miller, and D. E. Stokes. 1960. *The American Voter.* Ann Arbor, MI: University of Michigan Press.

Carpini, M. X. D., and S. Keeter. 1996. *What Americans Know About Politics and Why It Matters.* New Haven, CT: Yale University Press.

Clarke, H. D., D. Sanders, M. C. Stewart, and P. F. Whiteley. 2009. *Performance Politics and the British Voter.* Cambridge: Cambridge University Press.

Dalton, R. J. 2006. *Citizen Politics: Public Opinion and Political Parties in Advanced Industrial Democracies*. 5th ed. New York: SAGE Publications.

Dalton, R. J. 2008. "Citizenship Norms and the Expansion of Political Participation." *Political Studies* 56 (1): 76–98.

Gordon, S. L., J. Struwig, and B. J. Roberts. 2018. "The Hot, the Cold and the Lukewarm: Exploring the Depth and Determinants of Public Closeness to the African National Congress." *Politikon* 45 (2): 163–180.

Gouws, A., and C. Schulz-Herzenberg. 2016. "What's Trust Got to Do with It? Measuring Levels of Political Trust in South Africa 20 Years After Democratic Transition." *Politikon* 43 (1): 7–29.

Hooghe, M., and A. Kern. 2017. "The Tipping Point between Stability and Decline: Trends in Voter Turnout, 1950–1980–2012." *European Political Science* 16: 535–552.

IDEA (International Institute for Democracy and Electoral Assistance). 2019. *Voter Turnout Database*. Accessed August 13, 2019. https://www.idea.int/data-tools/data/voter-turnout/.

Inglehart, R., and C. Welzel. 2005. *Modernization, Cultural Change, and Democracy: The Human Development Sequence*. Cambridge: Cambridge University Press.

Kersting, N. 2007. "Electoral Reform in Southern Africa: Voter Turnout, Electoral Rules and Infrastructure." *Journal of African Elections* 6 (1): 134–151.

Kimmie, Z., J. M. Greben, and S. Booysen. 2010. "The Effect of Changes in Registration and Turnout on the Results of the 2009 South African Election." *Politeia* 29 (1): 101–123.

Lipset, S. M. 1960. *Political Man. The Social Bases of Politics*. Garden City, NY: Doubleday.

Nevitte, N., A. Blais, E. Gidengil, and R. Nadeau. 2009. "Socioeconomic Status and Nonvoting: A Cross-National Comparative Analysis." In *The Comparative Study of Electoral Systems*, edited by H. D. Klingemann, 85–108. Oxford: Oxford University Press.

Norris, P. 2000. *A Virtuous Circle: Political Communications in Postindustrial Societies*. Cambridge: Cambridge University Press.

Parry, G., G. Moyser, and N. Day. 1992. *Political Participation and Democracy in Britain*. Cambridge: Cambridge University Press.

Roberts, B., J. Struwig, and A. Grossberg. 2012. "A Vote of Confidence: Gender Differences in Attitudes to Electoral Participation and Experience in South Africa." *Journal of African Elections* 11 (2): 7–36.

Saunders, C. 2014. "Anti-politics in Action? Measurement Dilemmas in the Study of Unconventional Political Participation." *Political Research Quarterly* 67 (3): 574–588.

Schenkkan, N., and S. Repucci. 2019. "The Freedom House Survey for 2018: Democracy in Retreat." *Journal of Democracy* 30 (2): 100–114.

Schulz-Herzenberg, C. 2007. "A Silent Revolution: South African Voters, 1994–2006." In *State of the Nation: South Africa 2007*, edited by S. Buhlungu, J. Daniel, and R. Southall, 114–145. Cape Town: HSRC Press.

Schulz-Herzenberg, C. 2019a. "To Vote or Not? Testing Micro-Level Theories of Voter Turnout in South Africa's 2014 General Elections." *Politikon* 46 (2): 139–156.

Schulz-Herzenberg, C. 2019b. "Trends in Voter Participation: Registration, Turnout and the Disengaging Electorate." In *Election 2019: Change and Stability in South Africa's Democracy*, edited by C. Schulz-Herzenberg, and R. Southall, 44–65. Johannesburg: Jacana Media.

Schulz-Herzenberg, C. and R. Southall, eds. 2019. *Election 2019: Change and Stability in South Africa's Democracy*. Auckland Park: Jacana Media (Pty).

Struwig, J., B. J. Roberts, and S. L. Gordon. 2016. "*Amandla Awethu*: Public Attitudes, South African Democracy and Electoral Participation." In *State of the Nation: South Africa 2016 Who Is in Charge? Mandates, Accountability and Contestations in South Africa*, edited by D. Plaatjies, C. Hongoro, M. Chitiga-Mabugu, T. Meyiwa, and M. Nkondo, 140–159. Cape Town: HSRC Press.

Verba, S., and N. H. Nie. 1972. *Participation in America: Political Democracy and Social Equality*. New York: Harper & Row.

Verba, S., K. L. Schlozman, and H. E. Brady. 1995. *Voice and Equality: Civic Voluntarism in American Politics*. Cambridge, MA: Harvard University Press.

Addendum

Coding of indicators

Individual resource measures

Gender of respondent: (1) Male (2) Female. Age of respondent in years (at time of last birthday). Interviewer recorded respondent's race: (1) Black African (2) Coloured (3) Indian or Asian (4) White. Type of geographic location: (1) Urban formal (2) Informal urban settlement (3) Rural traditional authority areas (4) Rural formal (farms). What is the highest level of education that you have ever completed? (1) Junior primary schooling or less (2) Senior primary schooling (3) Incomplete secondary schooling (4) Complete secondary schooling (5) Post-secondary.

Psychological engagement measures

How interested would you say you are in politics? (0) Not at all interested (1) Hardly interested (2) Quite interested (3) Very interested. Political efficacy is measured through an index constructed based on responses to the following three statements - 'Whether I vote or not makes no difference'; 'After being elected all parties are the same, so voting is pointless'; 'Voting is meaningless because no politician can be trusted'. Responses were captured using a 5-point agreement scale: (1) Strongly agree (2) Agree (3) Neither agree nor disagree (4) Disagree (5) Strongly disagree. The items combined using an averaging approach to produce a reliable scale, with a Cronbach alpha of 0.8272, and the original 5-point scale was reversed and transformed into a 0–10 score, with (0) representing low political efficacy and (10) high political efficacy. 'Do not know' responses were coded as missing. Duty to vote is measured based on responses to a single attitudinal item: 'It is the duty of all citizens to vote' – 5 point scale, reversed for analysis (higher values = higher sense of duty): (1) Strongly disagree (2) Disagree (3) Neither agree nor disagree (4) Agree (5) Strongly agree.

Party closeness is a constructed measure based on the pattern of responses to two consecutive survey questions: 'To which political party do you feel most close?' and 'How close do you feel to this party?'. The first question included a coded set of 15 political parties followed by an 'other party' option. Additional categories were included for 'no party', 'refusal' and 'do not know'. If a respondent identified with a specific political party, they were asked the follow-up strength of partisanship. The variable was coded as: (0) Non-partisan (1) Not close (2) Quite close (3) Very close.

Regime evaluation measures

How satisfied or dissatisfied are you with the way democracy is working in South Africa? – reversed 5-point scale: (1) Very dissatisfied (2) Dissatisfied (3) Neither satisfied nor dissatisfied (4) Satisfied (5) Very satisfied. 'Do not know' responses were coded as missing.

The service delivery index is a measure combining responses to six questions evaluating government performance in one's local area of residence. How satisfied or dissatisfied are you with the way that the government is handling the following matters in your neighbourhood? 'Supply of water and sanitation', 'Providing electricity', 'Affordable housing', 'Access to health care', 'Cutting crime', 'Creating jobs' – 5 point scale: (1) Very dissatisfied (2) Dissatisfied (3) Neither satisfied nor dissatisfied (4) Satisfied (5) Very satisfied. 'Do not know' responses were coded as missing. The items combined to produce a reliable scale, with a Cronbach alpha of 0.7150, making use of a reversed satisfaction scale ranging from 1 to 5, where (1) represents strong dissatisfaction and (5) strong satisfaction.

Political trust was measured using an index constructed from three measures capturing confidence in core political institutions. Indicate the extent to which you trust or distrust the following institutions in South Africa at present: National government, Parliament, Local government. (1) Strongly trust (2) Trust (3) Neither trust nor distrust (4) Distrust (5) Strongly distrust. The items combined to produce a reliable scale, with a Cronbach alpha of 0.7580, making use of a reversed trust scale ranging from 1 to 5, where (1) represents strong distrust and (5) strong trust. 'Do not know' responses were coded as missing.

Conclusion: Quo Vadis South Africa?

Joleen Steyn Kotze and Narnia Bohler-Muller

The 2019 General Elections in South Africa proved to be pivotal moment in the country's electoral democratic history. As a dominant party system, the outcome of South Africa's elections was generally somewhat predictable where speculation often centered around *by what electoral margin the ANC would win*. While opposition strongly contests elections, they seem unable to penetrate a *protected core of ANC* voter that facilitates continued electoral hegemony. This is not surprising. Dominant party system generally emerges following major periods of "…nation-building, revolution, independence, or reconstruction after war" (Greene, 2007: 10). These periods of reconciliation and post-conflict reconstruction create a sense of legitimacy built on the idea of societal transformation for a better and peaceful future (Greene, 2007: 10). Legitimacy is built on the perception that the dominant party act as a proverbial custodian of some future political project to advance a just society. However, as other dominant party systems like Mexico had shown, the political capital dominant parties use to sustain their hegemony eventually runs out. For Mexico's PRI party, who ruled for 70 years, for example, their spectacular defeat in 2000 did not come overnight. Rather, it was a slow process as opposition parties were able to snatch away various governorships from the ruling party in the context of a lack of political efficacy, burgeoning corruption, and slack delivery of basic services.

Indeed, this volume demonstrates that it seems that the ANC's electoral capital as the liberator and the deliverer of freedom and democracy is waning; yet opposition parties are unable to rise a challenger parties to counter the electoral hegemony of the ANC. Instead, we find that South Africans are disengaging from electoral politics. This volume demonstrates that electoral behaviour and shifts in political partisanship and loyalties are fluid. However, opposition parties cannot capitalise on this fluidity in political partisanship as a result of discontent with basic service delivery and quality of governance. Citizens are increasingly turning to voter abstention and/or protest action to show political discontent.

Government performance is a means for dominant parties to sustain electoral dominance (Doorenspleet and Nijzink, 2010: 17). They note that dominance is created at the ballot box and as such the correlation between government performance and party dominance relates to reasons voters vote the way they do. Thus, "…voting for the dominant party could be a matter of institutional ties (I want to belong to the majority) or beliefs (I don't believe the value of competitive politics) or a lack of information (I don't know any better because my information is incomplete or manipulated)" (Doorenpleet and Nijzink, 2010: 17). A growing sense of dissatisfaction with performance opens the political space for socio-political discontent (Doorenspleet and Nijzin, 2010: 18), but also for opposition political parties to emerge as challenger to the dominant party. Furthermore, as highlighted by Doorenspleet and Nijzink (2010: 18), in the South African case, "deteriorating government performance might have more direct electoral consequences at regional or local levels, but at the national level, voters who are dissatisfied prefer to stay away or continue to vote for the ruling because the opposition fails to present itself as a viable alternative". Given the inability of opposition parties to capitalise on the weakening electoral dominance of the ANC, Africa (this volume) rightly concludes that

> … we can infer that political parties through their choices, behaviour and campaigns as well as concurrent political developments, are primarily responsible for the changes in these parties' political fortunes. If campaigns do matter, we should pay far more attention to the quality of choices offered to voters via campaigns. We should ask questions about the extent to which they provide voters with the basis to make informed choices and scrutinize the conditions under which campaigns enhance the quality of democracy.

The main opposition, the Democratic Alliance, in fact, lost a few votes in the 2019 General Elections. And, even though the Economic Freedom Fighters (EFF) managed to increase its electoral margins, it did not necessarily persuade those ANC voters who are dissatisfied with the party to head to the polls and cast their vote for the EFF. Indeed, Schultz-Herzenberg (this volume) demonstrates that partisan loyalties are declining and that there is a need for greater electoral competition given that political parties may attempt to capitalise on partisan loyalties to increase or maintain their share of the electoral pie. This strategy, as Africa (this volume) demonstrates, may not necessarily be viable to facilitate substantive electoral competition between political parties.

Boulainne (2018: 5) stresses that democracies increasingly face a crisis of legitimacy because of growing levels of distrust due to the "…gap between citizens' expectations for democratic governance and their satisfaction with the performance of democratic systems". For Boulainne the key to deepening democracy is the quality of deliberations between citizens and government, involving citizens in governance and decision-making, and the degree that inputs have an effect or influence on government decision-making. If there is a perception that community inputs has no bearing on government decisions, one may see a decline in political trust and democratic legitimacy of governance institutions. This may create a situation where communities will engage the state outside institutionalised process through protest action, for example. If we consider the number of service delivery protests, we note a significant increase over a 13-year period (Sadives, 2018). In 2005 South Africa recorded 35 protests related to service delivery failures, and by 2014, an election year, the number of protests escalated to 191. By 2018 there were 237 service delivery protests, and 218 in 2019. A possible explanation is detailed in Von Holdt's (2011) *The Smoke That Calls* where he details the rationale and action for, often violent and destructive service delivery protests and xenophobic violence. A central theme of his work is a sense that representatives (ward councillors) neither listen to community concerns nor do anything for the community. Similarly, Steyn Kotze (2018: 37 – 62) details increasing disillusionment with voting because of a sense that *democracy remains elusive* as life had not necessarily gotten better.

This links with another factor dominant political parties use to sustain electoral hegemony, that of political culture, interpreted as the "…widely shared, fundamental beliefs that have political consequences" (Doorenspleet and Nijzink, 2010: 14). Political culture extends not only to citizens' feelings of the quality of democracy, but also extends to how people see their role within the dominant party state and *vice versa* (Doorenspleet and Nijzink,

2010: 16). This would entail the perceptions people hold on whether dominant parties are accountable to the masses who keep them in power in the first place. Here Doorenspleet and Nijzink highlight that "…institutions like dominant parties are infused with cultural norms that are constantly being reinvented and redefined…cultural patterns could reinforce the position of dominant parties through the lived experiences of their leaders, members, and voters". We have often heard that the very public factional politics and leadership contestations at elective conferences amount to a *battle of the soul of the ANC* (Gumede, 2005; Mkentane, 2017).

A growing sense of dissatisfaction with performance opens the political space not only for social unrest and protest (Doorenspleet and Nijzin, 2010: 18), but also for challenger parties to emerge to capture power away from a weakened dominant party. We have seen the violent and destructive expression of dissatisfaction with government performance at local government level through protest action. Furthermore, as highlighted by Doorenspleet and Nijzink (2010: 18), in the South African case, "deteriorating government performance might have more direct electoral consequences at regional or local level, but at the national level, voters who are dissatisfied prefer to stay away or continue to vote for the ruling because the opposition fails to present itself as a viable alternative". Indeed, this found expression in previous local government and general elections in South Africa, where some highlighted that a vote for the opposition at the local level might not translate into a vote for that party in the next general elections. Slowly the ANC's grip on political power weakened in various local and metropolitan councils, and by the conclusion of the 2016 Local Government Elections, it was spectacularly evicted from the seat of political power three metros, that of Tshwane, Johannesburg, and Nelson Mandela Bay. The main opposition, the Democratic Alliance, could not attain a majority in these metros and the EFF seemingly struggled to penetrate ANC strongholds. This trend in declining electoral support for the dominant ANC continued with the 2019 General Elections. While the ANC emerged victorious with just under 57.50 % of the vote in 2019 its electoral dominance had declined from 62.15% and 65.9% in 2014 and 2009 General Elections, respectively. Yet, opposition political parties could not necessarily gained the vote of the disillusioned ANC voter, who rather opted out of the elections game and abstained from casting their ballot.

As South Africa progresses towards its fourth decade of democracy, political behaviour through protests have increased on various platforms. This includes economic protest activity through labour strikes, political protest through service delivery protest action, and socio-cultural protest activities in the form of various hashtag movements such as #FeesMustFall and #AmINext. South Africa is indeed a contentious democracy, but this contestation is not necessarily found at the ballot box and not only for ANC voters. Runciman *et al.* (this volume) show, although South Africa is a democracy of discontent where voting and protested are often seen a complimentary mechanisms of political participation, it is not necessarily limited to disillusioned ANC voters:

> we demonstrate that opposition parties are to a much larger extent representative of protesters. Moreover, voting protesters, as persons driven by circumstance to direct political action, have now found political homes to both the left and right of the ANC - and these may be considered, to some degree, as 'parties of protest'. This notwithstanding, it may still be true that 'bricks' are used as part of a dual repertoire of political signalling, albeit under circumstances of party loyalty being much less of a binding constraint on the voting protester's cross at the polls.

Runciman *et al.* (this volume) further highlight: "…while some voters who may be dissatisfied with the ANC are voting for the opposition parties; some are simply choosing not to vote". We see an increase of South African voters who stayed away from the polls in the 2019 General Elections. Only 49% of South Africa's Voting Age Population went to the polls (Schulz-Herzenberg, this volume). When we look at the youth population, only 49% of South Africa's young people registered to vote, and, for the age group 18–19-year old, only 19% registered to vote (Roberts *et al.*, this volume). At a glance, then, it seems South Africans are increasingly disengaging from formal electoral politics, and as such there should be a general disinterest in politics and a view that politics is not important. The World Values Survey found that approximately 45% of South African felt that politics is important in life and a little more than half did not regard politics as important (World Values Survey , 2020). The 2018 round of the South African Social Attitudes Survey conducted by the Human Science Research Council found that almost 30% of South Africans indicated that they were interested in politics compared to 44% who were not interested at all. How do we explain this decline in interest in politics?

A possible explanation is what Rosenberg (1954–1955: 354–361) refers to as the futility of political activity. This futility of political activity is determined by the outcome of political action:

> In most cases a precondition for political activity is what one does will make a difference, will have an effect of some sort…political activity beyond the level of discussion is probably has the aim of *getting one's will translate into action*. But people tend to be motivated to action only if they feel that this action leads to the desired outcome (p. 354).

For Rosenberg, thus, if the individual or group feels that a specific political activity will have no desired outcome, they will be less motivated to engage in that specific activity. And, given that generally speaking, people exercise political power through the vote, a person "feels a discontinuous sense of control over the political process. He has some power at the periodic intervals of election time, but most of the time he sees no relation between his desires and action and actual political results" (p.359). Looking at South African perceptions with regard to the act of voting, we note that there may be a sense of futility of action associated with voting. The 2018 South African Social Attitudes Survey found that just under half of South Africans demonstrated ambivalence to voting as a political activity; this even though almost two-thirds felt it their civic duty to vote.

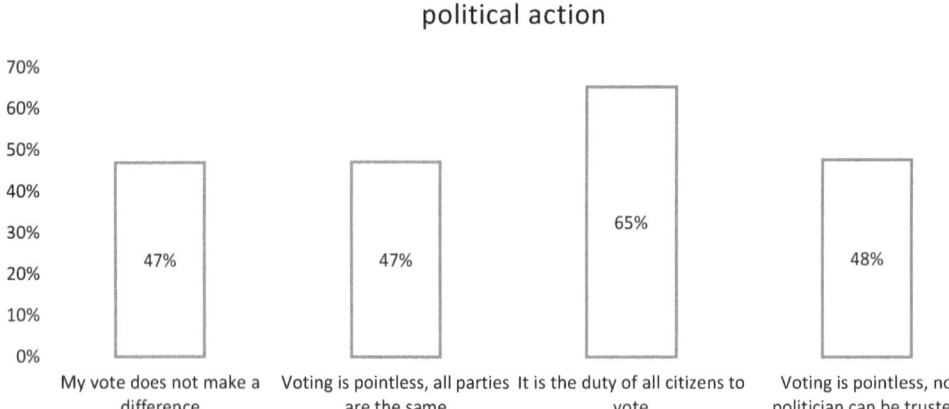

Figure 1. South African perceptions on voting as a political action (Constructed from the 2018 South African Social Attitudes Survey, Human Science Research Council)[1].

South Africans see voting as futile because of a sense of an *empty promise of democracy* premised on failures in basic service delivery and a sense that "...voting is useless... We vote for them and they don't deliver...[and] I have voted several times and my voice has not been heard" (Steyn Kotze, 2018: 58). Lekalake (2016) found that public satisfaction with democracy is at 48% because of high levels of dissatisfaction with political leadership, which "...spilled over into waning support for democracy". More worrying is the finding that half of South Africans feel that the country is undemocratic or a democracy with major problems and 61% of respondents would forego elections for a non-elected government who could provide basic services (Lekalake, 2016). This points to a crisis of democratic legitimacy in South Africa.

This democratic legitimacy gap results in an increase in populist politics that exploit social, political, and economic cleavages. Populist political discourse usually emerges when there is a perceived failure in the institutions of government. Consider the birth of the EFF. The story that this political party tells is one of ANC failures, one in which the ANC is accused of forgetting its core constituency – the poor. Malema's EFF engages in populist discourse to mobilise the poor against the perceived failures of the ANC government through, for example, going to Parliament in overalls and domestic workers' uniforms. This creates the idea the EFF is there to represent the forgotten poor. In this context, populist leaders portray themselves as providing a voice for the people (Vincent, 2011: 3). More importantly, populist leaders use a sense that the views of the people have largely been ignored by mainstream political elites as a means to generate a mass support base (p.3). The greatest political capital that populist leaders have is their appeal to the people as a legitimising force for a particular set of ideals or policy positions (p.3). In this context, consider the clarion call for nationalisation and radical land redistribution without compensation, which relates to symbolism and home-making as Bank and Hart (this volume) details. Julius Malema is very often the political face we equate with this particular discourse. He also capitalises on this discourse through the theatrical use of red overalls and hard hats to create the perception that he is the one who is truly concerned with the ANC's forgotten poor and working-class majority. Populist leaders accuse political elites of "having become increasingly removed from 'the people' and thus pursuing policies which run counter to those actually wanted by the people". Think of the theatrics of the EFF and Julius Malema in Parliament, such as chanting that then President Jacob Zuma must repay the money spent on Nkandla. This is meant to show the public that the EFF is taking on corrupt leaders on behalf of the forgotten poor and the "decent working class person" (p. 4). The EFF regularly engages in confrontational politics, using Parliament and other institutions of government to advance its political agenda. This includes threatening to disrupt parliament if ministers are not fired as well as disrupting state of the nation addresses,[2] holding municipal councils hostages through disruption and not voting on key issues such as budgets and integrated development plans to advance their national political programme,[3] and demonising political opposition and government institutions that seek to hold the party and party leaders accountable.[4] Increasingly, populist parties that present a danger to democracy are gaining electoral support, and South Africa is not necessarily the exception to this development. While the EFF's national share of the vote is only just over 10%, one cannot negate the fact that it was the only party that increased its share of the electoral pie, albeit with approximately 4%.

Populist politics increases political polarisation, where "... political opponents begin to regard each other as existential enemies, allowing incumbents to justify abuses of democratic norms to restrain the opposition, and encouraging the opposition to use 'any means necessary' to (re)gain power" (Ziblatt, no date). Second, sustaining diverse democracies or multi-ethnic societies where "... the politics of redistribution has also been notoriously

complicated by ethnic diversity…"and, due to migration and globalisation, "… have gener-
ated different forms of right-wing populist backlash and has exacerbated political polariza-
tion" (Ziblatt, no date). Third, economic inequality undermines democratic viability and the
quality of democracy (Ziblatt, no date). Fourth, the rise of populism, which sees populist
leaders with autocratic tendencies "… come to power speaking on behalf of 'the people',
but often doing so in ways that seem to challenge the basic norms of liberal democracy"
(Ziblatt, no date). Lastly, a form of institutional inertia that result in democratic institutions
not being able to withstand increasingly undemocratic and authoritarian political behaviour resulting in a diminishing democratic institutional core needed to sustain democratic
governance (Ziblatt, no date). Indeed, Levitsky and Ziblatt (2018: 23–24) highlight four key
behaviours within institutions that undermine democratic governance. These are rejection of or a weak commitment to democratic rules and norms, denying the legitimacy of
political opponents, toleration or encouragement of violence, and readiness to curb civil
liberties of opponents, including the media. In essence, at an institutional level, restricting
political space is a central driver of diminishing democracy. To a degree, some South African politicians from different parties have engaged in this behaviour.

South Africa has not been immune to a general global trend of decline in democracy
(V-Dem, 2019). In 2019, V-Dem demoted South Africa from a liberal democracy to an electoral democracy (V-Dem, 2019). The quality of South African democracy has declined in
three key areas: electoral democracy, liberal democracy, and participatory democracy. This
points to a general decline in both the quality of our democracy in terms elections, participation, and civil and political liberties, as well as quality of governance where corruption,
state predation, and a general disregard for the rule of law and constitutional democracy
impact on our performance as a democracy.

We have seen the rise of increased racial polarisation, the rise of populist parties, a ruling political elite that has undermined the rule of law and basic democratic norms, as
well as increased xenophobic violence, economic inequality, social marginalisation, and
a lack of engagement with formal political processes, most notably voting and elections.

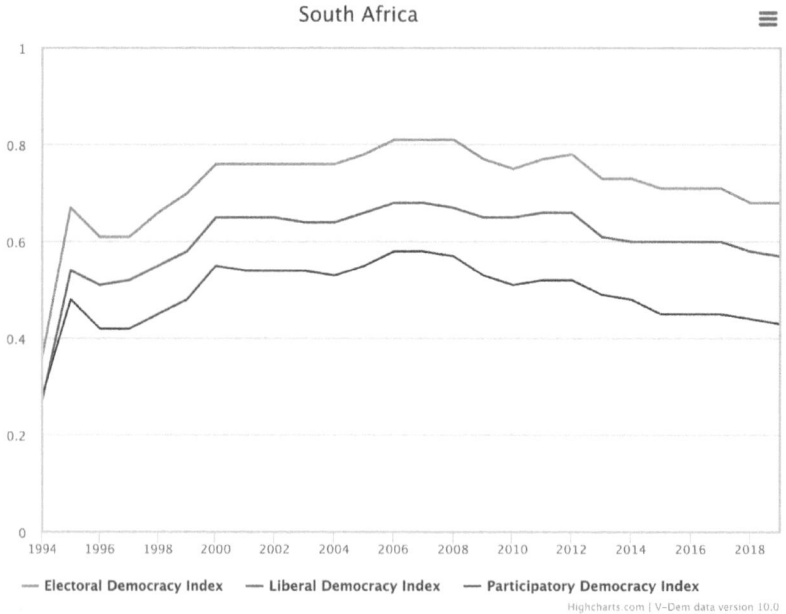

Figure 2. South Africa Democratic Performance: Varieties of Democracy, 1994–2019.

Satisfaction with democracy has declined, and increasingly, one finds a general disappointment that democracy has not delivered on the promise of a better life. A key period that resulted in this decline is commonly referred to as the *nine wasted years* under the Zuma administration. Under the leadership of former President Jacob Zuma, state institutions were increasingly being subjected to personal and political manipulation – a racialised political discourse that divided South African along both racial and class lines – state capture, and rampant corruption. Increasingly, one saw the creation of a parasitic neo-patrimonial state where political loyalty was rewarded at the cost of political efficacy and good governance. Press freedom came under fire as the Zuma administration wished to curb access to information through what was commonly referred to as the *Secrecy Bill*. Political opponents were depicted as enemies of the transformative agenda, and opposition political parties regularly vilified as proponents of an "apartheid agenda" that sought to safeguard "white monopoly capital". The impact of this was the overall decline of not only quality of governance, but quality of democracy in South Africa.

It opened the space for populist parties, such as the EFF, to increase their influence on the political agenda. Indeed, there is a perception that as an opposition, the EFF speaks "the power of truth" (Booysen, no date). In the 2019 General Elections, under the banner of a narrative of *regeneration and getting back on the moral path*, the ANC dipped below 60% in electoral support, and this with just under half of those eligible to vote going to the polls. With President Cyril Ramaphosa now at the helm of government, the challenge is to regain democratic gains made in the early period of South Africa's democracy. Key will be to address issues of corruption, poor governance, unemployment, and social and economic marginalisation, in order to facilitate a level of inclusive citizenship to advance social cohesion for democratic durability. If not, South Africa could potentially decline further, bringing a real threat to our democratic future with discontent being expressed through increased protest action and increased levels of disengagement from formal political processes such as elections.

Notes

1. Responses for I don't know or Refused to Answer not included in graph.
2. See https://www.timeslive.co.za/politics/2020-02-09-fire-gordhan-or-we-will-disrupt-sona-malema-threatens-ramaphosa/.
3. See https://www.iol.co.za/news/politics/eff-decision-to-abscond-from-councils-put-power-back-into-anc-hands-11048804.
4. See https://www.dailymaverick.co.za/article/2018-03-23-analysis-the-eff-vs-insert-next-enemys-nameacronymdescription/.

References

African Governance Index. 2015. *South Africa Data Portal*. Available online: http://southafrica.open-dataforafrica.org/naeetle/african-governance-index?indicator=ACCOUNTABILITY. (Accessed on 20 June 2017).

Baulainne, S. (2018). Building faith in democracy: Deliberative events, political trust and efficacy. *Political Studies* Vol. 67 (1): pp. 4 – 30.

Booysen, S. (n.d.). *Twenty years of democracy: Citizen views on human rights, governance and the political system*. Available at https://freedomhouse.org/sites/default/files/Twenty%20Years%20of%20South%20African%20Democracy.pdf. [Accessed 13 April 2020].

De Jager, N. & Steenekamp, C. 2019. 'Political Radicalism: Responding to the Legitimacy Gap in South Africa'. In Van Beek, U. (ed). *Democracy under threat: A crisis of legitimacy?* Palgrave.

Doorenspleet, R. & L. Nijzink. (2013). *One-party dominance in African democracies.* Lynne Rienner Publishers: Boulder.

Green, K.F. (2007). *Why dominant parties lose: Mexico's Democratization in comparative perspective.* Cambridge University Press: Cambridge.

Gumede, W. 2005. *Thabo Mbeki and the Battle for the Soul of the ANC.* Zebra Press: Cape Town.

Lekalake, R. (2016). *Support for democracy declines in South Africa amid rising discontent with its implementation.* Available at https://afrobarometer.org/sites/default/files/publications/Dispatches/ab_r6_dispatchno71_south_africa_perceptions_of_democracy.pdf. [Accessed 11 April 2020].

Levitsky, S. & Ziblatt, D. (2018). *How democracies die: What history reveals about our future.* Penguin Books: New York., pp. 23–24.

Mainwaring, S. & Pérez-Liñán, A. (2013). Democratic breakdown and survival. *Journal of Democracy* 24(2): 123–135.

Mkentane, L. (2017). *Battle for the Soul of the ANC gets more ugly.* Available online at http://www.iol.co.za/capetimes/news/battle-for-soul-of-anc-gets-even-more-ugly-9425192. (Accessed on 20 June 2017).

Mo Ibrahim Index of African Governance. 2016. *A decade of African governance: 2006 – 2015.* Available online: http://s.mo.ibrahim.foundation/u/2016/10/01184917/2016-Index-Report.pdf?_ga=2.79572183.2100150121.1497966226-2093360130.1490966877. (Accessed on 20 June 2017).

Pillay, D. (2015). 'Has the ANC lost its soul?' in *The Herald Online*, 12 August. Available online: http://www.heraldlive.co.za/opinion/2015/08/12/anc-now-lost-soul/. (Accessed on 20 June 2017).

Rosenberg, M. (1954–1955). Some determinants of political apathy. *The Public Opinion Quarterly* 18(4): 349–366, pp. 354–361.

Sadives, M. (2018). *More protests in 2018 than in any of the previous thirteen years…and it could get worse.* Available at https://www.timeslive.co.za/news/south-africa/2019-01-16-more-protests-in-2018-than-in-any-of--previous-13-years--and-it-could-get-worse/. [Accessed 11 April 2020].

Steyn-Kotze, J. (2018). *Delivering an elusive dream of democracy: Lessons from Nelson Mandela Bay.* (SUN MEDIA: Cape Town).

V-Dem. (2019). *Democracy facing global challenges.* Available at https://www.v-dem.net/media/filer_public/99/de/99dedd73-f8bc-484c-8b91-44ba601b6e6b/v-dem_democracy_report_2019.pdf. [Accessed 12 April 2020].

Vincent, L. (2011). Seducing the people: Populism and the challenge to democracy in South Africa. *Journal of Contemporary African Studies* 29(1): 1–14, p. 3.

Von Holdt, K. (2011). *The smoke that calls: Insurgent citizenship, collective violence and the struggle for a place in the new South Africa.* Centre for the Study of Violence and Reconciliation and Society, Work and Development Institute: Johannesburg.

World Values Survey. (2020). *V. 7: Importance in Life: Politics.* Available online: http://www.worldvaluessurvey.org/WVSOnline.jsp (Accessed 11 April 2020).

Ziblatt, D. (n.d.). *Global Challenges to Democracy.* Available at https://scholar.harvard.edu/dziblatt/challenges-democracy. [Accessed 12 April 2020].

Index